BROKEN, BANKRUPT, AND DYING

BROKEN, BANKRUPT, AND DYING

HOW TO SOLVE THE GREAT AMERICAN HEALTHCARE RIP-OFF

BRAD SPELLBERG

LIONCREST
PUBLISHING

BROKEN, BANKRUPT, AND DYING
How to Solve the Great American Healthcare Rip-off

ISBN   978-1-5445-0907-5   *Hardcover*
       978-1-5445-0906-8   *Paperback*
       978-1-5445-0905-1   *Ebook*

This book is dedicated to Catherine and Michael, who give your parents purpose—to leave the world a better place.

TABLE OF CONTENTS

TABLE OF FIGURES

FOREWORD

I am pleased to introduce *Broken, Bankrupt, and Dying*, by Dr. Brad Spellberg. I have known Brad for many years as an esteemed colleague and friend and have been constantly impressed by his presence as the Chief Medical Officer of a large academic safety-net hospital, a respected researcher, author, and erstwhile policy wonk, among other things.

When he told me he'd written a new book, I was only a little surprised. After all, even the busiest doctor/administrator/ lab researcher has to find something to do at 4:00 a.m. when insomnia kicks in. When he told me what the book is about, all I could say was, "Sounds like what I've been saying for the last decade—at least you've written it down!"

Healthcare is complicated, and healthcare policy and economics can be very difficult to understand. The debate about healthcare in the United States rages on—often becoming a political football—engendering highly partisan arguments, but rarely truly resolving these questions. If you are looking for a solid introduction to some of the key problems we face in American healthcare, *without* the partisan political rhetoric, this book is an excellent start by focusing on the practical win-win possibilities, rather than ideological arguments.

There are many concepts in healthcare policy that are complicated, but at least one is fairly simple—if you're going to pay for something, you should at least get your money's worth! This book explains in relatively simple terms why that's not true for the American healthcare system, why we should be bothered by it, and what we can do to fix it.

As Brad explains, despite the fact that many Americans insist that we have the best healthcare system in the world, it isn't true by most measures. Because of the hodgepodge system that we have let develop over time, the American healthcare system does not serve everyone, and the people that it does serve, it does so at a high cost. The thing that Americans should ultimately take offense to is not that our healthcare system costs as much as it does, but that it provides terrible value for doing so. And people die because of it. Fundamentally we have been paying Rolls-Royce prices for Kia-level luxury, and it doesn't have to be that way.

Brad then builds the case, piece by carefully constructed piece, for an optimal solution. That solution is probably somewhat different from some of the plans you've heard prominent politicians talking about. He walks us through the alternatives, including their pros and cons, and makes a strong plea for engagement. There are few individuals in the country who, when asked, will tell you that our healthcare system isn't broken. Nonetheless, we still struggle with the political willpower to make necessary changes to make our healthcare system effective and sustainable. If we want these changes to happen, we must rely on the power of the public to demand action.

We can actually make a better healthcare system, but to do so, we need all of us to understand the problems well enough to ask for the right solutions. This book will help put people on the path to that understanding.

Arun Patel, MD, JD, MBE, FAAP
Director of Patient Safety and Risk Management
Department of Health Services
Los Angeles County
Former Staff, US House Committee on Energy and Commerce

INTRODUCTION

The US healthcare system is the greatest rip-off perpetrated on the American people in the last century.

It's a powerful assertion, perhaps even off-putting. But it is an assertion born of substantial, objective data. As I will show you, Americans have overpaid for healthcare to the tune of trillions of excess dollars in taxes and lost wages compared to people who live in other countries. And Americans live shorter lives than people in those countries. It's hard to describe paying trillions of dollars more for health while dying younger than everyone else as anything other than the greatest rip-off of the last century.

In polls of prospective voters, Americans list healthcare as the top domestic agenda item that they want to see the government fix. Patients and their families are fed up with their continuously rising healthcare costs, which force them to choose between receiving care and eating or paying rent. And healthcare workers are fed up with mind-numbing insurance authorizations, relentlessly rising paperwork burdens and Byzantine care networks.

We are at a crossroads. Americans have choices to make about what to insist on from their elected officials. But people are confused about which healthcare plan would be best able to meet our national needs by lowering costs and improving outcomes. That's where this book comes in.

Indeed, as we will see, it is not clear that any of the commonly discussed plans to fix US healthcare are exactly the right solution. They all have strengths and weaknesses. But, most importantly, they all may have sufficient detractors to preclude practical implementation. International models point the way to a sort of compromise between proposed models, which can allow us to achieve universal healthcare coverage while retaining choice for the public.

And we can do this with improved healthcare outcomes at a markedly reduced cost. We can even do this while benefitting corporate competitiveness by relieving businesses of the crushing costs of employee health insurance benefits. Think it can't be done? Keep reading. I'll show you that we actually know it can be done. Because systems like this already exist elsewhere in the world.

One of the central premises that I will be laying out for you is that the problems in our healthcare system are not the fault of one person or one group. The blame can't be laid at the feet of corporate greed any more than hospital ineptitude, physician inefficiency, or patient noncompliance. The fault lies within the system itself.

The US healthcare system needs to be redesigned. Or rather, it needs to be designed in the first place. Because as I will explain, the healthcare system we have now is an accidental outgrowth of efforts to combat post-World War II inflation. It was never purposefully designed to deliver healthcare. Yes, seriously. No, I'm not making that up.

I hope to stimulate your thinking about how a healthcare redesign could be accomplished, and what the final product might look like. Any healthcare system that we adopt must fit US cultural norms. It can't work to impose something upon people that they viscerally dislike. That would be setting the system up for failure. But there is so much middle ground here. There are multiple possible paths forward, and that's the key. Our system performs so badly, virtually any modification is bound to improve it.

In 2009, I published a book, *Rising Plague: The Global Threat from Bacteria and Our Dwindling Arsenal to Fight Them*. I had spent years working on national policy issues related to the crisis of antibiotic resistance. What I learned from this experience was that the public did not have a solid grasp on what caused antibiotic resistance, what its effects were, and how it could be combatted. This lack of knowledge hampered effective dialogue about implementing solutions, which required both political and regulatory changes to be made. I wrote the book to help educate the public about the crisis, which would then enable solutions to be implemented.

Rising Plague was widely circulated on Capitol Hill among key congressional staffers. I also did extensive media outreach to further the message. I made numerous television appearances, gave dozens of news and radio interviews, and even appeared in a documentary movie on the topic titled *Resistance*. The book and all the surrounding media effort helped lay the groundwork for the establishment of legislation known as the Generating

Antibiotic Incentives Now or GAIN Act. GAIN was passed in 2012 as part of the FDA Safety and Innovations Act. Thanks in part to these efforts, we have considerably more antibiotics available today than we did ten years ago. And we are seeing major gains in implementing programs to protect antibiotics. In short, I learned that public outreach works. Arm the public with information, and they will help drive change.

Then, in 2014, I moved to Los Angeles County + University of Southern California (LAC+USC) Medical Center to become chief medical officer. LAC+USC Medical Center is one of the largest public hospitals in the US. And in my new role, boy, were my eyes opened to the gaping maws, catastrophic inefficiencies, and frankly outrageous costs of the US healthcare system.

So, in the summer of 2017, I chose healthcare reform to be the focus of my yearlong American Association for the Advancement of Science, Leshner Public Engagement Fellowship. After completing that Fellowship, I decided that the *Rising Plague* experience was instructive with respect to engaging the public. I wanted to put together a book that tells the story of how bad the US healthcare mess is, how we got here, and how we can move forward to make it better.

In this book, I am going to share with you real patient stories, just as I did in *Rising Plague*. These patients are the core of the issue. Their stories reveal the human toll our healthcare system takes, day in and day out. Every day, Americans experience trauma, feel pain, suffer stress, go bankrupt, get sick, and even die due to the dysfunction of our healthcare system. People are indeed broken, bankrupt, and dying.

The patient stories told in this book are based on real events. I have altered details to assure patient anonymity, but the thrust of their stories is real. Without their stories, all we have is cold, hard numbers. And politics don't move based on cold, hard numbers. It takes a human touch to drive home real damage and trauma.

I wrote this book because I'm at the front lines with patients, with my physician colleagues, with my nursing staff, physical therapists, phlebotomists, patient financial workers, and appointment schedulers. And, frankly, every one of the more than 10,000 employees and contractors who make our hospital work. And you know what? We're *all* frustrated. We're *all* mad. Our national healthcare system isn't working for our patients. And it isn't working for our staff. And it isn't working for our taxpayers. Or our businesses. We need a change.

I don't care what your politics are. This isn't about politics. Whether you are on the right or the left or in the middle (like me), we're getting a raw deal. My perspective is born from being a taxpaying healthcare executive, who also is a doctor who treats patients, and who has had patients, friends, and colleagues who have suffered at the hands of the US healthcare system.

My focus is on what we get in return for the money we spend on healthcare, plain and simple. I'm talking hard outcomes here. If we spend more money, we should die less often and at older ages. That is the central theorem of this book. If we are spending more money to get worse outcomes, something is wrong and needs to be fixed.

Again, I will reiterate, the issues I'm talking about cut across all party lines. If you're a fiscal hawk, pro-business Republican, read on, because you should want a different healthcare system.

If you're a Green New Deal, community-minded left-winger, read on, because you should want a different healthcare system. If you're an independent, a Libertarian, a centrist, or a populist, read on, because you should want a different healthcare system.

You may be surprised at what you learn. You may be surprised at how conceptually simple it is to overcome this great healthcare rip-off. Because US healthcare may be the one issue that has the potential to cut across all political lines and unite us in a cause. The cause is making things better for patients, for employees, for businesses, for taxpayers, and for people working in the healthcare industry.

This book is about the great rip-off that is the US healthcare system. It's about all the ways in which we, as a society, have accepted crippling limitations and been slowly lulled into thinking everything is fine, and we really can't do better. Most importantly, it's about the fact that we know we can do better, for our patients, for our families, for our businesses, and for our society as a whole. All we need to do is stand up and tell the people we elect to federal office that the time has come.

CHAPTER 1

|||||||||||||||||||||||||

THE HUMAN COST OF US HEALTHCARE

Mr. A was a fifty-year-old man who was at the end. He was at the end of his rope, and near the end of his life. His heart had acutely failed. It had been slowly failing for years. Years of high blood pressure had taken their toll. Medications helped when he could afford them. But Mr. A worked in construction as a handyman, or wherever he could get work. So he had been on and off medications over the years due to the resulting, intermittent insurance coverage.

The prior evening, Mr. A had come to the LAC+USC Medical Center emergency department complaining of shortness of breath, inability to walk, and leg swelling. After a night receiving treatment in the emergency department, he had not improved enough to go home. So he was admitted by one of the emergency department physicians to my internal medicine team with a diagnosis of advanced heart failure.

As I reviewed his medical record before going to meet him, I noted that this was his first trip to my hospital. Which was a little strange—it should've raised a flag for me that something else was going on. Because we are the largest safety-net hospital for Los Angeles County. While 90 percent of our patients have some form of insurance (mostly Medicaid), LAC+USC Medical Center takes care of more uninsured patients than any other hospital in Los Angeles. Why had he never come to us before, if he had been on and off health insurance for years? And why come to us this time, if he was previously getting his care somewhere else? I pondered these questions as I walked downstairs to meet him.

"Good morning," I said, as I entered Mr. A's room in the emergency department. "I'm Dr. Spellberg, and I'll be the attending physician for you when you get upstairs into a hospital bed."

I found him resting on a gurney, with his eyes closed. Oxygen was being administered to both nostrils by nasal prongs. He lay on his side in a fetal position, and his eyes were squeezed shut. He appeared worn and disheveled, with bags under his eyes. A blanket covered him, so I couldn't see anything other than his face. He grunted in response to my greeting.

"What's going on?" I asked. "Are you in pain?"

"Didn't sleep last night," he said. "Legs hurt. They're swollen. And I can't breathe."

I paused for a moment, confused. Mr. A was connected to electrodes and measurement devices that displayed his vital signs on a monitor next to his gurney. The monitor to which he was connected showed that his heart rate and blood pressure were only mildly elevated. And the level of oxygen in his blood, detected by an infrared monitor on his finger, was reading close to normal. It was a little low, but not unnervingly so, and he was only on a couple of liters of oxygen per minute. Really sick patients would be on oxygen by a face mask at ten liters per minute.

"Huh," I said, and pondered this discrepancy between his objective physiological measures, and his description of how he said he was doing.

I changed tact. "I understand you have heart failure?"

He nodded, eyes still closed.

"Are you taking medications?"

He shook his head and grimaced, still not turning to lie on his back to face me. "Ran out. Can't afford them."

The more I talked to him, the odder the scene seemed. Something felt wrong. Or as I like to say, my "spidey" sense was tingling, like when Spider-Man's intuition tells him something is off. Mr. A was attempting to act very, very sick. But he appeared more chronically ill than acutely in crisis. He wasn't gasping for breath. And I could tell from across the bedside that while the veins in his neck were swollen, indicative of heart failure, they weren't the worst I had seen. When heart failure gets very bad, those veins bulge out all the way up the jaw. And that wasn't the case here. It wasn't adding up.

I grabbed his hand. "My friend," I said. "Are you okay?"

He opened his eyes and looked up at me in surprise. "What do you mean?"

"I mean, you don't quite appear as sick to me as you sound. Is something else going on here?"

He gave me a sheepish look and scrunched his head down into his neck. "Well, I am sick. I do have leg swelling, and I can't walk very far."

"I believe that." I pulled the bedsheet back and noted the prominent swelling in his legs. I pressed on them and my fingers sunk an inch, easily, into his boggy, swollen skin, sort of like pushing into a wet sponge. I would have called it three-plus edema, or swelling, out of a scale of four (with higher being worse). So, it was pretty bad, but again not the worst case I had seen. "But you look like you're breathing okay. Is that true?"

He sort of shook his head, but not convincingly. "As long as I'm lying down, I can catch my breath. But I can only walk a few steps before I get too short of breath to go on."

"Did you pee a lot of water out overnight with the medications?" I asked. "Maybe that made you better?"

"I've been making a fair amount," he said. "I filled that container up twice." He pointed to his portable urinal.

"Huh," I said again. "That's about two liters of fluid you got rid of. It's a good start, but I think you've got six or seven more liters to go. It doesn't seem like two liters would account for such a dramatic improvement in appearance." I paused and just looked at him. "So, do you want to tell me what's really going on?"

He stared at me for a few more moments. Then I saw his eyes

begin to water. My own watered almost reflexively. I squeezed his hand. "What's up?" I asked. "How can I help?"

"I…didn't think you'd help me unless…"

"Hey, you're here, and you're my patient, and we're going to take care of you. Tell me what's going on."

"My heart is at the end. It won't ever recover. That's what my doctors told me. They said there was nothing else they could do. I'm not from around here. I came from out of state last week. I have no insurance. I make too much money for Medicaid. But I can't afford blood pressure medications. So I came to Los Angeles for help. I need help. I thought I needed to make you feel I was really sick, or you'd turn me away."

He began to cry. So did I.

Wow. Talk about a kick in the gut. How do you process something like that? Here was a man who had worked hard his whole life, doing unglamorous jobs, working where and when he could to make a living. And he lived in the wealthiest nation in the world, with no insurance. And he couldn't afford his medications. And he was told he was at the end and nothing more could be done.

No one had been there to help him figure out how to get care all along to prevent his heart failure from getting this bad in the first place. So he had picked up and moved to another city, and thought he had to exaggerate how sick he was at the current moment so that doctors at the public hospital would take pity on him and find some way to care for him.

And hardest of all? Our county hospital is only supposed to

provide emergency care for patients who live outside our county. We're not supposed to provide long-term care to "out of county" patients. What were we going to do with Mr. A?

⚕ ⚕ ⚕ ⚕ ⚕

Now, meet Mr. B. He was a big, ruddy, gray-haired, bear of a man. When I met him, he had a severe breathing condition caused by both heart and lung disease, and he couldn't easily walk due to injuries to his limbs. And his disheveled appearance bespoke his current living situation—he was homeless.

Mr. B had also recently moved to LA from out of town. He now lived on a street corner in a tent with his wife. On his street corner, in his tent, he had gradually become more and more wheezy, and more and more short of breath. One day, he began gasping for breath and turning blue, and his wife called 911. The ambulance came to his street corner, picked him up, and rushed him to one of the busiest emergency departments in the US for care: LAC+USC Medical Center.

The emergency physicians stabilized Mr. B. They put him on oxygen by face mask and gave him medications for chronic obstructive pulmonary disease (COPD) and heart failure to allow him to breathe better. Then they admitted him to my internal medicine team.

I met Mr. B upstairs in his hospital room. When I walked into the room, the first thing I saw was him breathing very heavily, sitting bolt upright in bed. In fact, he was "tripoding." This is a classic position for people who can't breathe, where they sit forward and brace their arms against their legs to try to decrease the pressure on their chest wall as they inhale. The second thing

I saw was the severe swelling in his legs. The third thing I saw was the military tattoo on his arm.

"Good morning, doc!" he wheezed at me from beneath his oxygen mask with a big smile. "Are you…here to fix me? Cuz I ain't…easy to fix!"

I laughed and introduced myself. "Yes sir, I am going to do my best."

He lifted the oxygen mask off his face. He spoke haltingly, as he could only get a few words out at a time before stopping to breathe. "Well…I need some medicine…to help me pee…all this water out. And I need…some breathing treatments…for the COPD. Right?"

"Sounds like you know what's going on," I said to him. "You've been through this before, eh?"

"Long time…" he wheezed at me. "Years…I been dealing with illness…and injury since…I was blown up. In Desert Storm."

"You were in Desert Storm?" I asked.

"Yes sir…I was. And I was…brought back from the dead…by the medics. I've had more…surgeries than I can count. Probably two dozen. I got heart failure…I got damage…to internal organs…I've got spinal damage…leg injuries…I've got chronic pain…from the injuries…and COPD."

"He's a tough one," his wife piped in. She was sitting at the bedside, tending to him. "He's a fighter."

"And my wife…here…puts up with it…for some reason…"

"I do," she replied. "For some reason. But don't let him push you around," she advised me. "He's really just a big teddy bear underneath all that gruff."

I looked down at his arm tattoo again. "You were a Marine?" I asked.

He gave me a look like I had insulted his mother. With grim determination on his countenance, he pulled that oxygen mask away from his face again and sat bolt upright. "*Were?* Hey...I'm still a Marine. Once a Marine...always a Marine." He put his mask back on and took a breath.

"Semper Fi," I said.

"Oorah!" he wheezed through his mask and then lay back down on the bed, appearing satisfied. His wife and I exchanged a grin. Mr. B was quite a character, and impossible not to like.

I examined Mr. B and found that, as with Mr. A, he had advanced heart failure. Fluid had extensively built up in his lungs and the soft tissues of his body behind his failing heart. He had high blood pressure. He also had had a major cardiac injury when he was blown up in combat years earlier. He had never fully recovered from it. And he had smoked, a habit picked up in the military. He had quit a few years back, but the damage to his lungs was done.

His chest X-ray showed that Mr. B had likely acquired pneumonia, which triggered an acute exacerbation of both his heart failure and his chronic obstructive pulmonary disease. He was living on the street, in unsanitary conditions, his immune system was already stressed from his underlying illness, and he wasn't exactly getting the best nutrition in his tent. Something had to give, and that thing was an infection in his lungs—pneumonia. The infection put a strain on Mr. B's heart and lungs, causing both to acutely fail.

Mr. B was not in good shape. He needed serious long-term care. Yes, we could help Mr. B with his heart condition and his breathing condition. We could give him antibiotics to treat his pneumonia. We could give him other medications to help him get rid of all the excess water in his body. We could lower his blood pressure, so his heart didn't have to fight so hard to pump blood around his body. We could give him bronchodilators to open his airways and help him breathe. But he needed much more than that.

Could we find him a home to live in? As a vet, he should have been receiving his long-term care in the VA system. But he was new to the LA area, and his homelessness situation and chronic injuries had given him mobility problems. If we couldn't get him some form of housing, how could we get him plugged into the local VA system, figure out how to help him get to his appointments there, and help him navigate how to secure medications?

The outcomes for Mr. A and Mr. B and his wife were not the best. It turned out Mr. A had only been in the LA area for a few days. He had no permanent address. He was officially "out of county." Mr. A would need to obtain a permanent address in Los Angeles for us to be able to continue seeing him, after we stabilized his acute condition.

Only after he had an address could we give him the paperwork he would need to complete to become eligible to be seen by us in our primary care clinics. In the meantime, he could come back to the emergency department for emergency care anytime, but he couldn't be seen in our outpatient clinics for primary care. His alternative? That would be to go back to his actual home and take his chances.

Until his living and financial situations were sorted out, the best we could do was give him a thirty-day supply of medications at discharge and tell him to return if he got worse again. I honestly do not know what happened to Mr. A. I never saw him again. I fear he went back home to make peace with where he was in life, which was not far from the end.

The outcome for Mr. B was a little happier. We were able to find a temporary housing solution for him and his wife, which hopefully would buy them time to get their finances and transportation in order, and then get plugged into the VA for long-term care.

I would estimate that the resident physicians with whom I worked, and the social workers and the care coordinator on our team probably spent 80 percent of their time dealing with the psychosocial and living situations Mr. A and Mr. B had. I think we spent no more than 20 percent of our time dealing with actual, traditional hospital medical care.

I figure that at least twenty hospital employees worked to sort out our patients' financial statuses, determining if we were allowed to see them and if so, for what type of care, and trying to figure out a living situation for them. Imagine the number of person-hours spent on these activities, none of which actually involved delivering hospital-based, traditional healthcare.

Imagine the sheer scope of money spent on staff hours for these matters. The US healthcare system requires us to do such things before we are allowed to provide medical care.

US healthcare in the twenty-first century is not facile, not efficient, and not at all patient-centered.

Let's talk about the US healthcare system. Do the experiences of Mr. A and Mr. B and countless other patients translate into overall bad performance for our healthcare system?

I often hear people say that the US has the best, most sophisticated healthcare system in the world. I would generally agree that the technology available in the US is second to none. The training and technical expertise of our physicians and nurses are second to none. We spend years in medical school, and then postgraduate training in residency programs, and then subspecializing in fellowship programs. We have a constant, lifelong need to maintain our skills with continuing medical education, and continually need to take more medical board exams to keep our certification current.

I work every day with some of the most amazing people I could ever imagine meeting. They are my heroes. I would trust my life to them as to few others. So there is no doubt in my mind that our physicians and nurses in the US are world-class.

Yes, we can treat heart failure and COPD and many diseases when patients present to the hospital with emergencies. Yet, there is more to keeping people healthy than having brilliant doctors and nurses who can treat patients' severe diseases once they are bad enough to result in hospitalization.

People need to be able to get to a physician to receive healthcare in the first place. It does little good to have highly trained, extremely skilled physicians if patients can't afford to go see them.

People need to be able to afford the treatments offered to them so they can take medications regularly. It does no good for us to prescribe the right medications for patients only to have them not fill the prescription because they can't afford it, or their insurance plan won't cover it or will only cover part of the costs. We run into this problem all the time. It is a constant source of frustration for our patients and our staff.

The fragmentation of the US healthcare system is difficult to describe in words. You almost have to experience it to understand, viscerally, how disruptive it is to our ability to care for patients. And how baffling and infuriating it is for sick patients and their families, and providers alike.

Not only does our healthcare system not provide a smooth and coordinated process to enable care for sick patients, it does little to keep people from getting sick in the first place. People need to participate in their healthcare in a coordinated way, which helps encourage them to live a healthy lifestyle to keep from getting sick. Our healthcare system does not do an effective job of promoting such healthy living, instead waiting until patients get sick enough to where they can no longer avoid having to come see us, expense or no. In fact, as we will see, our healthcare system almost prefers it when patients get sick. Because that's how entities that provide healthcare get paid.

So, what do the numbers say about how we do in the US? Do we have the best healthcare outcomes in the world? Or, as suggested by the anecdotal evidence of Mr. A's and Mr. B's stories—and the stories shared among my colleagues of many other patients like them—is there objective evidence that our healthcare system is suboptimal? Is there evidence that, despite all of our technical expertise, training, and advanced technologies, Americans' healthcare outcomes suffer due to poor access, lack of continuity, and lack of preventative care?

Indeed there is such objective evidence. In fact, the evidence is overwhelming and not really disputed.

There are many ways one can evaluate how effective a healthcare system is. And there are professionals who do this for a living. One of the most sophisticated groups is the Commonwealth Fund.[1]

The Commonwealth Fund was founded by a US philanthropist, Ms. Anna Harkness, in 1918. This nonpartisan, nonpolitical, independent think tank focuses on studying healthcare systems in the US and abroad, with a goal of working to improve them. Their mission is to "promote a high-performing healthcare system that achieves better access, improved quality, and greater efficiency."[1]

To support this mission, the Commonwealth Fund conducts research on the US and international healthcare systems. They publish their findings in publicly available reports on their website (www.commonwealthfund.org), which I would strongly encourage anyone interested in to review.

In conducting their research, the Commonwealth Fund accesses data from primary sources by interviewing and surveying patients and doctors from around the world. They also access data from other sophisticated sources, such as the World Health Organization (WHO), and the Organisation for Economic Co-operation and Development (OECD).[2]

The OECD is a member organization of countries that pool their data resources together to enable global comparisons. Theirs is another of those websites that if you are a healthcare data junkie, you can't live without. They accumulate primary data on the economies and healthcare systems from across their thirty-six member countries, which span the globe. A staggering array of data from those countries is available for download from their website (www.oecd.org/health), including data relevant to many of the Commonwealth Fund rankings that we will discuss.

One of the publicly released reports that the Commonwealth Fund regularly updates is a ranking of healthcare systems among wealthy nations, again based in part on OECD data.[3] These healthcare rankings are widely cited and highly respected.

According to the Commonwealth Fund, where does the US healthcare system rank compared to those of ten other wealthy nations (US, Canada, the United Kingdom, the Netherlands, Norway, Sweden, Switzerland, Germany, France, Australia, New Zealand)? Eleventh. Dead last (Figure 1-1).

Those overall rankings are based on an aggregate assessment of several individual parameters, which themselves are also individually ranked. These individual components include: Care Processes, Access to Care, Administrative Efficiency, Equity, and Healthcare Outcomes. The Commonwealth Fund report, "Mirror, Mirror 2017," gives detailed descriptions of how these measures are defined (and see Figure 1-1 legend for brief descriptions).[3]

Now, some people may try to argue that actual healthcare outcomes are what they care about, and the other individual components are just not as important to them. They may say, "Who cares what the overall rankings are, if those are based in part on things like equity of care, access to care, or efficiency of care? All I care about is living and dying." Such folks may try to argue that while the US does poorly on efficiency and equal access, because our doctors are so highly trained and our technology is so sophisticated, surely we must lead the world in actual health outcomes.

Countries	UK	Aus	Net	NZ	Nor	Swe	Swi	Ger	Can	Fra	US
Overall Rank	1	2	3	4	5	6	7	8	9	10	11
Care Processes	1	2	4	3	10	11	7	8	6	9	5
Access	3	4	1	7	5	6	8	2	10	9	11
Admin. Efficiency	3	1	9	2	4	5	8	6	6	11	10
Equity	1	7	2	8	5	3	4	6	9	10	11
Outcomes	10	1	6	7	3	2	4	6	9	5	11

Figure 1-1. Commonwealth Fund rankings of healthcare system performance among eleven wealthy, peer nations. UK = United Kingdom, Aus = Australia, Net = the Netherlands, NZ = New Zealand, Nor = Norway, Swe = Sweden, Swi = Switzerland, Ger = Germany, Can = Canada, Fra = France, US = United States. The Overall Rank is shown first, followed by the individual subcategories. Care Processes includes preventative care measures (such as using mammography to screen for breast cancer and influenza vaccination to prevent infection); avoiding preventable admissions for chronic diseases such as diabetes, asthma, and heart failure; medical and laboratory error rates; and care coordination. Access to Care reflects data on how expensive care was, how frequent and how big gaps in coverage by insurance were, and how long it took to get an appointment to see a physician or obtain elective surgeries. Administrative Efficiency (Admin.) reflects wasted time, effort, and cost spent dealing with medical records, awaiting test results, dealing with paperwork, and resolving disputes. Equity reflects whether similar care was provided for people across higher and lower-income levels. Healthcare Outcomes are based on "mortality amenable to healthcare," which means death from specific diseases that are typically treatable with proper, effective care, as well as infant mortality and life expectancy after age sixty years. Data are adapted and reproduced with permission from the Commonwealth Fund at www.commonwealthfund.org/chart/2017/health-care-system-performance-rankings.[3]

Nope. The US ranks eleventh out of eleven in actual Healthcare Outcomes (Figure 1-1). This outcome measure is based on the rate of death from diseases that can be prevented or treated with healthcare. What are such diseases? They include, for example, diabetes, heart attacks, heart failure, acute infections like pneumonia, appendicitis, etc. But they don't include sudden death, for example from getting hit by a bus, which healthcare is unlikely to be able to change.

It is embarrassing how badly the US system ranks. On death, we rank dead last. We also rank dead last overall, in Access to Care, and in the equal care provided to all people irrespective of socioeconomics. We are next to dead last in Administrative Efficiency. The only category we do somewhat better in is Care Processes, which includes patient engagement in prevention and health and wellness—we rank fifth there.

The Commonwealth Fund has been doing these rankings for some years now. So it is possible to look back on how we've changed over a ten-year period compared to our peer nations. Maybe our bottom rankings are a new thing, and for years were better, and then just got worse recently? Perhaps we used to be ranked number one, and just fell over the years?

Nope. Ten years earlier, our Healthcare Outcomes (death amenable to healthcare) were second to last (Figure 1-2). The US fell one notch to dead last (pun intended) in the intervening decade. What's even more depressing is that every other peer nation improved their mortality rates much more effectively than we have. As a result, we have fallen further behind everyone else in the intervening ten-year period. Things are getting worse, faster.

Of all the things to get worse at—and to be the worst at among all your peers—death is not the one to pick. In general, we tend to frown on dying in the healthcare profession. We prefer it when healthcare helps to avoid death. I suspect our customers (that is, you, the patient) also prefer to avoid death.

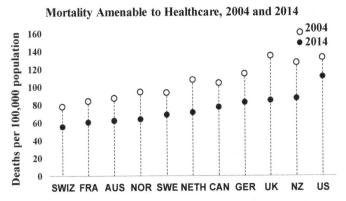

Figure 1-2. Changes in Healthcare Outcomes from among eleven peer nations between 2004 and 2014, as assessed by the Commonwealth Fund. SWIZ = Switzerland, FRA = France, AUS = Australia, NOR = Norway, SWE = Sweden, NETH = the Netherlands, CAN = Canada, GER = Germany, UK = United Kingdom, NZ = New Zealand, US = United States. Outcomes are based on "mortality amenable to healthcare," as described in the text. Data are adapted and reproduced with permission from the Commonwealth Fund at www.commonwealthfund.org/chart/2017/mortality-amenable-health-care-2004-and-2014.[3]

The Commonwealth Fund rankings are objective and highly respected. And there are plenty of other data from other sources to back up their rankings. For example, if you want other evidence, we could just look at average life expectancy, plain and simple. Bloomberg, the business and financial media conglomerate, keeps track of average life expectancy among 195 nations across the globe. In October of 2018, they reported that the US—the wealthiest country in the world—ranked sixty-fourth (!) out of 195 countries in average life expectancy.[4]

Similarly, in 2017, the highly respected medical journal, *Lancet*, published a remarkable study conducted by a consortium of nearly 700 scientific collaborators, who scoured through mortality data from numerous countries as part of the "Global Burden of Diseases, Injuries, and Risk Factors Study."[5] The study was funded by the Gates Foundation. They found that the US was tied for thirty-fifth place out of seventy-five total countries in death rate amenable to healthcare. Thirty-fifth place, people. Ouch.

Who did the US tie with on the rate of death amenable to health-care? Estonia and Montenegro. Yeah. Seriously.

The good news for the US is that it was ranked more highly than Lebanon, which achieved thirty-sixth place. The bad news? Well, the US was outperformed by Croatia and Kuwait, which tied for thirty-fourth place.

Yet another analysis conducted by the OECD found that the US ranked dead last in life expectancy compared to other economically advanced peer nations (Western European nations, Canada, Japan, Australia, and New Zealand), and twenty-sixth out of all thirty-five OECD member countries.[6] It wasn't just wealthy nations that beat the US on life expectancy. Chile and Slovenia had longer life expectancies than the US.

The US also ranked dead last among wealthy, peer nations in infant mortality and in average life span remaining for adults who are already forty years old. This latter finding is important. It means that our shorter-than-average life spans in the US are not merely the result of more babies dying as newborns, with their very short life spans tragically dragging down the overall average. Rather, our shorter-than-average life span in the US also reflects shorter life spans for those who make it into adulthood. We're bad at caring for the very young, and we're bad at caring for those who are older. It's actually not at all clear who we are good at taking care of.

Dr. Don Berwick is one of the most respected healthcare system experts in the world. He has served in numerous high-profile roles, including as CEO of the Institute for Healthcare Innovation, and also for a time as Director of the US Centers for Medicare and Medicaid Services. He has said, "It is, I guess, politically correct, [and] widely believed, that American healthcare is the best in the world. It's not."[7]

Dr. Berwick went on to add, "There's a much more complicated story there…If you need very complex cardiac surgery or very advanced chemotherapy for your cancer or some audacious intervention with organ transplantation, you're pretty lucky to be in America…But most health care isn't that. Most health care is getting people with diabetes through their illness over years or controlling the pain of someone with arthritis or just answering a question for someone who is worried or preventing them from getting into trouble in the first place. And on those scores: chronic disease care, community-based care, primary care, preventive care. No, no, we're nowhere near the best. And it's reflected in our outcomes."

Dr. Berwick made those comments in an interview he gave in 2009. More than a decade later, things have not improved. In fact, they've gotten worse.

What's wrong with this picture? There is this great disconnect. How can it be that the country with the most highly trained medical professionals and the most sophisticated medical technology in the world ranks dead last on Healthcare Outcomes, including rate of death, compared to peer nations? And ranks in the middle on life expectancy compared to 195 nations, none of which are even close to as economically wealthy and well developed as the US? And has been this bad for decades?

The healthcare quality and safety movement in the US can be traced back to a highly influential report published in 1999 by the Institute of Medicine (now the National Academy of Medicine): "To Err Is Human: Building a Safer Health System." That report was followed a few years later by a companion report from the same national expert body, "Crossing the Quality Chasm." The essence of these reports from leading experts in healthcare safety and quality is that merely having highly trained individuals and expensive, sophisticated technology does not result in safe and effective care. Putting excellent experts into a broken system of care leads to inefficiencies, waste, harm to patients, and overall bad care and bad outcomes.

Healthcare is a team sport. Having brilliant physicians and highly trained nurses does not intrinsically make a highly functioning team. It's like a professional sports team with a roster of superstars who are all acting as individuals and share no common playbook or system, and thus cannot get on the same page with one another and keep losing championships.

Indeed, the more sophisticated the technology and expertise is, the higher the stakes are, and the greater is the need for coordination of care. Yet, the US healthcare system wasn't designed with any of this in mind. Indeed, as we will learn in chapter 4, our system wasn't designed at all. It just organically came to be, as a side effect of fighting two world wars.

Having a healthcare system made up of a hodgepodge of myriad insurance companies, government programs, and healthcare providers does not support coordination of care. The chaos is exacerbated by the fact that the hospitals and doctors and other healthcare professionals are all using different electronic medical records, which don't talk to one another. And each "network" of providers is allowed to take care of different sets of patients and is prevented from taking care of others. None of this affords coordination of care. None of it affords timely care. It all distracts from patient care. It fosters errors to occur. It prevents focus on the things that actually affect patients' health and well-being.

In the US, you have to receive your care "in network." If you go to a hospital that is outside your insurance carrier's network, you will get turned away. Or if it is an emergency, you will get stabilized and then told you must find your way back to an in-network hospital. Even in public, safety-net hospitals, like LAC+USC, we have networks. People think public hospitals can care for whoever shows up at the door, but as the story of Mr. A illustrated, we can't.

I can't tell you how commonly patients come to us, wanting to be seen by us, but find out after they arrive that we can't care for them because we are not "in network" with their insurance. This is nearly a daily event for us. These patients come to us because they believe they will get better care from us. But we have to turn them away and send them back to their in-network hospital as soon as their emergency condition has been treated and stabilized.

But they still keep coming for emergencies whenever they are in real trouble. So we keep providing emergency-only care because that's all we're allowed to do. And we keep sending them back to their in-network provider, which keeps not knowing what we've done for them. And we keep not knowing what they've done. And it's a giant mess of a system, which leaves our patients confused and angry, and our doctors and nurses in the dark and unable to make coordinated care decisions. The result is that our patients keep getting sicker and sicker.

This messy, hodgepodge system leads to uncoordinated care and bad outcomes. We see it again and again. It is incredibly frustrating for our staff. It is even more frustrating for our patients and their families.

☤ ☤ ☤ ☤ ☤

Ms. C was yet another homeless patient I cared for just as I was finishing this book. Ms. C was a diabetic. Over the years, the diabetes had ravaged the blood vessels, bones, and tissues in her feet and legs. She had multiple toes amputated in prior years because of uncontrolled infection. But her diabetes had never been well controlled. So these complications kept happening.

She had come to the emergency department at my hospital several times over the prior year with recurrent, persistent infection in her feet. Each time she was given antibiotics and seen by surgery. But each time, it was rediscovered that Ms. C was not a patient for whom we were allowed to provide longitudinal care. Despite being homeless for well over a year and living on the streets in a tent, Ms. C actually had good insurance. Her insurance required her to receive her care at a private hospital network elsewhere in Los Angeles. Ms. C was "out-of-network" for us. So each time she came to LAC+USC Medical Center, we could only provide emergency care to stabilize her. And each time, Ms. C was treated, stabilized, and then discharged with antibiotics and instructions to return to her primary care physician in her primary hospital network.

But then weeks or months later, her infections would recur. So she kept coming to us either because ambulances took her to our emergency department, or because her tent was physically closer to our hospital than her private hospital, making it more feasible for her to reach us. On her most recent admission to my team, we relearned all of this information. Fed up with this cycling of readmissions, we actually tried to transfer Ms. C directly as an inpatient to her assigned, in-network hospital. Our care coordinators and utilization review managers spent many hours submitting forms and documents and getting on the phone, trying to dialogue with the other hospital. But, in the end, they would not take Ms. C as an inpatient transfer. They instructed us to once again finish the care for the inpatient stay and then refer the patient back to her in-network doctor as an outpatient.

Why would they refuse the transfer? Maybe the receiving hospital was full and had no beds at the moment. Or maybe they realized that it would be very difficult to find a place for Ms. C to go so she could be stably housed, and they wanted us to do that work instead of them having to do it.

When patients are no longer sick enough to require an acute inpatient bed, the insurance payer will not cover the additional costs of hospitalization. So there is tremendous time and cost pressure to move patients out of inpatient beds as soon as they are no longer in immediate need of them. That pressure does not allow the hospital the days to weeks it can take to find even temporary housing. Those days to weeks typically are not paid for by insurance payers. Could this be why the receiving hospital would not accept her transfer? Better that the public hospital and taxpayers eat the costs of the prolonged hospitalization to help Ms. C find housing?

We took care of Ms. C the best we could. We gave her local wound care. We gave her antibiotics. And, we chose to keep her in the hospital until we could find temporary housing for her. It wasn't a permanent solution—she would only be able to stay for a few weeks in the housing. But it would give her, for the first time, a place of her own, where she could recuperate, have medications that wouldn't be stolen or go bad due to lack of refrigeration, and get transported to and from her private medical care. It was by no means an ideal solution. But we hoped it would be a start for her to have a shot at finding permanent housing and stable medical care.

Ms. C's situation highlights the desperate straits Americans can find themselves in, trapped in a broken, hodgepodge, multi-payer system that completely lacks coordination or continuity. And a system that prioritizes profit, so payers act to limit their exposure to costs of patients with extensive medical and psychosocial care needs, and hospital networks try to shift those costs to the public system.

⚕ ⚕ ⚕ ⚕ ⚕

And as bad as the situation was for Ms. C, all of the above presumes that a patient has some form of insurance and a healthcare provider who is willing to see them. A more basic problem, rampant in the US, is the lack of access to care in the first place. Patients like Mr. A have no employer-sponsored health insurance, and/or make too much money as independent contractors or working for small businesses to qualify for federal subsidies for public insurance. Patients like Mr. B and Ms. C have insurance coverage and a network of providers they can go to but are homeless, have difficulty transporting themselves, and are in such unstable living conditions that they move around and aren't sure where they are supposed to go next.

When uninsured patients who live in Los Angeles County need care, they tend to come to us at LAC+USC Medical Center, or one of our sister county hospitals. We are the safety net for the largest county in the country. The cost of their care is paid for by the taxpayers primarily because, as we will discuss further below, only the ultrarich could afford to pay a hospital bill without insurance.

Let me reiterate this point because it is important, and it foreshadows recurrent discussions throughout this book. If you think that you, as a taxpayer, are not already paying for healthcare for uninsured patients, you're wrong. Hospitals are not legally allowed to refuse to give care to patients with emergencies, irrespective of their ability to pay. We care for them, the cost is enormous, and if patients have no insurance, the taxpayers foot the bill. So, the question is, why not put these patients on public health insurance to keep them healthy in the first place, so they won't progress to develop emergencies, and the tax bill will be lower?

Los Angeles County does do this with support from the state of California. Uninsured patients who reside within LA County (sadly Mr. A did not have a permanent address in LA) can get access to our primary care clinics for routine and preventative care to try to keep them from getting sick in the first place. But in many states and counties in the US, no such program exists—the place Mr. A came from did not, and look how that ended up working out.

Perhaps more surprising is that many patients who have some form of insurance still can't afford their healthcare because insurance typically has gaps in coverage, such as deductibles and co-pays. We will discuss these financial gaps in health insurance extensively in chapters 2 and 3. For now, the key point is, just having insurance doesn't mean that you will be able to afford to receive the medication, physical therapy and rehabilitation, emergency room visit, or inpatient or other care you need. You may think you are fully covered by the health insurance policy you pay monthly premiums for, but most policies have sizable coverage gaps that can leave you vulnerable to very expensive medical bills.

As we will see, these problems are largely nonexistent in other wealthy, industrialized nations that have universal healthcare in one form or another. In those countries, your costs would either be fully covered or covered with only small co-pays.

⚕ ⚕ ⚕ ⚕ ⚕

If you can't get in to see a doctor, or you can't afford to take your medications, or you are homeless and have no transportation, you don't get to see a doctor until you have an emergency. Similarly, if you have other factors that preclude regularly accessing the healthcare system (e.g., mental illness, substance abuse problems, violence, or trauma from which you are hiding), we will only be seeing you in an emergency. As a result, we miss all of the possible times and ways to intervene earlier, to preclude an illness or disease from progressing to the point of becoming an emergency. All of the opportunity to promote health and wellness is lost.

It is a sad fact that in 2017, the US ranked thirty-fifth out of the thirty-six countries reporting data to the OECD on what proportion of their population has health insurance[8,9]—this is even after implementing the Affordable Care Act, which increased health insurance coverage by about 18 million people in the US (in other words, we used to be much worse!).[10] The Affordable Care Act absolutely did decrease the uninsured rate in the US, and from that perspective, it did achieve one of its principle aims. But the Affordable Care Act was never intended to achieve universal coverage in the US, and it, of course, did not do so.

Even after insuring those 18 million more Americans via the Affordable Care Act, the US is still ranked thirty-fifth out of thirty-six OECD member nations with respect to its uninsured rate. The first twenty countries on the list cover 100 percent of their population with health insurance. The first twenty-six countries cover at least 99 percent of their population. Countries that may surprise you as providing more health insurance coverage for their residents than the US include Greece (100 percent), the Czech Republic (100 percent), Slovenia (100 percent), Turkey (99.2 percent), Slovakia (94.6 percent), Estonia (94.1 percent) and Chile (94 percent). How does the US do? We cover 91 percent. That leaves nearly 28 million people still uninsured in the US.

So, merely having highly trained medical professionals and sophisticated technology does not a highly functioning healthcare system make. Especially if people can't get to the highly trained medical professionals and their sophisticated technology in the first place.

If we wait to provide care until the moment someone has an emergency, our death rate will not improve. If we continue to confuse people about where they should get their care, our death rate will not improve. If we continue to fail to coordinate care, so one hand doesn't know what the other is doing, our death rate will not improve. All the fancy medical technology in the world and the most highly trained providers are at the mercy of these factors.

⚕ ⚕ ⚕ ⚕ ⚕

What's even worse is that our healthcare system likes it that way. Unlike most healthcare systems in the world (we will discuss international models of healthcare at length in chapter 6), the US remains largely a fee-for-service healthcare system. What that means is that those who provide the care get paid for each episode for which they provide care. The more care they provide, the more they get paid. And the more sophisticated, emergent, and invasive (and hence dangerous) the care, the more they get paid. This fee-for-service system provides a financial incentive to wait until people get really sick and need complex, emergency care before care is given.

Imagine if our fire stations were funded this way. What if we paid firemen per episode, for each fire they responded to? They would have no incentive to prevent fires from happening. In fact, their pay would go up if they actually started setting fires just so they could respond to them. Isn't it more logical to fund fire stations and firemen a prespecified amount, such that they are incentivized to help reduce the number of fires in the first place?

Of course, this is how we fund fire stations in the US, using "global budgeting."[11] Global budgeting provides a total annual budget to a facility using a prespecified cost target, forcing the organization to work to stay within that budget. Funds are allocated up front for the cumulative work to be done, rather than per each episode of work. The incentive then is to work hard in the first place to prevent bad outcomes and reduce the episodes for which interventions will be needed.

We don't pay firemen per fire they respond to because that would be silly. We give them global budgets annually and tell them they must do their job within that budget, which incentivizes them to prevent fires and to keep fires from becoming severe in the first place.

Why on earth would we choose to fund healthcare the other way, based on paying in response to each episode of care, and paying more money for doing more procedures to sicker patients? Why would we want to encourage our healthcare system to let patients get sick enough to require expensive, emergency care rather than trying to keep people healthy in the first place, so they don't need such care?

It turns out that, in contrast to the US, several peer nations do use hospital global budgeting, including Canada, Scotland, and Wales.[11] As we will discuss further in chapter 6, Taiwan also uses global budgeting to keep its costs down, with great effect.[12] Each of these countries has figured out that global budgeting financially aligns the interest of the hospital with the interests of society. The societal interest is to keep people healthy in the first place and to only provide expensive care when it is necessary, rather than as often as possible to rack up charges via fee-for-service encounters.

This approach is not taken virtually anywhere in the US. But perhaps there is hope for the future. The US Centers for Medicare and Medicaid Services worked with the state of Maryland to conduct a demonstration project in which all acute care hospitals in the state were switched to a global budgeting model.[13] The project is pioneering for the US—it would be old news in Canada, Scotland, Wales, and Taiwan, of course. Nevertheless, the result of the demonstration project has been fairly dramatic. An analysis of the program found that switching all forty-six acute care hospitals in the state to a global payment model, away from a fee-for-service model, resulted in a 48 percent reduction in preventable complications, a reduction in hospital readmissions, and a remarkable $429 million in hospital savings.[14] All of this was achieved in two and a half years.

The power of global budgeting is to encourage and incentivize the hospital to keep people healthy and reduce admissions to the hospital. To the contrary, in a fee-for-service model, hospitals make more money when they admit more patients to the hospital. Indeed, in a fascinating report, journalist Tara Golshan interviewed a hospital executive in Maryland who admitted that he used to get very nervous when his emergency room and hospital wards weren't full.[15] Because empty beds meant his hospital was giving up revenue, and that put his operating budget at risk. That means, perversely, he could be perceived to have been subconsciously rooting for more patients to get sick. So they would need to be admitted to his hospital, and his hospital could get paid more.

But global budgeting completely changed his world around. With a fixed global budget, his hospital gets paid whether his beds are full or empty. In fact, he *loses* money when patients come to the hospital because he gets no extra revenue from his global budget, but his costs go up. So now, his motivation is to work to keep people healthy in the first place, so patients don't get sick and don't have to come to the hospital. I mean, come on. Doesn't that sound like how our system should operate?

Ms. Golshan also described a significant limit to the global budgeting program rolled out in Maryland.[13] Specifically, she reported that because only the hospital is globally budgeted, it is possible for costs to be shifted from globally budgeted hospitals to outpatient care centers, which remain fee-for-service providers. These outpatient centers include, for example, same-day surgery centers or outpatient infusion clinics. Moving patients to outpatient centers saves the hospital money by reducing the number of patients they need to care for but doesn't save society (or taxpayers) money overall. It just shifts the costs from a capped, global-budgeted inpatient to an uncapped, fee-for-service outpatient location. In fact, the outpatient centers are happy to get the business sent to them since they remain fee-for-service operations. So the taxpayers are paying for the care either way. If the outpatient centers were also globally budgeted, they would not want to accept such transfers, and they would be equally motivated to keep people healthy in the first place.

Also, since the state doesn't negotiate or govern drug costs, exploding drug costs have been out of control in Maryland, as in all other states, irrespective of global budgeting. These problems reflect flaws in a system in which global budgets are implemented in one piece while leaving other pieces as fee-for-service entities.

The article that Ms. Golshan wrote was part of a series of articles published by *Vox*, titled, "Everybody Covered."[15] This investigative reporting project was funded by a grant from the Commonwealth Fund. We will return to it in chapter 6, as several other very important articles reveal critical international insights into how to improve healthcare systems. We will also discuss the issues of fee-for-service versus population-based or global healthcare payments more in coming chapters.

In the meantime, broader efforts have been made more recently by the US Centers for Medicare and Medicaid Services to shift to a value-based model of care and away from fee-for-service. Yet these value-based models have really been, at best, incremental tweaks. Don Berwick has referred to them as "timid,"[16] and I couldn't agree more.

I actually think timid may be a generous descriptor for the paltry steps taken thus far. Medicare and Medicaid have, at best, dabbled in these efforts and have not in any way truly emphasized them. The bottom line is, Medicare expenditures on fee-for-service medicine continue to increase year over year.[17,18] Private insurance is even worse and remains virtually entirely fee-for-service.

We have not yet fundamentally transformed the financial incentives in the US healthcare system away from a fee-for-service model. At the end of the day, our healthcare system has a deeply ingrained streak of allowing patients to get really sick and needing to come to the emergency room before we provide care. Thus any meaningful redesign of our healthcare system must not only deal with the structure of how we pay for care (e.g., via private or public insurance), it must also fundamentally switch the payment model so that we are incentivized to keep people healthy, rather than being incentivized to let them get sick.

To many of us, there are moral problems with the existing fee-for-service model, of course. It seems immoral to allow people to wait until they have an emergency before we offer them care. This causes terrible suffering for the patient and for their family. It causes tremendous psychological strain. It causes lost productivity for society.

If you are not swayed by the moral argument and think more

in terms of capitalism and finance, you should still be aligned with the thinking that this is a bad idea. Because there are also huge economic problems with this fee-for-service model. As Benjamin Franklin famously said, "An ounce of prevention is worth a pound of cure." Healthy people are inexpensive to care for. Sick patients are very expensive. It makes no sense, financially, to tell people we won't provide cheap preventative care and will choose to instead provide much more expensive emergency care.

You may be a fiscal hawk (I certainly like to think I am!). You may think, "I don't want my tax dollars spent on getting everyone healthcare, I want lower taxes!" But if you think that it is too expensive to give people preventative care up front, you are actually favoring a system that will ultimately cost you more money in taxes in the long run over a system that would have lowered your costs.

You may also believe, "Look, why should I have to pay for preventative care for people who have brought their poor health upon themselves? I am responsible for myself. Why do I have to pay for care for people who eat unhealthy foods, or don't exercise, or smoke, or drink, or use drugs?"

But we then come to a critical dilemma. What should the physician and nurse do in the emergency room when the uninsured patient comes to the hospital dying of an emergency? Or the patient who smokes or drinks, or is obese and doesn't exercise, comes to the emergency room? Should the physician, who has taken the Hippocratic Oath, be expected to turn the patient away to die in the street because they have no insurance? Or because they smoked or drank, or used drugs, or are overweight, and therefore they don't deserve to have their emergency treated?

Physicians and nurses will almost uniformly tell you, I'm sorry, we cannot do that. It is a violation of the most sacred principle of our profession. Aside from these professional responsibilities, most of the public doesn't want people with emergency conditions turned away and left to die in the street either. Indeed there is a law in the US called the Emergency Medical Treatment and Labor Act (EMTALA). EMTALA makes it illegal for hospitals and emergency rooms to turn away anyone who presents to the hospital with an emergency condition, irrespective of their ability to pay or any other factor.

That law exists for a reason, and the public, by and large, supports the concept. People may be comfortable saying that an individual has to pay their own way for nonemergency care. But few argue that people who will die without emergency care should be left to die in the street due to lack of funding or unhealthy living habits.

If you accept that patients with emergencies can't be turned away, you are precluding the argument that you don't want to be responsible for other people's healthcare. You are creating the very paradox that plagues us if you say that patients without emergencies should be turned away based on lack of funding or unhealthy habits, but that patients with emergencies must be treated no matter what. Because withholding care from patients who don't yet have emergencies means they will often progress to an emergency condition. And it will be much more expensive to care for them then. And since you won't let us turn them away then, you will pay the cost for that care.

The cost of care for the uninsured is covered by public taxes, and also by charging higher rates to insurance companies, which then pass those costs on to your and my insurance premiums.

So, ultimately, the costs of healthcare for the uninsured are covered by those who pay taxes and pay for private health insurance.

You choose. Do you want to pay less up front to prevent disease, or pay much more later, when the condition progresses to an emergency?

One final point. Ironically, the one way you might be able to cause individuals to be responsible for their own care is to give them health insurance. Here's a seeming paradox, but completely true. Even as the costs of caring for uninsured patients drive up the price of premiums for people who have insurance, the sick, uninsured patient will not notice. Because they have no insurance, and pay no premiums.

In contrast, if we implemented universal coverage so that individuals did have insurance all along, they would be paying their way in premiums, and whatever other regular costs we build into the system. As our costs went up, so would theirs. In other words, giving people insurance causes them to be financially responsible for their own healthcare. Not giving them insurance makes other people who have insurance responsible for the costs of the uninsured's healthcare. Ironic, isn't it?

Furthermore, it is possible to assign differential rates to people based on their own behavioral choices. It is possible to have an extra premium payment for smoking, or being overweight, in order to account for the extra financial risk the patient is asking society to take on their behalf. That is only possible to do if they have insurance in the first place.

Note here that I am not specifically advocating for charging higher premiums based on unhealthy choices. I am just saying that it is possible to do this. It is possible to have people take financial responsibility for their own health if we ensure that they have healthcare. If we leave people without healthcare, they will get none until they have an emergency, at which point society gets stuck with the bill. So the paradox is, if we want to hold people accountable for their own health, we have to ensure that they have some form of health insurance.

Let me summarize. Refusing to provide access to care for everyone results in bad outcomes. It is immoral. And it is financially stupid. It is the trifecta of bad healthcare.

⚕ ⚕ ⚕ ⚕ ⚕

The bottom line is that if you want to know why the death rate is so high in the US relative to other countries and why the average life span is shorter, you don't have to look far. We have poor access to care in the US, with a higher rate of uninsured people than in all other wealthy nations, and higher than in many poorer nations as well. As we will see in the next couple of chapters, even Americans who have health insurance have much bigger gaps in coverage than people in other countries, leaving them on the hook for healthcare costs they can't afford.

We also have inequitable care in the US, where the lack of access is not evenly distributed across sociodemographic strata. We have highly inefficient care, with bloated administrative costs that are driven by the poor coordination between myriad health plans and confusing healthcare networks. We have uncoordinated care, with patients bouncing around our healthcare networks and providers like in a pinball machine. And we have a financial payer system that rewards most lucratively care that is provided in emergencies by physicians who do intensive procedures and surgeries. And rewards giving more care more often to sick patients rather than preventing problems in the first place.

Indeed, as we will see, in our fee-for-service healthcare system, doctors who do invasive procedures are paid at a much higher rate than physicians who try to prevent disease. Those who work to keep people healthy in the first place, and spend more time thinking, educating, and talking to patients, rather than doing procedures on them, are paid substantially lower salaries.

⚕ ⚕ ⚕ ⚕ ⚕

Dr. Paul Batalden is a famous US expert in healthcare quality. To him is attributed one of the most insightful, pithy quotes I have ever heard about healthcare quality. He said, "Every system is perfectly designed to produce the result it gets."[19]

The point of this quote is that when an outcome is reliably bad from a system of care, it isn't an accident. The system is doing exactly what it was designed to do. If you want to change the outcome, the very system has to be fixed. Don't blame the people who are trapped in the broken system. Don't blame bad luck. Don't blame some special interest group. The blame belongs to the very design of the system itself.

Our healthcare system results in the shortest life expectancy of any peer nation, and lower than many poor nations, because the system is poorly designed. It's very simple, really. Why it is so poorly designed, and how it can be redesigned to result in better outcomes are subjects of coming chapters. But the entire conversation must start with an acceptance of the reality as demonstrated by the data. People in the US die younger than they should because our healthcare system is poorly designed and as a result, functions poorly.

Alternatively, you may posit, perhaps the problem lies in under-resourcing. Maybe other countries invest more resources into their healthcare systems, which is why they have better outcomes. Thus, perhaps if we simply "throw more money at the problem," it will get better.

Let us proceed to chapter 2 to determine if this alternate hypothesis is correct or, rather, if the US healthcare system is indeed a catastrophic rip-off of the American people.

CHAPTER 2

⸾⸾⸾⸾⸾⸾⸾⸾⸾⸾⸾⸾⸾⸾⸾⸾⸾⸾⸾⸾⸾

THE FINANCIAL COST OF US HEALTHCARE

Mr. D was an elderly man who fell and seriously fractured his hip. His family called 911, and the ambulance brought him to LAC+USC Medical Center for care. Our trauma team stabilized him, and he was rushed into major surgery to repair the injury. Unfortunately, the surgery left him immobilized. And he also had other serious, long-term medical problems. So he still needed care.

Now Mr. D had insurance and a series of doctors who had been caring for him at a private hospital closer to his house. That private hospital was not a trauma center, which is why he ended up in our hospital. After our experts stabilized him and repaired the fracture, we attempted to transfer the patient back to his private hospital, so the doctors who had known him for years could resume caring for him.

But, just as with Ms. C in chapter 1, the private hospital would not accept Mr. D for transfer. At first, we could not get a hold of his primary physician. And the hospital said that they could not take him without an accepting physician. So the next day, Mr. D's family helped get us the contact information for all of his physicians. We sent that information along to Mr. D's private hospital.

After another day, they responded, "We can only take him if you get authorization for transfer from his insurance." So, off our team of care coordinators went to get a hold of Mr. D's insurance and get authorization, which eventually they were able to secure. And then the receiving hospital said, "But you've had him for so many days already, he seems stable. There's no reason to transfer him now. Just keep him and place him in a skilled nursing facility, so he can heal."

This didn't seem a very satisfactory answer to us, to Mr. D, or to his loved ones. Mr. D and his family really wanted him to go back to where all the doctors had known him for years. But our hands were tied. We could not transfer him if his hospital, where he had gotten all of his prior care, refused to accept him. So Mr. D's loved ones took matters in their own hands. They hired a private ambulance to transport Mr. D to the private hospital. They figured, we'll check him out of the hospital against medical advice, and just drive him over to the private hospital, which can then admit him. But the ambulance company checked with the private hospital, and the hospital told them that Mr. D did not meet criteria for admission and he would not be admitted. So the ambulance company refused to take him. Back to square one—after another week of futile effort.

Meantime, our social workers were calling skilled nursing facilities day after day. But all of the facilities would not take Mr. D because his insurance had incomplete coverage for nursing home care. He was fully covered for inpatient care in a hospital, but not for a nursing home. Mr. D was quite literally trapped in our hospital.

He needed chronic medical care, but he no longer needed acute care. And we couldn't find anyplace for him to go for that chronic care. His family worked during the day and couldn't be there to take care of him at home. The limited home nursing support his insurance would cover (two to three hours per *week*) made it impossible for him to be safe at home. So day after day, he lay in bed at a large, public hospital that serves as the busiest trauma center for the largest county in the country. Day after day…week after week…

Let's say, ballpark, that it costs about $5,000 per day to care for a patient in one of our regular hospital beds. For half that cost, we could've put Mr. D in the fanciest room at the Ritz Carlton Hotel in LA. And, in contrast to our hospital, at the Ritz Carlton, there aren't patients in a busy emergency department who are acutely ill and need to get into that room. Trapping Mr. D in the hospital was bad for Mr. D. And it was bad for other acutely ill patients who needed to get into the bed Mr. D was occupying in the hospital. Why not cover the much less expensive cost of sending him to a nursing home for recuperation? Or better still, robust nursing care at home, which would be the least expensive option? Wouldn't that make more sense?

In fact, on any given day, between fifty and ninety patients occupy acute care beds in our hospital *because they have nowhere else to go*. They come to us acutely ill or injured. We treat and heal them. At that point they no longer need to be in our hospital. But they can't leave. They are trapped in our hospital, just as Mr. D was. And who eats the cost of that? The taxpayers. What kind of madness is this?

Patients also get trapped in private hospitals. You know who eats the costs of their care? As we discussed in chapter 1, people who pay health insurance premiums. Because when a patient is no longer acutely ill, the hospital is not going to be paid for care from that time forward. So they increase the rates they charge to other patients' insurance companies to make up for the lost revenue. And the insurance companies in turn, increase their rates to their customers (that would be you and me). Does this sound like an efficient, rational healthcare system to you?

We began this book by positing that the US healthcare system is the greatest rip-off of the American people of the last century. We then reviewed numerous lines of objective evidence on US healthcare performance. The evidence unanimously demonstrated that the US healthcare system delivers poor outcomes compared to peer nations. Indeed, US healthcare outcomes are poor compared to many nations that are economically much less well developed. But to qualify as a rip-off, it isn't enough to be getting bad results. We also have to be paying as much money as our peers while getting poor results in return.

So, are we sure we are getting ripped off? The story of Mr. D and the countless patients like him would certainly seem to support the idea that we overspend on healthcare, at least at the individual patient level. The question is, do these myriad and innumerable anecdotal experiences translate to overall excessive healthcare costs in the US?

At the end of the last chapter, we considered another opposing hypothesis. We considered the possibility that we aren't spending enough on healthcare in the US, and as a result, we are getting what we pay for. If this hypothesis is correct, we should find that the US is spending less on healthcare than peer nations do.

So, how much do we spend on healthcare in the US? Is it less than other countries, or more? And, do countries that spend more money have better outcomes?

Before we show the numbers, let's make something clear. Financial data are complicated, and there are many ways to look at costs. Certainly, the total amount of money a country spends on healthcare is important. But comparing the total amount of money spent doesn't account for different population sizes between countries. Intuitively, countries with larger populations will likely tend to spend more money on healthcare than less populous countries. So, just looking at absolute expenditures might not tell the entire story.

If we want to compare across countries with different population sizes, we might also look at their healthcare costs divided by their population sizes. This cost term is known as "cost per capita," or "cost per person." It allows us to determine if countries are spending more or less for each individual resident than their peer nations.

We also might want to account for the relative wealth of various countries. Countries with more wealth tend to have employees with higher incomes. This can make healthcare affordable within the country, even if the care is more expensive compared to other countries. It is also intuitive that wealthier countries might spend more on healthcare because they have access to more sophisticated healthcare technologies and have more money to spend. We, therefore, might want to account for relative economic productivity and wealth of nations when comparing healthcare spending across nations.

Each of these ways of analyzing healthcare spending helps clarify our overall understanding of the issue. Total expenditures are informative to absolute out-of-pocket dollars spent. Adjusting the total expenditures per person allows for apples-to-apples comparisons across countries with vastly different population sizes. And adjusting the total healthcare expenditures for the economic productivity/wealth of the nation allows us to account for the amount of money available to spend on comparable services and technologies in those countries.

So it will give us a more complete picture if we look at all of these analyses, rather than just selecting one to focus on. Another advantage of doing this is it precludes the argument that the numbers have been cherry-picked to disadvantage the US, for example, by hiding information that makes the US healthcare system look good.

Never fear. We are going to look at each of these analyses, and, as we will see, no matter how we slice and dice the data, the US has a problem.

According to the US Centers for Medicare and Medicaid Services, in 2018, the US spent $3.65 trillion on healthcare.[1,2] That staggering sum of money includes public spending by government sources funded via tax dollars, private spending on health insurance, and private spending by individuals on out-of-pocket costs.

Let's just for a moment step back and appreciate the sheer magnitude of that number, $3.65 trillion.

$3,650,000,000,000.

That's a lot of zeroes to spend. In one year. Just in the US. Just for healthcare. Let that sink in.

Let's see what we can compare that number to for scale. The total economic value of all goods and services produced in a country in one year is known as the Gross Domestic Product (GDP). The GDP accounts for *everything* made and *every* service provided in a country. It is economically all-encompassing. It is the most commonly used indicator to compare the economic productivity of nations. It is also an often-used surrogate for the relative cumulative wealth of nations.

And it turns out that the $3.65 trillion that the US spent on healthcare in 2018 is greater than the entire GDP of the United Kingdom, which is about $3 trillion.[3,4] Let me underscore that astonishing fact. In 2018, we spent more on healthcare in the US than the entire value of all goods and services produced in one of the wealthiest nations in the world.

That $3.65 trillion we spent in 2018 was also more than the entire GDP of oil-laden Brazil, which is $3.3 trillion.[3,4] It was more than twice the GDP of Spain and Canada ($1.8 trillion).[3,4] It was very close to the entire GDPs of Russia and Germany.[3,4] In the US, we spend more money on healthcare than the entire value of all goods and services produced by most countries in the world. Mull that over.

In terms of total expenditure, the $3.65 trillion spent in 2018 placed the US far greater than any other country in the world when it came to healthcare costs. When graphed against forty-four other countries for which data are available from OECD, it is embarrassing how much more money the US spent (Figure 2-1).

The closest competitors for total expenditures? China is the most populous country in the world, with a population four times larger than the US.[5] They spent the next most per year on healthcare, not surprisingly, given their enormous population. But their total expenditures on healthcare were slightly under $1 trillion in 2018, almost 75 percent lower than US expenditures.[6] I'll reiterate this point. In 2018, China spent nearly fourfold less to provide healthcare to fourfold more people than the US did. Rounding out the top five, Japan spent close to $600 billion per year, Germany spent $500 billion per year, and France spent $320 billion.[6] Which means the US spent nearly fourfold more than the second-biggest spender, and six-, seven-, eleven-, and thirteenfold more than the third through sixth-highest spenders in the world.

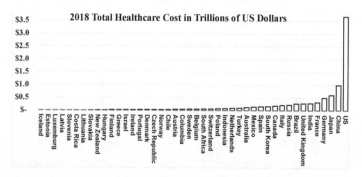

Figure 2-1. Total healthcare costs in 2018 among member nations in the Organisation for Economic Co-operation and Development (OECD). Expenditures for each country are shown after being converted to US dollars. The US spent far more money on healthcare than any nation on Earth, including nearly fourfold more than the country with the next largest expenditure (China), and 2,500 times more than the lowest-cost country (Iceland). Data are from OECD.[6]

Remember our comparison of the performance of healthcare systems of wealthy nations from chapter 1? The United Kingdom was ranked first, Australia second, the Netherlands third, and Norway and New Zealand were tied for fourth/fifth place. To achieve the top rankings, these countries respectively spent 13-, 29-, 39-, 110-, and 195-fold less than the US, the latter of which performed the worst. It's hard to digest this complete dichotomy of terrible performance versus astronomical cost.

So, just by looking at absolute costs, we can disprove the hypothesis that the US performs poorly on healthcare because it underspends and is just "getting what we pay for." Since the US is clearly not starving the healthcare system of resources and is not underspending, we can conclude that "throwing more money at the problem" is likely not a good solution to our healthcare problems. Other countries do much better than the US while spending much less. Clearly, spending more isn't the secret to doing better on healthcare.

By looking at objective outcomes and cost data, we have gained considerable evidence to support the premise that we, the US taxpayers, have been getting ripped off, and catastrophically so. We overspend to the tune of one to two trillion dollars per year compared to other countries. Again, can you think of any other factor of life, any other purported scam or rip-off, for which the US public has ever overspent by one to two trillion dollars annually?

Of the $3.65 trillion the US spent on healthcare in 2018, there was a relatively even mix of public versus private dollars. Specifically, private healthcare spending (for health insurance plus out-of-pocket) in the US in 2018 totaled $1.8 trillion, while public spending totaled $1.85 trillion. So, overall, there was very close to a 50/50 percent split for private vs. public expenditures.

Public spending included federal, state, and local government health insurance, including Medicare and Medicaid, Veterans Affairs (VA) services, and the Children's Health Insurance Program (CHIP), totaling $1.49 trillion.[1,2] Other costs, including medical research, public health costs, Indian Health Services, general assistance programs, and federal maternal/child health programs added another $360 billion in public spending ($1.49 trillion + 0.36 trillion = $1.85 trillion in public healthcare costs).

By comparison, private health insurance expenditures were $1.24 trillion, which did not include $376 billion in out-of-pocket expenses spent by individual people who had gaps in their insurance coverage, or who were uninsured. Thus, adding together private health insurance and out-of-pocket expenditures totaled $1.62 trillion in the US in 2018. The remainder of the private healthcare costs included, among other items, spending by employers for on-site health units for their employees, worker's compensation insurance, and philanthropic costs, collectively totaling $180 billion ($1.62 trillion + $0.18 trillion = $1.8 trillion in private healthcare costs).

If we only include in the calculation the costs of public insurance (Medicare, Medicaid, VA, CHIP), private insurance, and out-of-pocket costs, US total expenditures in 2018 were $3.1 trillion. Of this $3.1 trillion total, $1.62 trillion were private and out-of-pocket expenditures and $1.49 trillion were public expenditures, still close to a 50/50 percent split (with slightly more private than public spending). That is a very important piece of background information, which will repeatedly come up as we evaluate what makes the US healthcare system different from other countries in coming chapters.

The other very important piece of background information relates to the high cost of out-of-pocket spending. As alluded to in chapter 1, the US has unusually large gaps in health insurance coverage relative to other countries. Of the total of $1.62 trillion of private healthcare spending in the US in 2018, 76 percent ($1.24 trillion) was covered by private health insurance. As mentioned above, that leaves 24 percent ($376 billion) of private health costs paid by Americans directly out of pocket, because of gaps in their insurance coverage.

So people with private health insurance in the US had to cover a quarter of their own healthcare costs from their own wallets, despite paying their insurance premiums. That massive amount of out-of-pocket spending is driven by myriad gaps in private health insurance coverage in the US, which, as we will see in coming chapters, is a problem unique to the US among peer nations.

What are these health insurance gaps that leave us vulnerable to medical costs, despite paying our premiums and having active insurance? Let's review this terminology because we're going to talk about these insurance gaps repeatedly throughout the book.

The monthly cost to purchase and maintain a health insurance policy is the so-called insurance premium. Paying the premium entitles the policyholder to have many of their healthcare costs covered by the insurance. Those who actually deliver the healthcare (e.g., physicians, hospitals, etc.) typically bill the insurance company directly, so the patient is not in the middle. However, insurance policies do not cover all healthcare costs. There are gaps built into policies, which vary in type and scope from policy to policy.

In general, in the US, there are three common forms of gaps that exist even when you pay your monthly premiums: deductibles, co-pays, and coinsurance. An insurance deductible is the amount of money you have to spend first before your insurance will cover the remainder of your bill. A co-pay is the amount of money you have to spend at the same time your insurance covers your bill. Coinsurance creates a situation where, even after the deductible is spent and the co-pay is paid, you still owe a fraction of the bill that is left. Coinsurance is essentially the fraction of the healthcare cost you are on the hook for even after you have paid the deductible and co-pay.

The question is, how frequent and how large are these gaps in insurance coverage in the US?

The Kaiser Family Foundation recently surveyed more than 2,000 private and public employers to calculate the average health insurance costs to American families, and delineate the extent of their gaps in coverage.[7] The study found that the average annual health insurance premium for a single member (that is, covering only the worker and no dependents) was $7,188. The average annual premium for family coverage was an astounding $20,576.

That $20,576 average annual health insurance premium reflects an increase of 5 percent from the prior year. Meantime, the study noted that inflation was only 2 percent, and workers' wages only increased on average by 3.4 percent. Which means health insurance premium costs are continuing to rise at more than twice inflation, and at a rate 50 percent higher than workers' income is rising. As one cheeky study member noted, the annual cost of employer health insurance premiums is now more than the cost of a new car, every year, spent for each employee.[8]

The costs of health insurance premiums are borne *both* by employers and by employees. The Kaiser Family Foundation survey found that employers are covering an average of $14,551 per employee for health insurance premiums. This employers' share of their workers' health insurance premiums increased by 50 percent between 2009 and 2019 (from $9,860 in 2009). That is a huge, hidden, internal "tax" on those companies. Workers in other countries rely on national insurance, and so don't impart that large benefit hit to their employers. Imagine having those funds freed up to reinvest in growing businesses.

Even more concerning, the average share that the individual worker paid out of pocket for their premiums was $6,015. That cost reflects a near doubling of the employees' share of cost between 2009 and 2019 (from $3,515 in 2009). Again, imagine having those funds freed up, which would mean higher take-home pay for workers.

Remember, those costs are just for the premium. They don't include all of the many other out-of-pocket costs driven by gaps in coverage in insurance policies. The survey found that the average deductible of these insurance plans for single members was $1,655. That number had doubled between 2009 and 2019. So, insurance plans that cost more than $20,000 per year in premiums still leave uncovered an average annual deductible of $1,655. For those enrolled in Health Maintenance Organization (HMO) insurance, the average deductible was even higher, at

$2,905. The deductibles for catastrophic-only insurance coverage ranged up to a whopping $4,779 per year.

I was also shocked to learn that 66 percent of health plans had coinsurance for in-hospital care. Coinsurance used to be very rare, but as insurance companies have sought to squeeze more profit from their customers, coinsurance has apparently become commonplace. The average coinsurance rate was 20 percent— that means after paying your deductible, you would owe 20 percent of the remaining hospital bill. Given how expensive hospital care is (e.g., $5,000 per day for a regular bed, $15,000 per day in the intensive care unit), coinsurance creates a massive out-of-pocket expense despite being covered by insurance. Good luck paying that. No wonder Americans are going bankrupt.

Another 14 percent of workers had a flat co-pay for inpatient costs. The average co-payment was $326 per hospitalization, on top of the deductible. Still, others had flat "per diem" payments for inpatient care, meaning you pay an out-of-pocket fee for every day you stay in the hospital. The average additional charge was $475 per day in the hospital, on top of the deductible. And 7 percent of patients had to pay combinations of both co-pays and per diem payments for inpatient stays. Are you sufficiently confused yet?

Then there is cost-sharing for outpatient care, for when you go to your doctor's office, for example. Co-pays are more common in the outpatient realm, and two-thirds of covered workers' plans included co-payments for outpatient care. In addition, 25 percent had coinsurance, which means many plans had both co-pays and coinsurance.

Finally, there are variations in coverage for prescription drugs.

These variations are so complex, I dare not try to describe them, lest I risk putting you into a coma. As complex as my brief overview of all of these matters is here, believe it or not, I've greatly simplified. The Kaiser Family Foundation survey report is 238 pages long. So, if you're totally into data, download it and knock yourself out.

We will discuss the impact and trauma to individual people caused by these gaps in health insurance in the next chapter. As we will see, these gaps leave patients very vulnerable to sudden, crushing healthcare costs. In the meantime, my purpose in this chapter has been twofold. First, I sought to give you hard numbers on the extent of the sizable gaps in coverage Americans have—and may not understand—despite paying premiums for their health insurance. And second, I sought to illustrate for you how incredibly complex all of this is.

Is it any wonder that patients have a hard time understanding their health plans? Does that seem like a good thing to you? Is there not merit in simplification?

Another major problem of healthcare costs in the US is the sheer amount of waste we pay for. Of the $3.65 trillion total spent in 2018 on healthcare in the US, how much was waste? I previously mentioned Dr. Don Berwick, who is one of the most respected experts in healthcare systems in the US and the world. In 2012, he and a colleague, Andrew Hackbarth from the economic think tank, the RAND Corporation, published a report in *JAMA*, the *Journal of the American Medical Association*, estimating the amount of waste in the US healthcare system.[9]

Berwick and Hackbarth's analysis estimated that poor execution of care delivery and lack of adoption of known healthcare best practices cost the US an excess of $100 to $150 billion per year in waste. Poor care coordination and fragmented care, which we will come back to in a future chapter, cost another $25 to $50 billion per year. Overtreatment and unnecessary treatment (such as excessive and unnecessary care and surgery, and unnecessarily intensive care at end of life) cost between $150 and $225 billion per year. Administrative waste cost between $100 and $400 billion per year. Overpricing, for example, due to poor price transparency and lack of negotiations to lower pricing, cost $85 to $180 billion per year. And fraud cost between $80 to nearly $300 billion per year.

All told, adding up the midrange of the values from each category, Berwick and Hackbarth estimated the US spent more than $900 billion dollars in 2012 on wasteful, unneeded healthcare costs.[9] Thus waste accounted for one-third of all healthcare dollars. Keep in mind, the $900 billion in waste was in 2012 dollars—just applying the consumer price index inflation guide puts that number in 2018 at over $1 trillion. But healthcare costs in the US have risen at more than double inflation, so the true cost of waste currently is likely considerably above $1 trillion. If one-third of the $3.65 trillion we spent on healthcare in 2018 was waste (as it was in 2012), that means we set fire to more than $1.2 trillion in hard-earned cash in that one year alone.

Name me anything else in our society—anything—that costs the US taxpayer more than a trillion dollars in pure waste. That's a trillion-dollar rip-off in just one year. And it happens every year. That has to be the biggest rip-off to ever hit US taxpayers.

The US suffers from poor healthcare outcomes, and yet spends so much more than everyone else in the world that it is embarrassing. What would you call this, if not a rip-off?

Ah, but the skeptics may say, it isn't fair to look at total cost. As we mentioned, countries have different population sizes, and it is intuitive that it will be more expensive to provide healthcare to more people. The US is one of the more populous countries on the planet. So, let us adjust for these differences by dividing the total cost by the number of people living in the country. As mentioned earlier, this is called "per capita cost" or "cost per person." This would be a fairer way to compare healthcare costs among countries with larger and smaller populations. As I mentioned at the beginning of this chapter, all such adjustments show the same result.

When we compare cost per person, we find that once again, the US is embarrassingly ahead of every other country (Figure 2-2). Interestingly, several major shifts in the data occur when adjusting cost per person. For example, the most populous nations, China and India, move from near the top of cost in Figure 2-1 (total cost) to near the bottom in Figure 2-2 (cost per person).

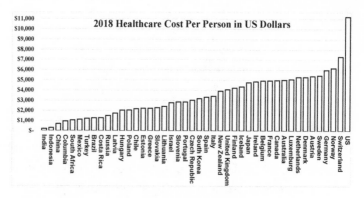

Figure 2-2. Healthcare cost per person in 2018 among nations participating in the OECD. Expenditures for each country are again shown after being converted to US dollars. To calculate cost per person, the total expenditures in each country are divided by the total number of people living in the country. Data are from OECD.[6]

In contrast, the least expensive healthcare system in Figure 2-1, Iceland, moves to the middle of the pack. In fact, virtually all wealthy, Western European nations move up higher on the scale when adjusting for population. Their total costs are lower than China's and India's because they have much smaller populations, but their costs per person are much higher than China's and India's.

But there is one nation that doesn't budge an inch. From our perch in the lead, and by an embarrassing amount, the US dominates the world in healthcare cost, even after adjusting costs for population.

The US spent $11,212 per person on healthcare in 2018.[1,6] That is $4,000 more per person than was spent in the second most expensive nation, Switzerland, and an astounding $8,000 more per person than in the least expensive Western European nation, Portugal.

Rounding out the top five, the nations with the next most

expensive healthcare per person were Switzerland, Norway, Germany, and Sweden. They spent 35 to 50 percent less per person on healthcare than the US. As mentioned, the least expensive Western European nation was Portugal, which spent a remarkable 75 percent less per person on healthcare than the US. At the other end of the scale, Columbia, China, Indonesia, and India spent an astounding 92 to 98 percent less per person on healthcare than the US.

Let's go back to our healthcare system rankings among peer nations from chapter 1. Overall, the UK, Australia, the Netherlands, New Zealand, and Norway were the highest ranked. Respectively, they spent 64 percent, 55 percent, 53 percent, 65 percent, and 45 percent less per person than the US did while roundly beating us in performance rankings. And all Western European countries, including Portugal, had average life expectancies that were substantially higher than the US's.

To underscore this point, let's look at one of the most striking graphs I've ever seen. It plots national healthcare expenditures per person in US dollars on the X-axis (bottom horizontal line) against average life expectancy on the Y-axis (left vertical line) (Figure 2-3).

The data are plotted from 1970 through 2018. Each line plotted represents one country. For the most part, the countries by and large cluster together reasonably closely. All except for one. There is that one strange outlier. It starts off looking the same as other countries through the 1970s, but from 1980 on, it splits off and deviates from the pack in a bad way. On a plot of cost (X-axis) versus life expectancy (Y-axis), you want to be up and to the left. The higher the line goes up, the longer people are living. The further to the left, the less money is being spent to achieve those longer life spans.

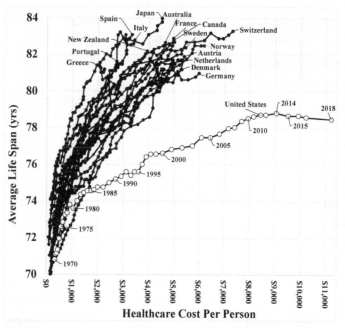

Figure 2-3. Healthcare cost per person in US dollars (X-axis) compared to average life span (Y-axis) in 2018 among OECD nations. Values are graphed for each country for each year between 1970 and 2018. Countries in the upper left of the graph spend less money to achieve longer life spans—that's where you want to be. Countries in the lower right of the graph spend more to live shorter lives. That's where the US is, as a remarkable outlier. Note also that the US experienced a steady decline in average life span from 2014 through 2018, even while increasing per-person healthcare costs by $2,000, or 22 percent. Data are from OECD and the World Population Review.[5,6]

Now, let's go back to that one rogue, straggly line, which diverges so dramatically from all the others, bending down and to the right. Going down and to the right is the worst place to be. A line that bends down and to the right means people are spending more money for the privilege of dying younger. That's what the US does, in dramatic fashion.

And one final, truly striking finding. You'll note that the continual trend for virtually all the lines on the graph is to move steadily up and to the right. The rightward progress of the lines reflects growth in costs, which is expected due to inflation. The upward progress reflects the steady increase in average life span throughout the twentieth and twenty-first centuries achieved in all of these countries.

Except for one. The US's progress to the right outpaced all others—US costs grew faster. But, more importantly, while US costs have been growing, the US is the only country for which progress in living longer lives stopped and persistently reversed. Starting in 2014, the average life span in the US actually has steadily *declined*. US life spans peaked in 2014 at 78.8 years. We've lost almost half a year of average life span since that time. While we were losing that half a year of average life span, our per-person cost for healthcare in the US has *increased!* By a lot! In 2014, the per-person healthcare costs in the US were a tad over $9,000. In 2018, they rose to over $11,000. So, as we are dying younger, we're paying 20 percent more! What a deal! That is to say, what a rip-off. It's hard to imagine a more ringing condemnation of a broken system.

Yet still, the skeptics may want more adjustments and evaluations, perhaps desperately clinging to the hope that if we just use the proper analysis, the US will end up, somehow, someway, looking okay. The US is the wealthiest country on Earth. "Of course we spend more because we have more to spend," the thinking may go. "And we have better technology, and that technology costs money." To account for this, logically, the thing to do is to adjust total spending by dividing it by the GDP of the country. This will allow an apples-to-apples comparison for wealth, as opposed to population.

Fair enough. Let's do it.

It has long been known that the US leads the world in the cost of healthcare as a fraction of its GDP (Figure 2-4).

In 2018, Canada, wealthy Western European and Asian nations, Australia, and New Zealand all spent between 7 to 12 percent of their GDP on healthcare. The US was by far the most expensive, spending 18 percent of its GDP. The next most expensive was Germany, which at 12 percent, was still one-third less expensive than the US. The least expensive healthcare system by this measure in 2018 was Norway, which spent two-thirds less money per GDP than the US.

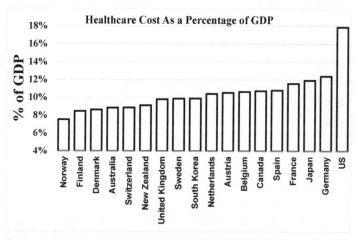

Figure 2-4. Healthcare cost per Gross Domestic Product (GDP) in 2018 for wealthy OECD nations. The US dominates in cost per GDP among wealthy, peer nations. The peer nation with the second most expensive healthcare, Germany, spends one-third less than the US does. The peer nation with the least most expensive healthcare by this measure, Norway, spends nearly two-thirds less than the US does. Data are from OECD.[6]

As I mentioned, those data were from 2018. But the Commonwealth Fund has been tracking cost per GDP for many years. The US has been in the lead since the 1980s (Figure 2-5).[10] And that lead has been growing steadily over time. For example, the last year graphed in Figure 2-5 is 2014. At that time, the US's cost per GDP was 16.6 percent, and the next most expensive country was Switzerland at 11.4 percent. So between 2014 and 2018, the US cost per GDP increased to 18 percent, while Switzerland's fell to under 9 percent. In 2014, the US cost per GDP was 5.2 percent higher than Switzerland's, while in 2018, the US cost per GDP was more than 9 percent higher than Switzerland's.

Clearly the US is much more expensive—as assessed by cost per GDP—than wealthy, peer nations, and has been for many years. And the gap is widening.

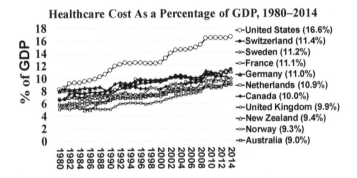

Figure 2-5. Healthcare cost per GDP over time for nations ranked by the Commonwealth Fund. The US has dominated in cost per GDP for over thirty-five years from among the eleven wealthy, peer nations the Commonwealth Fund ranks in healthcare performance. Data are adapted and reproduced with permission from the Commonwealth Fund, https://www.commonwealthfund.org/chart/2017/mortality-amenable-health-care-2004-and-2014.[6,10,11]

But then I got curious. The graphs you see others using to evaluate cost per GDP typically only plot the US compared to economically advanced, peer nations. I wondered what would happen if I compared all OECD nations, including the less wealthy ones. So I added in all the OECD countries and replotted the data, and something interesting happened (Figure 2-6).

Adding in less economically advanced nations still left the US as the most expensive in the world as a fraction of its GDP in 2018. But a dramatic shift did occur. What was it? Well, in Figure 2-6, I've filled in the bars representing the wealthier nations against which the US was compared in Figure 2-4. Notice where they tend to cluster?

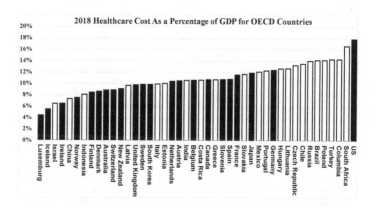

Figure 2-6. Healthcare cost per GDP for OECD nations in 2018, including wealthier and less wealthy nations. Even when compared to all OECD nations, the US continues to dominate in cost. However, the other wealthy, peer nations from Western Europe, Canada, Australia, New Zealand, and Japan are shifted to the left side of the graph—these nations are marked by filling their bars in with black color. They are replaced on the right side of the graph by numerous less economically advantaged countries. In essence, the costs of the US healthcare system, as a fraction of GDP, more closely resemble the costs seen in poorer, less economically developed nations. Data are from OECD.[6]

When we include the poorer nations, like South Africa, Columbia, Turkey, Brazil, Chile, Mexico, Slovakia, etc., we see that they tended to have higher costs as a fraction of their GDP. The US did not behave like its own peer nations. Rather, the US behaved like the poorer nations do, but worse (that is, an even higher fraction of GDP is spent on healthcare in the US).

Clearly, other wealthy nations have figured out something about their healthcare systems that we have not. Despite having wealth, they have figured out how not to bankrupt themselves staying healthy and living longer lives. And they've done it much better than the US. They live longer lives and spend much less doing it, and that is reflected even when we adjust costs per GDP. The US? Well, we've been left in the dust.

Americans are clearly broken, bankrupt, and dying younger. Something is very wrong in our healthcare system. As Shakespeare wrote in *Hamlet*, there is something rotten in the state of Denmark. But it ain't Denmark's healthcare system! As the figures in this chapter show, theirs is among the least expensive and generates longer life spans than the US system. The totality of the evidence is hard to argue with, showing that the US healthcare system is ripping Americans off, costing hugely more than other countries while delivering poorer outcomes.

In chapter 1, we found that objective data from multiple sources demonstrate that the US healthcare system performs poorly across a number of measures, including death amenable to healthcare, and average life span. We wondered, is it possible that our bad outcomes in the US are the result of us just not putting enough resources into healthcare? Or are we getting ripped off in the US?

In chapter 2, we have found that the problem in the US is not a lack of spending money. We are not "getting what we pay for" in the US. To the contrary, the US spends more than every other country in the world on healthcare, and it doesn't matter how the data are sliced and diced. In fact, when compared to economic productivity, the US healthcare system behaves much more like the systems found in poorer, less economically advantaged countries. For the high cost the US spends, we achieve poor outcomes. So, we go back to our initial hypothesis, which has been confirmed. People living in the US are getting a raw deal. They pay much more, and in return, get worse healthcare, and live shorter lives.

Before we ask the questions how did we get to this place and where do we go from here, we need to spend some time really understanding the consequences. In the next chapter, we will look at the crushing financial burden individual people and families face from healthcare costs in the US and the implications for the future of the US as a world economic and military leader.

CHAPTER 3

||||||||||||||||||||||

US HEALTHCARE HURTS

Mr. E is a personal friend. For years we lifted weights together at the same gym. Whenever I or other regulars missed days, he was there on our return to tease us for our laziness. Mr. E was sort of the unofficial mayor of the gym.

He was healthy as a horse and built like a linebacker. He loved being physically active. Every chance he got, he went hiking. He ate healthy food, he didn't drink, and he didn't smoke. He had no vices.

He was also a successful businessman and had health insurance through his employer. He lived in a solid, middle-class neighborhood, had a car, and a house. And he was a single dad, raising a teenage daughter whom he loved very dearly, and who was the pride of his life. Mr. E just had a vibe of positivity about him. He was almost larger than life. He was living the American dream.

And then one day, things changed.

The trouble began at a weekend barbecue. Just as he sat down to eat, Mr. E suddenly felt terrible cramping in his abdomen. He doubled over in pain. He felt woozy and nauseous. All around him his friends were enjoying their barbecue, but he couldn't eat. The pain grew worse. Not long after, he couldn't take it anymore. He apologized and left. He spent the evening in bed in cramping pain.

After a relatively sleepless night, he went to the doctor the next day, who diagnosed him with a probable case of diverticulitis. Diverticulitis is a very common disorder that causes inflammation in the intestines of people who have "diverticulosis." Diverticulosis occurs in at least a third of US adults and is a condition in which people develop out-pouches in the walls of their intestines, called diverticula. Why diverticula develop is not entirely clear, but there is likely a genetic component to it. And it turns out, Mr. E's mother had diverticulosis.

Unfortunately, once the out-pouches develop, sometimes food particles can get clogged in them, trapping bacteria behind them. The bacteria can then begin growing out of control behind the bottleneck, resulting in an infection in the intestinal wall. These infections are what we refer to as "diverticulitis" (literally, inflammation of diverticula). Diverticulitis is quite painful and causes nausea and vomiting. Sometimes it goes away on its own, but sometimes treatment requires taking antibiotics. And sometimes, when it gets really bad, or the infection is resistant to antibiotics taken, the infection can become life-threatening, and major surgery can be required.

The first time Mr. E developed diverticulitis, it responded well to treatment, and he only had to pay the co-pay to see his physician and to obtain a prescription for antibiotics. By the morning after he began his treatment, his symptoms had resolved, with no apparent health consequence. The healthcare system did its job for him.

All was well for a few months. Mr. E had no other medical problems, so he didn't give the diverticulitis a second thought. And then, his world came crashing down.

The pain came back. He was out at the mall doing Christmas shopping and he felt that same, horrible cramping come back. It halted him in his tracks and he staggered to a bench to sit down. *"Uh oh,"* he thought. *"Here we go again."* The wave of intense cramping pain passed after a few minutes, but then quickly returned. Not long after, he couldn't take it anymore, and he asked his daughter to drive him home. There he rode out the night, as the pain kept getting worse and worse. He figured, *"No problem, I'll just get that same antibiotic I took last time and it should be fine."* First thing in the morning, Mr. E went back to his physician and got the same prescription. But this time, the antibiotics did not make the pain go away.

All day he waited for improvement and got none. He kept taking the medications, and the pain kept growing worse. Overnight the pain began to spread to his back. He couldn't get comfortable in any position. He kept taking the medication. He kept getting worse. By midday the following day, the pain became intolerable. He literally couldn't stand up. Now Mr. E is very stoic. He doesn't do a lot of complaining. But in that moment, he was in despair and was starting to get really afraid.

Doubled over on his couch, he picked up the phone and called his daughter and asked her to drive him to the emergency room.

Mr. E had never been hospitalized before. This would be his first trip through the heart of the US healthcare system.

At the emergency room, Mr. E's vital signs were taken. They weren't good. Based on the initial evaluation, the nurses right away took him from the triage area back to the main treatment area. There his treating doctor ordered a CT scan (known colloquially as a CAT scan), which is a fancy set of X-rays that allowed the physicians to see in great detail inside Mr. E's abdomen. The CT scan showed that the inflammation in Mr. E's diverticulitis had eroded entirely through the wall of his intestine. He had developed a hole in his intestine, which was spilling its contents into his abdomen. Mr. E was quite literally leaking stool from his intestine into his abdominal cavity.

"Frankly, I don't know how you are still alive," the doctor told Mr. E. "You need to go to surgery right now."

They rushed Mr. E back to the operating area and began to prep him for surgery. He was facing death, and he was afraid he would never see his daughter again. He thought of his family, and all of the time he could miss with them if he died on the table. As Mr. E got put under anesthesia, his daughter began calling family, who began to gather at the hospital and started their vigil for him.

Mr. E was taken back to the operating room. There, for several hours, his highly trained surgeon cleaned out the mess in his abdomen.

Fortunately, Mr. E survived his trip to the OR. He was moved to the recovery area and then ended up in a hospital bed, on strong medications, and with highly skilled nursing. He was connected to monitors, had tubes coming out of his body, and had a steady stream of IV fluids running into him. He was disoriented and did not understand what had happened.

Imagine his shock when Mr. E woke up enough to begin poking around his abdomen with his hands, and his fingers stumbled over a plastic bag protruding from his skin. "What the heck is that?" he wondered.

It wasn't until the following morning that his surgeon found Mr. E lucid enough to explain. Ultimately, the surgeon said, he had decided that to save Mr. E's life, he had to remove more than six inches of Mr. E's colon. That left Mr. E with a colostomy bag. A colostomy bag is an opening where a disconnected colon empties through the abdominal wall into the outside world. A plastic bag is placed over the opening to catch the stool as it comes pouring out.

The part of Mr. E's colon where the diverticulitis had occurred had been so badly damaged by the infection that it was not salvageable. It had to come out. And that left the surgeon with a dilemma. After he cut out the diseased area, he was left with two parts of the colon, open at each end, missing their center connecting piece. Because those two ends had been next to the infection and were also inflamed, they could not be stitched back together. They would not heal properly together in their inflamed state. Rather, if stitched together, they could scar down and cause a bowel obstruction, or the connection could simply fall apart at the suture line.

The infection had to cool off with treatment before the two ends of the colon could be reconnected. Eventually, after months, Mr. E could go back to have a second surgery to reconnect the intestines and remove the colostomy bag. For now, he was going to have to deal with changing a colostomy bag every day. Mr. E's life had undergone a catastrophic change, completely unexpectedly, in the blink of an eye. And there was nothing he could have done to prevent it.

⚕ ⚕ ⚕ ⚕ ⚕

Mr. E spent several more days in the hospital, recovering. Just as he was getting strong enough to go home, he learned he was not done with his trip through the healthcare system. The bacterium causing his infection had been highly resistant to most antibiotics. And, it had spread from his intestines into his bloodstream. Mr. E was going to need a couple of more weeks of antibiotic treatment. And, unfortunately, there were no oral antibiotics that could be used. The bacterium was resistant to all of them.

The only effective antibiotic option for his infection had to be administered intravenously. Mr. E had a long-term IV catheter placed in his arm that wound all the way up into the great blood vessels in his chest. That long-term catheter would stay in his body for weeks while he kept taking antibiotics at home. A nurse would bring the antibiotic bag to the house every few days. The nurse trained him on how to infuse the drug himself through the long-term IV line.

Slowly, week after week, Mr. E began to recover. He needed physical therapy. He needed home nursing. A month later, he had recovered enough to gingerly come back to the gym. And then after a few more weeks, he returned to work and began to resume his life.

But then after a couple of more months, he went back to the hospital, this time electively, to have his colostomy bag removed, and have his intestines reconnected. And he had to take more time off work to recover from the second surgery.

Fortunately, Mr. E did recover. He survived because he had been in excellent physical shape before his illness. His life began to return to normal, at least physically. But the emotional and psychological toll of his illness remained with him.

And then the financial trouble began.

Remember, Mr. E had no bad habits, was healthy as a horse, exercised regularly, and ate well. His illness hit him completely out of the blue. Yet, as a result of that illness, Mr. E needed intensive and prolonged medical care.

What was the cost of all of this care? It's hard to say exactly. Heck, even Mr. E probably can't say exactly. Healthcare costs are Byzantine and murky. Patients almost never see actual costs in the US. But we can ballpark them. The emergency room care likely ran around $5,000. The CT scan alone probably cost $1,000. Major surgery? That'll run you $20,000 to $30,000 easy. Time spent in OR recovery followed by days in a regular hospital bed? That's like $5,000 per day. All the medications and fluids and IV tubing? That's hundreds more per day. The many laboratory tests that were sent? That's easily $1,000 per day. Home nursing and home antibiotics? Another $5,000 to $10,000. Followed by a second hospitalization for elective surgery. There's another $20,000 to $30,000.

In total, Mr. E was easily looking at $100,000 in medical bills.

Obviously, only an ultra-rich person could possibly pay such bills out of pocket. Fortunately, Mr. E had insurance. It was actually pretty good private insurance, too, provided by his employer.

Mr. E paid his premiums faithfully month after month and year after year. He had done his part. But as we discussed in chapter 2, US health insurance comes with coverage gaps. Mr. E's insurance was no different. While he had good health insurance, he had a standard deductible and a coinsurance term. Factor in these costs and Mr. E was facing a hospital bill well over $10,000 that he had to pay out of pocket, despite having insurance.

What's more, the costs for home care were only partially covered. So Mr. E was not off the hook to pay bills to cover some of these costs, despite having fully functioning insurance. Mr. E also missed work for several months as he recovered from his surgeries, and that caused a substantial decline in his income.

Mr. E had car payments. He had a mortgage. He had personal expenses, some of which were unexpected, unplanned costs that life sometimes causes us to have to bear. And of course, he also had regular living expenses. You know, the normal costs the rest of us all deal with every day. Stack on many thousands of dollars of healthcare bills and reduced pay for several months and Mr. E was in trouble financially. He couldn't make his home payments. His debts began to spiral. A year or two later, this downward spiral ended with him declaring personal bankruptcy. And then, the final insult added to injury? Mr. E lost his home. His other friends and I watched all this happen, standing there helplessly, wondering how this could be.

Mr. E's entire world had been turned upside down by a totally unpredictable ailment. The US healthcare system failed him.

Even when it was being provided to a middle-class, successful American with good health insurance, it continued to punish beyond the physical and emotional. It punished financially, too, in very personal ways. It was like being victimized all over again.

✡ ✡ ✡ ✡ ✡

Mr. E's experience was certainly not unique. In 2019, a survey of people living in the US who filed for personal bankruptcy was published in the *American Journal of Public Health*.[1] The study found that a shocking two-thirds of Americans who had filed for bankruptcy reported that medical expenses were the key trigger for their bankruptcy. That translates to an astonishing 530,000 Americans per year who indicate healthcare costs led to their eventual declaration of bankruptcy. A similar rate was found by the same authors in a study ten years earlier.[2]

The authors of the study also pointed out that in the prior year, 250,000 GoFundMe campaigns were conducted specifically around helping with costs of medical care.[3] They also cited data from the US Consumer Financial Protection Bureau showing that medical bills accounted for more than half of all unpaid bills sent to collections annually.[3] These other findings appear to provide a form of external validity to the frequency with which medical expenditures contribute to substantial financial distress for Americans.

However, other academics have questioned the validity of the survey data, which are based on asking people their feelings about what led to their bankruptcies, rather than on some form of objective financial or other data. These skeptics argue that people may overestimate the impact of medical costs on driving bankruptcies.[4,5]

Either way, the bottom line is that even if people are overestimating the direct impact medical costs have on their downward spiral into bankruptcy, the survey results tell us what is weighing on the minds of Americans. People's perceptions of what led to their bankruptcies are at a minimum reflective of severe psychological stress caused by medical costs. That is not something to brush off due to academic concerns about possible imperfections in data collection or analysis.

Furthermore, two more rigorous academic analyses conducted by some of these same skeptics did find a substantial but lower (perhaps 10-20 percent) proportion of bankruptcies can be directly attributed to healthcare costs.[4,5] Frankly, even 10-20 percent of personal bankruptcies due to medical care is a serious problem. And these academic analyses have flaws of their own, in that they were drawn based primarily on data from hospitalizations. In-hospital costs tend to be covered more robustly by most insurance plans than outpatient costs (e.g., those due to clinic visits or emergency visits that don't result in hospitalizations, and drug costs). Outpatient costs tend to have more frequent gaps in coverage, such as co-pays and lack of coverage for drugs (especially expensive ones). Outpatient visits are also much more frequent events than hospitalizations. Thus, the more rigorous analyses may have inadvertently excluded the bulk of the drivers of bankruptcy.

In the more rigorous analysis, people's risk of bankruptcy steadily increased for several years from the time they had a substantial healthcare cost, just as it had for Mr. E. He had unquestionably begun his spiral into eventual bankruptcy due to a combination of lost income and high, unexpected, and uncovered healthcare costs. So even if bankruptcies are not immediately triggered by unexpected medical costs, the healthcare costs deplete whatever savings people may have accumulated. This confluence of decreased income and increased cost can set off a cascade of financial pressure, making people more susceptible to bankruptcies when additional life stressors arise in the future.

At the end of the day, it matters little whether healthcare costs are directly or indirectly responsible for 20 percent or 66 percent of personal bankruptcies—the truth is likely somewhere in between. In the US—but not in any other wealthy, peer nation—such costs certainly contribute to bankruptcies at alarming rates, and trigger huge psychosocial stress and trauma among Americans of all socioeconomic strata.

Interestingly, while implementation of the Affordable Care Act expanded health insurance coverage to 18 million more Americans, it does not appear to have reduced the proportion of bankruptcies attributable to healthcare. After all, the two survey studies showing similar, high rates of bankruptcies triggered by healthcare spanned the pre- and post-Affordable Care Act era (2009 and 2019).[1,2]

If you want to know why, all you need do is look at Mr. E's experience. Lacking insurance is bad—more on this below. But as we've seen, just having insurance in the US doesn't necessarily mean you're out of the woods. Deductibles, co-pays, coinsurance, and other gaps in coverage add up, causing considerable out-of-pocket expenses even for patients with health insurance. And the insurance plans are so complex and varied, people may not understand this when they sign up for their plan. They may think they are fully covered when very few of them actually are. And these gaps in coverage, resulting in out-of-pocket costs, are on top of the cost of the insurance premiums we all pay in the first place to buy and maintain the insurance. Even after we've paid these premium costs to acquire and maintain health insurance up front, we typically still have to pay more to access actual healthcare.

That's when the rubber meets the road. Among people who are employed, up to 75 percent say they live from paycheck to paycheck and have virtually no ability to absorb extra costs without having to give up something basic in return (food, heat, healthcare).[6-8] The majority of Americans (60 percent) say they could not possibly come up with enough money to pay for a sudden, unexpected $1,000 expense. Any hospitalization is almost certain to trigger a cost above that threshold. Indeed, even a visit to an emergency room will. And visits to urgent care or receipt of prescriptions for expensive medications can as well.

And that's for people who have health insurance. What about for people who don't? They could never, possibly, in any way, pay hundreds of thousands of dollars of healthcare costs triggered by major hospitalization, or even the tens of thousands of a brief hospital stay. Who could? What happens to such people? Most hospitals squeeze what they can out of patients and what they can't squeeze they sell to collection agencies, which of course, ruins a person's credit and greatly increases the likelihood of triggering bankruptcy.

But before you go ranting at the evils of hospitals and blaming them for the problem, remember that most hospitals live on operating margins of less than 3 percent. In fact, the median operating margin for nonprofit hospitals in the US in 2018 was a razor-thin 1.7 percent.[9] That means, they are barely squeaking by, unlike, for example, pharmaceutical companies, which routinely run 10-20 percent profit margins.[10] If hospitals don't collect on their bills, they go into debt themselves, and then may have to close. We've had a rash of hospitals closing in the US in the last twenty years due to financial strains.[11] It is the healthcare system that is creating these strains, and we are all trapped in it, patients, doctors, nurses, and hospitals alike.

None of us, save for perhaps the truly ultra wealthy, are immune from the vicissitudes of sudden and unexpected healthcare costs. A study by the Commonwealth Fund found that an astonishing 79 million Americans, accounting for more than 40 percent of Americans who work, were paying off some form of medical bills.[12] Surprisingly this problem spanned multiple strata of income, including those making well above the median income and in the realm of professionals with advanced degrees. Healthcare is devastatingly expensive.

Even more concerning is the truly astounding finding by the study that nearly two-thirds of American adults had foregone some form of medical care because they could not afford it. This included both uninsured people and people who had insurance but whose insurance left gaps in coverage, as discussed above. As you might imagine, choosing not to get care because you can't afford it is likely to cause health problems that will become much more severe, and even life-threatening—and thus much more expensive—over time.

A 2018 study published in the policy journal *Health Affairs* evaluated credit reports of more than 4 million Americans.[13] They found that nearly 20 percent of Americans had been sent to collections over medical bills. One in ten had been sent to collections over bills under $200, and half under $500. That gives you a sense of how closely Americans are living from paycheck to paycheck, and how little buffer they have to absorb unexpected healthcare costs. It also underscores how medical bills lead to crisis for American families with alarming frequency.

⚕ ⚕ ⚕ ⚕ ⚕

As alluded to above, aside from gaps in coverage, another problem that plagues Americans is the complexity of our health plans. People may incur unexpected healthcare costs because of sudden injury or illness, as did Mr. E. But people may also incur unexpected costs because they don't understand the coverage their insurance plan offers.

Indeed, the Kaiser Family Foundation has conducted surveys that have confirmed most Americans are deeply confused about the benefits they get from their health insurance.[14-16] Three-quarters of those surveyed did not understand the gaps in their coverage and admitted to being confused about what benefits they actually had and what was not covered.

It's no wonder Americans are confused by what is covered and what isn't. I'm not only a physician but a healthcare executive in charge of a substantial proportion of the budget of a giant public hospital. And even *I* find it confusing to figure out what is covered and what is not. You might wonder why it is that we can't just come up with a simple master table that shows Americans how much insurance costs in premiums, deductibles, and co-pays. Why can't we just summarize exactly what healthcare services are covered by insurance plans, and which services are completely excluded from coverage?

It's very simple. There are innumerable health plans out there in the US, and every one of them differs on all of these details. Heck, there are numerous health plans offered even by the same insurance company. So, it all varies enormously depending on which health plan you pick.

Adding to the complexity, in California, patients are allowed to change their Medicaid health plans once per month. They often do so because they want to access one specific service at one specific clinic or hospital, which their current plan does not cover. When they make this change, they completely lose the ability to receive all other care outside that new network, including all the care they were receiving before the change. But they often don't understand this consequence when they make the change.

The health plans and benefits are so complex and confusing, patients have a hard time understanding the implications of the changes they make, and what is covered and what is not. We regularly are forced to cancel surgeries for patients who changed their health plan because they wanted to switch so they could see a particular doctor, not realizing the downstream cascade effect that would have. Their changed health plan will no longer cover their surgery with us. This always happens at the beginning of the month, because changes in the health plan go into effect the first business day of the month.

Thus, we see a spike in canceled surgeries and canceled clinic visits for our advanced specialty clinics during the first week of every month. This is accompanied by a spike in angry and confused patients not understanding why they can't have their surgery or specialty care visits with us that were scheduled months ago. They don't understand that this is a side effect of making what they thought was a simple and minor tweak in their health plan. The confused patients take it out on the doctors and clinic staff. That is then followed by a spike in angry doctors calling my staff and me and taking their patients' and their own frustrations out on us in administration, even though we have no control over any of this. I totally understand why they all are furious. It is incredibly frustrating for everyone.

⚕ ⚕ ⚕ ⚕ ⚕

Of course, the only thing worse than being insured is not being insured. Not being insured is more than just annoying or financially risky. It can be fatal.

The fact is, patients who are not insured are much more likely to die from diseases amenable to healthcare intervention. According to one study from 2009, people without insurance had a remarkable 40 percent increased risk of death compared to those with insurance.[17] This was true across all socioeconomic strata, and even when adjusting for ethnicity, income, education, baseline health status, body weight, and habits (exercise, smoking, alcohol intake). After adjusting for all of these other factors using sophisticated statistical methods, being uninsured was a separate, independent risk factor for death.

This same finding has been observed repeatedly in a variety of large-scale studies conducted by many different investigators over many years. In 2017, Drs. Steffie Woolhandler and David Himmelstein systematically reviewed these studies in an article in the *Annals of Internal Medicine* titled, "The Relationship Between Health Insurance and Mortality: Is Lack of Insurance Deadly?"[18] They actually found that there had been a randomized, controlled trial conducted addressing the question of how being uninsured affects personal health, which quite frankly astounded me. But it's true. In 2008, the state of Oregon expanded their Medicaid program, but they knew that far more people were uninsured than they had funds to cover. So they conducted a random lottery and assigned Medicaid to the lottery winners. Nearly 75,000 Oregonians entered into the lottery, hoping to gain health insurance (which is amazing and dismaying in and of itself).

Oregon studied the outcomes of those who won the Medicaid expansion lottery and got insurance versus those who remained uninsured. About half of those who applied won spots. Not surprisingly, the lottery winners who obtained insurance had better control of diabetes and blood pressure during the following year than patients who remained uninsured. As a result, by as early as one year of follow-up, the investigators found that those who had randomly been assigned to receive insurance had approximately a 13 percent decline in the rate of death compared to those randomly assigned not to receive insurance.

It is critical to remember that these patients were random winners in a lottery. So those who won insurance had the same background mixture of illnesses as those who did not. Thus the excess risk of death was due to lack of insurance and not some other confounding factor. A subsequent review of expansion of Medicaid in three other states (New York, Arizona, and Maine) confirmed the observation and found that making insurance available to individuals reduces their risk of death compared to remaining uninsured.[19]

Drs. Woolhandler and Himmelstein also reviewed more than a dozen other studies evaluating the impact of being uninsured on risk of dying.[18] They concluded that the cumulative body of work published over many years and by many different groups of experts uniformly confirmed an excess risk of death in uninsured people compared to those who are insured. Summing the results across these studies, they found a 3 to 30 percent increased risk of death caused by being uninsured compared to people who have health insurance.

When one considers that the US has a higher uninsured rate than all peer nations and higher than many nations who are much less economically productive and less wealthy, this certainly must explain much of the excess mortality in the US.

⚕ ⚕ ⚕ ⚕ ⚕

I have personally been relatively fortunate to not have to use the US healthcare system much thus far in my life. I have had little care needs to date. But I have known many friends who have not been so fortunate. These are people who are professionals and very sophisticated about their own health and healthcare. Yet the experience again and again has been one of confusion and frustration.

Trying to figure out who you are allowed to see and getting referred to the right specialists is challenging enough. Now try to figure out what treatments and services are covered by insurance and which ones are not. Most inpatient care is covered, except for the deductible, which varies dramatically by the individual plan purchased. But inpatient care is only covered at an in-network hospital.

I have a friend whose insurance company tried to bill him more than $10,000 for a two-day inpatient stay at an out-of-network hospital. But he was in the hospital because he got hit by a car, so he was brought there by ambulance. He had no choice in the matter. It took numerous phone calls and an iron will to convince his insurance company to cover the hospital bill. Someone who continued to be ill and was too exhausted to fight or someone who was not so sophisticated at maneuvering through the maze of complexity might have just given up and been sent to collections. Which, of course, would have ruined their credit and risked a downward spiral into bankruptcy.

And if you have a coinsurance term in your policy, you will share in the cost of hospitalization or outpatient care even after spending your deductible. Get hit with a $30,000 hospital bill, and you will end up paying 20 percent of that bill, even after paying your deductible, and even at an in-network hospital. Are you prepared to pay thousands of dollars for an unexpected hospitalization?

And that doesn't even begin to cover care at a nursing facility or nursing home. Coverage benefits for such services tend to be time limited or capped at a certain amount per year. Once you've exceeded the amount of time or total cost covered, the rest of the cost is on you. As illustrated by Mr. E's story, gaps in health insurance coverage often force patients and their families to have to subsidize that care out of pocket beyond the insurance coverage.

As another example, when I was in the final stages of readying this book for publication, I had a patient in the hospital who needed to receive intravenous antibiotics at home. He was elderly and had Medicare, so you might have thought he was covered. But…no. He had Medicare Parts A and B (which pay for inpatient care and nursing home care), but not Parts C and D (which, respectively, close inpatient and outpatient coverage gaps and pay for outpatient drugs). He had chosen not to pay the extra required to purchase the additional coverage provided by Parts C or D. So, he had no coverage for home health nurses or home antibiotics. The cost to give him six weeks of an intravenous antibiotic at home was just about $6,000. Which he would've had to pay out of pocket. So, yeah. He said no dice to that.

Keep in mind that the wholesale cost of the drug he was receiving was $10 per day. So it should've cost $400 to give him forty days of antibiotic. But what with retail markup, and the cost of the nursing time, etc., he was told he would've had to come up with $6,000 out of pocket, which he obviously could not afford to do.

Guess what we had to do for him? We had to place him in a skilled nursing facility, which his Medicare did cover, so he could receive the antibiotics without paying out of pocket. That's our healthcare system at work, folks. It forced us to take a man out of his home and put him in a nursing home surrounded by sick people. And Medicare likely paid well over $15,000 for his nursing home stay, rather than the much less expensive cost of the home antibiotics he needed (wholesale price, $400).

We experience this kind of insanity over and over. Just as another example, I have a brilliant physician colleague who requires infusion of an expensive treatment for a chronic illness. This colleague gets these infusions every few months. After working out if their insurance covered the treatment and how to get it scheduled and administered, they received several treatments without problems. And then, suddenly, out of the blue, they received a bill for many thousands of dollars for one of the treatments. Completely confused, they called the insurance company. And got nowhere. They called again. And got nowhere. It took several weeks and multiple phone calls to get the insurance company to correct their error.

Honestly, as far as my friend could tell, only the personal intervention of their treating physician got the insurance company to change the bill. And it was never clear what triggered the bill to be generated in the first place, or how to keep it from happening again. Now if a very experienced physician has to go through all that to keep from paying a very expensive healthcare bill, what chance do people with no healthcare background have to maneuver through our system?

⚕ ⚕ ⚕ ⚕ ⚕

As we have seen, individual patients with gaps in their healthcare coverage or with no coverage at all are harmed. They are harmed medically, psychologically, and financially. What's more, they are harmed collectively, and in ways that are difficult to understand unless we take a big step back so we can see the big picture.

As discussed in the last chapter, our total healthcare spending in the US in 2018 was $3.65 trillion, of which about half ($1.8 trillion) was spent by private sources (workers, employers, and individual out-of-pocket costs). Public/government funds covered the remaining half of US healthcare costs. That amounted to around $1.85 trillion in 2018. Those public funds came from your and my taxes.

Of the $1.85 trillion, $1.49 trillion were spent directly on healthcare (with the other $360 billion spent on public health programs, biomedical research, etc., as delineated in chapter

2).[20,21] And of the $1.49 trillion spent directly on healthcare, $226.5 billion was spent by state and local governments.[20,21] The remainder, $1.26 trillion, reflects direct federal government expenditures in 2018 on healthcare (Medicare, Medicaid, VA, Children's Health Insurance Program).

What proportion of the overall US federal budget is taken up by that $1.26 trillion directly spent on healthcare? Well, the US government spent $4.11 trillion overall in 2018.[22] That means one-third of all federal dollars were spent on direct healthcare costs in 2018 (Figure 3-1). The fraction of total federal spending on healthcare has massively increased over the last several decades, from less than 5 percent in 1970 to 10 percent in 1980, 12 percent in 1990, 20 percent in 2000, and about 30 percent in 2020 (Figure 3-1). *That's a greater than 600 percent increase in the fraction of the federal budget spent on healthcare in the last half century.*

The US federal government spent about 1.5 percent of GDP per year on public health insurance in the 1970s. These costs have risen to 6 percent of the $21.5 trillion US GDP in 2018 (total healthcare spending was 18 percent of GDP; the 6 percent of GDP just included direct federal spending on healthcare, excluding public health, biomedical research, etc.). Direct federal healthcare spending is projected to nearly double, to 10 percent of GDP within two decades.

The real importance of Figure 3-1 is that it shows not only the growth of federal spending on healthcare, but also the erosion of all other aspects of the federal spending due to the rise in healthcare spending. Note how the defense spending, and the "Other" category, which reflects discretionary, non-military spending, have shrunk as healthcare spending has risen.

What happens to roads and infrastructure, education, science and technology, and the various domestic and foreign departments and agencies when healthcare costs take more and more of the federal budget to cover? What happens to the military and homeland security?

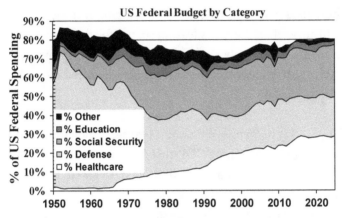

Figure 3-1. US federal budget spending by category over time. This graph shows the proportion of the US federal budget that is spent directly on healthcare (i.e., Medicare, Medicaid, VA), defense, social security and federal pensions, education, and other spending (not including interest on federal debt). As healthcare spending increases, it is eroding into all other spending, limiting what other programs (such as Department of Defense, Homeland Security, education, infrastructure, research, etc.) can be spent on. Data are adapted from the Congressional Budget Office and with permission from www. usgovermentspending.com.[23]

The projected increases in total healthcare spending over time in the US are rather terrifying. The US Centers for Medicare and Medicaid Services has projected that US healthcare expenditures will grow in the coming two decades at an annual rate of 5.5 percent.[24,25] That growth in spending is occurring in an era of historically low interest rates, with under 2 percent annual inflation. Annual wage growth for workers in the US is running at 2.5 to 3.5 percent per year (0.5 to 1.5 percent above inflation).[26] Thus, US healthcare costs are growing at nearly thrice the rate of inflation, and 50 percent above average US workers' wage increases.

By 2027, less than a decade from now, US healthcare expenditures are projected to hit $6 trillion per year.[24,25] That number reflects a doubling over a decade. With costs rising this dramatically, there will not be enough funds to maintain critical elements of US society and security.

These rises in healthcare costs are occurring at the exact time in history when the US is least prepared for them. Figure 3-2 shows US federal debt since 1900. In 2020, we are projected to reach $24 trillion in debt as a nation; we will exceed $30 trillion within a decade.

Figure 3-3 is perhaps even more sobering. It shows US federal debt as a proportion of GDP throughout the history of the country. Federal debt as a fraction of GDP spiked during and in the immediate aftermath of the War for Independence, the Civil War, and World War I, as the federal government spent to arm troops and fight wars. In those cases, the spike in debt peaked at below 40 percent of GDP. Then, in the run-up to and aftermath of the Great Depression, followed by World War II, the US broke new ground in debt spending. Debt spiked to levels that peaked near 100 percent of GDP. But in the aftermath of World War II, the debt was quickly paid down.

Until the current era. Our current debt is rising back to levels not seen since World War II. And it is projected to rise substantially higher than the peak seen during World War II. We simply can't keep spending ourselves into higher levels of debt. Something has to give.

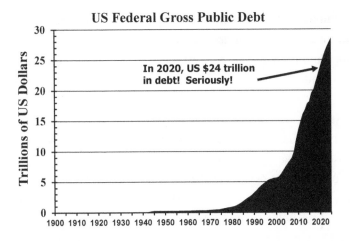

Figure 3-2. US federal debt over time. Total US federal debt, projected through 2020, in trillions of dollars. Adapted from Congressional Budget Office data[23] and with permission from www.usgovermentspending.com.

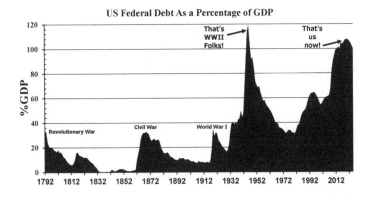

Figure 3-3. US federal debt graphed as a proportion of GDP over time. US federal debt is approaching levels proportionate to GDP not seen since World War II and is projected to exceed World War II levels within the coming decade. Adapted from Congressional Budget Office data[23] and with permission from www.usgovermentspending.com.

Back in 2012, the then chairman of the Joint Chiefs of Staff, Admiral Michael Mullen, said, "A nation with our current levels of unsustainable debt…cannot hope to sustain for very long its superiority from a military perspective, or its influence in world affairs."[27]

His boss, highly respected Defense Secretary Robert Gates, echoed this sentiment. He added, "At some point, financial insolvency at home will turn into strategic insolvency abroad. We are not there yet, but the longer the United States government delays in dealing with the country's long-term fiscal problems will only make dealing with them later more painful and potentially more risky in terms of national security."[27]

These comments were made a decade ago when healthcare spending was substantially lower. And spending is projected to rise further in the future. Our debt is driven by our spending, of which healthcare is the biggest chunk and the one rising at the fastest rate. As healthcare spending continues to rise, it chokes off the ability to spend federal dollars on other critical elements of life in the US, including education, infrastructure, and even national security.

In fact, remarkably, Don Berwick has pointed out that the US annually spends more on healthcare waste (>$1 trillion) than on the entire Department of Defense.[28] The US healthcare system can therefore be seen as a destabilizing influence at the federal level, with respect to the federal budget and to other costs we need to cover. Ultimately, US healthcare costs serve as a destabilizing threat to national security.

Finally, there are costs to American corporate competitiveness of our healthcare system. In countries with universal healthcare funded by a federal or regional system, businesses do not bear the cost of employees' health insurance. In the US, companies do bear such costs.

Corporate employee benefit costs include components other than health insurance, too, such as life and disability insurance. But health insurance is clearly the biggest cost driver of employee benefits. According to an annual survey conducted by the US Department of Labor, average employee benefits account for more than 30 percent of employees' total compensation packages.[26] The largest single chunk of the benefits package is the cost to the employer of the employee's health insurance. On average in the US, that amounts to more than 10 percent of total compensation for an employee. As discussed repeatedly above, that only accounts for the employer's contribution to the employee's health insurance.

The employee also typically has to cover part of those costs via shared premium costs, co-pays, deductibles, coinsurance, etc. Overall, that means employees are giving up more than 10 percent of their wages to cover healthcare costs for themselves, *not* including the taxes that are also taken out of their paychecks to pay for federal, public healthcare programs (e.g., Medicare, Medicaid).

In essence, the way we fund health insurance in the US amounts to a hidden 10 percent tax on businesses and on employees. We don't consider this to be a "tax" because it is not collected by federal or state tax collectors or by the government. Rather it gets paid to private insurance companies. But it is nevertheless a tax on employee income and employer costs.

That 10 percent hit to employer costs puts US businesses at a competitive disadvantage compared to businesses based in countries that do not have to pay for their employees' insurance. This is an example of why legendary investor Warren Buffett declared in 2017 that, "Healthcare has become the tapeworm of the American economy."[29]

In an excellent summary of this problem written in June, 2019, reporter Timothy Denney started with the story of a three-year-old child who had to have an MRI scan.[30] The child's family received a bill for $16,000 for the MRI. Yeah. $16,000. Including the costs of pre-medication to sedate the child and technical fees, the total bill they received was an eye-popping $25,000. How much did their insurance cover? Only $1,547, leaving the family on the hook for $23,795. Yes, seriously. And that's a family *with* health insurance!

Denney went on to cite a Harris poll of corporate Chief Financial Officers (CFOs) from around the country.[31] Ninety percent of the CFOs surveyed said that if their companies' healthcare costs were lower, they would be able to both raise their employees' pay and invest more in growing their businesses. Ninety-three percent of CFOs said that US healthcare costs put their businesses at a disadvantage to international competitors.

Similarly, a 2018 article in the *Harvard Business Review* addressed the corporate competitive disadvantage caused by the US healthcare system.[32] Authors Mark Kramer and John Pontillo pointed out that US companies paid $327 billion in income taxes to the federal government the prior year, but paid $1.1 trillion in healthcare costs. *That means companies paid threefold more in healthcare costs than income taxes!*

Let me reiterate this point. We constantly hear business leaders complaining about corporate taxes being job killers. And we constantly hear conservative, elected officials claiming corporate tax cuts will grow the economy. *But corporate taxes amounted to one-third the cost of employee health insurance costs.*

To pretend that these healthcare costs are not a crippling tax just because the money is paid to insurance companies and healthcare providers rather than to Uncle Sam is to put your head in the ground like an ostrich. The authors went on to make a very pithy, pro-business, and pro-health statement. I don't think I can write it more clearly than they did, so let me just quote them.

"Eliminating this tax by shifting all responsibility to the federal government under a single-payer system would create a massive economic stimulus, providing Democrats with the universal coverage they seek while offering corporate America a far greater stimulus than any proposed Republican tax cut…Transferring all responsibility for health care to the federal government would eliminate their spending on employees' benefits, providing an additional $773 billion a year in immediate bottom-line corporate profits that would be available for new investment."[32]

The authors then emphasized that while the economy has been in continual growth for years since recovering from the Great Recession, employees' take-home pay has not risen as expected.

The authors estimate that shifting healthcare costs to the federal government and off the backs of industry would result in an increase in take-home pay for more than 150 million workers of more than $1,400 per year. The result, they estimate, would be a marked stimulus of economic activity, including higher stock prices.

There are very few win-win-wins in life. But the idea of intervening in our healthcare system such that workers take home more pay, companies increase their capital to reinvest in their businesses and compete better on international markets, and people have better health seems like a win-win-win. We will discuss more about how this could be done, practically speaking, in the penultimate chapter.

The healthcare system in the US doesn't lead to good outcomes for Americans. But Americans pay far more than any other people on the planet for their healthcare. And after paying premiums for healthcare insurance, Americans still get hammered by the out-of-pocket financial cost of it. They also get hit by the psychological trauma of dealing with the maze of approvals needed, and the rules about what is covered and what isn't. When people are really sick, they are having the worst days of their lives, as are their loved ones. Putting this kind of deep psychological trauma on them regarding their insurance coverage is like squeezing lemon juice in a wound. Instead of promoting healing, it exacerbates fear and anxiety.

Adding insult to injury, American businesses are also being harmed by the "parasitic" costs of healthcare for their employees (playing off of Warren Buffett's tapeworm analogy).

The US healthcare system delivers bad service at an outrageous price for its customers. Those customers are you and me. And our families. And our friends. And our businesses. Nor does our healthcare system work well for the people who provide the care Americans need. Rates of healthcare professional burnout continue to rise ever higher in the US, driven by crushing paperwork burden, bewildering and convoluted provider networks, and myriad insurance plans with incessant authorization requirements.

Really, our system isn't working well for anyone. We can do better. We must do better.

I keep saying that we need to design a better, more rational, more effective healthcare system. You may be wondering, well, who the heck designed the one we have now?

In short, the answer is: no one. It was not designed. It simply organically came into being as a by-product of a series of events that had nothing to do with healthcare. That's right. Our massive $3.65 trillion healthcare system in the US is, by and large, an accidental by-product of history. That story follows in chapter 4.

CHAPTER 4

‖‖‖‖‖‖‖‖‖‖‖‖‖‖‖‖‖‖

OOPS! LOOK AMERICA, WE ACCIDENTALLY MADE A HEALTHCARE SYSTEM!

Mr. F had been getting progressively more short of breath for several weeks. Finally, it got to the point where he couldn't take so much as a step without stopping to gasp for air. At that point, his son drove him to our emergency department at LAC+USC Medical Center. Our doctors quickly diagnosed him with a very large pleural effusion. That is a collection of fluid between the lung and the chest wall, which compresses the lung so it cannot oxygenate blood. A CT scan also showed that Mr. F had a number of masses in the lung, consistent with cancer.

The emergency medicine doctors inserted a tube through Mr. F's chest wall, enabling the fluid to drain out so he could breathe. They then admitted him to the hospital. After a brief stay in the Intensive Care Unit (ICU) to stabilize him, he was transferred to my internal medicine team.

As I reviewed Mr. F's chart before going to see him, I noted several strange things. First, Mr. F had been diagnosed with cancer by an outside physician many months earlier. Second, Mr. F had really good private insurance and had no records at our hospital before this visit. I wondered why he had come to our hospital this time. I was guessing that Mr. F was only going to be staying with us temporarily until we could get him back to his own oncologist at his private hospital.

When I went to see Mr. F, he was already feeling better. "Good morning," I said as I walked in and introduced myself to Mr. F and his son. "How're you feeling?"

"I feel much better, Doctor, thank you."

"That's great! That tube taking all the fluid out is what did the trick. You had a lot of fluid in there, around your lung." I pointed down to the device on the floor that was collecting all the fluid as it still slowly drained down the tube from inside his chest. "The good news is that we found no evidence of infection in the fluid. But it does seem likely that this fluid is caused by your cancer. Unfortunately, the cancer is likely progressing."

They both nodded. They had been expecting this news.

"We're starting to think about the next steps for your care," I continued. "You're going to need chemotherapy to try to slow the cancer down. But the private insurance you have is not going to allow us to continue caring for you here. So we need to make arrangements to transfer you back to the hospital you've been getting your care at."

Mr. F exchanged a glance with his son.

"Where were you going before you came to us?" I asked.

His son named a fancy private hospital in the Los Angeles area. "But we don't want to go back. We want to stay here."

"Really? But your insurance isn't contracted with us."

"I know, they told us that when I got admitted," Mr. F said. "But I've had more care here in the last few days than I got for the last six months in my private network. They kept giving us the runaround, with more forms to fill out. I kept getting my treatments denied and then approved and then denied. I've been driving all over the city, and I still haven't gotten any chemotherapy. I'd like to stay here."

"We want to change the insurance," his son said. "Dad gets it through work, but we can change it out."

"Uh, okay," I said, a little surprised. "We can do that if that's what you want. When you are discharged, you can turn in a form to change your insurance. That will mean giving up your private insurance and replacing it with MediCal. Is that what you really want to do?"

"Yes. I don't care what kind of insurance it is. I just want to be at a place where I won't be having to jump through a bunch of authorization hoops. My primary doctor is in one part of the city and I have to drive to a completely different part of the city to get hospital care. And the offices don't talk to each other. And they're always giving me more forms. I just want to be in one place for all my care."

"Well, I can certainly understand that," I replied.

We briefly discussed his plan of care. Then, as I walked out of the room, I thought about how bad things have to be for a patient to insist on giving up posh private insurance through his employer, giving him access to one of the top private hospitals in the city, in favor of public insurance for poor people.

☤ ☤ ☤ ☤ ☤

Mr. F learned the hard way that even high-end, private insurance doesn't necessarily guarantee you a smooth ride in the US healthcare system. We have seen in prior chapters that the US healthcare system is far more expensive, and in return, delivers far worse outcomes than healthcare systems in other countries. The question is, why? As we will see, the answer to this question may not be so simple. Some of it is likely structural, and some of it may just be cultural.

Contrary to what you may think, the US is not the only peer nation that relies on private insurance companies rather than government-sponsored health insurance. As we will see in chapter 6, Germany, France, Switzerland, and the Netherlands rely primarily on health insurance from private entities (companies or cooperative funds) rather than government to achieve universal coverage of their populations. Thus, our reliance on private companies to provide health insurance is not in and of itself unique. The primary differences between those countries and the US are that: 1) the other countries do achieve universal coverage, whereas the US does not; and 2) all of the other countries mandate that all residents participate in the universal health plan.

When the Affordable Care Act was originally passed in the US, there was a so-called "individual mandate" somewhat similar to mandatory participation laws governing healthcare in peer nations. However, in contrast to other countries, the individual mandate was very controversial and incredibly politically charged in the US, and thus not as effective as intended. The individual mandate in the US was challenged in courts repeatedly. While it initially survived a Supreme Court challenge, it was ultimately made moot when Congress legislatively rescinded its tax penalty, effective in 2019. And even after it has been legislatively rescinded, people are still using its presence in the Affordable Care Act to try to invalidate the law as a whole. It is likely heading back to the Supreme Court for yet another ruling. Clearly, the individual mandate has been a lightning rod for relentless partisan controversy in the US.

Apart from the lack of mandatory participation, the other aspect of the US healthcare system that is unique is the sheer amount of private money spent on healthcare. A fascinating study published in *JAMA*, the *Journal of the American Medical Association*, evaluated this issue in 2018.[1] We will come back to this study again later in this chapter. In the meantime, the study compared many different aspects of the US healthcare system to international models. One of the aspects that they specifically evaluated was the percent of healthcare costs (adjusted per GDP) that was spent using public money (i.e., taken from taxes) versus private money (i.e., health insurance company payments to doctors and hospitals, insurance premiums, and out-of-pocket costs).

Surprisingly, many countries spent the same amount of public money (as a fraction of GDP) on healthcare compared to the US. Indeed, the study found that the US was the seventh biggest public spender on healthcare among eleven peer nations. That is rather shocking, isn't it, given how much more we spend in total? The difference was entirely in the amount of private money the US spent compared to those peer nations.

The study found that the US spent twice as much private money (adjusted per GDP) on healthcare as the second-biggest spender, which was Switzerland. The US spent four to five times more—that is 400 to 500 percent more—of private money on healthcare than most peer nations.

As we saw in chapter 2, in the US, there is close to an even mix of public versus private spending. In all other countries, much more public money is spent than private money. That is a primary structural difference between the US and other nations' healthcare systems.

So why is it that the US spends so much more private money on healthcare than other countries do? As we will see, there are likely two categories of reasons for this discrepancy. There are structural reasons. And there are cultural reasons. And both derive from far back in American history.

⚕ ⚕ ⚕ ⚕ ⚕

To understand the origins of the current US healthcare system, we must go back in time to World War I. World War I resulted in the conscription of more than 4 million Americans into military service, accounting for nearly 4 percent of the total population. And they weren't just any random sampling of Americans. They were able-bodied young men who comprised the bulk of the labor force. And this happened at the very time when industry needed to markedly ratchet up manufacturing the weapons and tools with which to fight a war.

This massive conscription of young adults, quite naturally, led to a very tight labor market and a shortage of goods and supplies in society. The shortage of labor, goods, and supplies had a natural tendency to increase prices. It's simple supply and demand, really. As supply falls, prices tend to rise. Indeed, due to this supply-demand concern, strict government controls were put in place on the prices of goods sold in the US to prevent out-of-control inflation from occurring.

But when the war ended, those price controls were lifted, and conscripted Americans rejoined the labor force. Companies began to compete to hire these workers, driving up salaries and wages. And with price controls lifted, companies also began to increase pricing on goods and services.

And so began an upward spiral of employees' salaries and wages along with the prices of goods and services, which led to a huge inflationary spike. US inflation hit 15 percent between 1919 and 1920. That inflation led to economic turmoil, and ultimately to labor strife, including large, national union strikes, which were highly disruptive to the US economy and society. This chaos and disruption left a traumatic imprint on those who lived through it. None of this had anything to do with healthcare. But the national tumult was seared into the memories of those who would lead the US through the next Great War.

Twenty years later, the US geared up to enter World War II. And those in government remembered the effects of post-war inflation after World War I. During the beginnings of World War II, massive conscription again created a huge shortage in the labor market. But this time, the US government was determined to prevent a recurrence of the post-war inflationary spike.

In 1942, President Roosevelt and Congress passed the Stabilization Act to try to head off post-war inflation, and the traumatic consequences thereof.[2-5] President Roosevelt also issued an executive order to reestablish the War Labor Board, which had price-fixed goods and services during World War I, but had been shut down at the end of that war. This time, instead of just fixing the prices of goods and services, the Stabilization Act authorized the president to also fix salaries and wages, which he did through executive order. He then entrusted oversight of this process to the War Labor Board.

Since salaries and wages were frozen by the War Labor Board, companies struggling in a tight labor market to compete for hiring workers could not simply escalate pay to convince employees to work for them instead of their competitors. Companies began to try to find other ways to lure employees, aside from raising salaries and wages.

If it is not clear at this point how any of this relates in any way to our healthcare system, keep reading. We're nearly to the nexus point.

⚕ ⚕ ⚕ ⚕ ⚕

When did modern medicine truly begin? Modern understanding of anatomy dates to the Renaissance. The germ theory of disease was described in the late nineteenth century, as was the beginning of modern understanding of the epidemiology of diseases. Diagnostic tools, such as X-rays and stethoscopes came into general use clinically at the beginning of the twentieth century. But these theories and technologies really only influenced diagnosis and prognostication of illness. None of these things actually enabled doctors to do anything to treat diseases.

The first really meaningful therapeutic interventions were surgical in nature, thanks to anesthetics such as chloroform. Enabled by effective anesthesia, surgeries began to be useful, therapeutic interventions in the middle of the nineteenth century. By the time of the Civil War, many limbs were lost—but we hope lives saved—by the combination of anesthesia and scalpel. Thus, perhaps in the sense that medical care intends to treat people's disease, not just diagnose the disease, we can consider this the beginning of modern medical care.

The historical lack of effective treatments for diseases may explain the relative dearth of health insurance until after surgery came along in the mid-nineteenth century. Without having a meaningful therapeutic armamentarium, there really wasn't much point in having medical care delivered to you. So, before we could treat diseases, why would you have even wanted health insurance?

By contrast, during and after the industrial revolution, as industrial accidents rose, there was increasing demand for ways to replace lost wages from injured workers. Thus, the insurance industry increasingly made available insurance policies focused on injury and illness to replace lost wages from time off work.[2-4,6] These wage-replacement policies were far more meaningful than health insurance policies would have been at the time. Indeed, one study conducted in Chicago found that when workers of that era went off work for injury or illness, their lost wages were four times larger than the cost of the rather ineffective healthcare they received.[5]

When a form of "health insurance" was to first come along in the US, it was the US railroads that brought it into being.[2,3,5,6] The railroads were dangerous places to work, and industrial accidents occurred regularly. The railroads were the dominant businesses in mid- to late-nineteenth-century America, controlling huge economic empires of resources. Losing workers to injury was a common source of strain on these economic behemoths. So the railroad companies began to hire physicians and guarantee "healthcare" for their employees. The funding for paying for this on-site healthcare service was drawn from employees' salaries and wages. These were really the first type of health plans in the US intended to provide healthcare to a population.

But because these employer "health plans" began in an era of medical care where we had no really effective drugs to treat disease, the healthcare covered was mostly surgical and procedural in nature. Thus, the primary focus of the railroad industry's healthcare was to deal with mechanical injury and surgically amenable illness, with a goal of returning employees to work as soon as possible.

One could argue that these plans were intended more for the benefit of the employer than the employee. Indeed there were tensions that arose among company-employed physicians and their patients, as the physicians attempted to push patients back to work. Whose interests were the doctors serving, their patients, or their employers?

But finally, early in the twentieth century, insulin became available, as did purified digoxin to treat heart failure. And then of course, the real revolution began with the availability of antibiotics.[7] Eventually, these employer-sponsored healthcare programs morphed into a more robust form of medical insurance, and this happened in parallel with advances in medical care in the twentieth century.

Health insurance plans began sprouting up organically thereafter.[2,3,5,6] The retail giant Montgomery Ward offered a form of health insurance policy to its employees in 1910. In 1929, a group of teachers in Dallas, Texas formed a group health insurance plan and paid Baylor Hospital a monthly fee to guarantee medical care for any sick members. That same year, the Los Angeles Department of Water and Power set up the first Health Maintenance Organization (HMO) to provide healthcare to its workers.

In 1932, a conglomerate of hospitals and doctors formed Blue Cross of Sacramento to provide a network of healthcare providers and cover the costs of healthcare for workers. Blue Cross plans slowly began to spread to other civic communities. And in 1939, the Kaiser Foundation Medical Plan was set up. It still exists today as Kaiser Permanente, one of the largest and most successful Health Maintenance Organizations in the US. It was set up to provide healthcare for the Kaiser Construction Company, funded by having employees pay premiums for the services by voluntary deduction from their paychecks.

But still, these health insurance offerings remained sporadic, not widespread. All of them were corporate-based or started at the grassroots level by the consortia of individual workers. In aggregate, they covered very few Americans. This then, was the backdrop of the healthcare system leading into World War II, and the 1942 Stabilization Act, which is when things changed.

The Stabilization Act of 1942, which was passed by Congress and signed by President Roosevelt to prevent post-war inflation, had several important impacts. As mentioned, the first thing it did was authorize the president to freeze salaries and wages, which forced companies competing for workers in a tight labor market to find other ways to lure employees. In addition to freezing salaries and wages, the Act also froze bonuses, gifts, and fees, and almost anything that could be considered a direct form of employee compensation.

However, in 1943, the War Labor Board ruled that insurance and pension funds did not count as wages or direct income to employees, and hence were exempt from the law. Suddenly insurance plans, including health insurance, could be ramped up by companies as benefits to compete for workers. Thus, companies began to improve their benefit packages to lure new hires.

The *coup de grace* was then delivered by the IRS, which also ruled that premiums spent on health insurance were tax deductible for the worker. So workers were delighted to be hired by companies that had developed benefit packages enabling the employees to receive both health insurance and a tax deduction. The existing insurance infrastructure in the US rapidly took note of these developments. It aggressively began to create and push health insurance plans that companies could add to their benefits packages in the frenzied competition to hire workers.

Yet another Congressional Act in 1942 further fed the frenzy. The Revenue Act was critical to the US government's efforts to raise money to fight the war. It markedly increased income tax rates, up to 90 percent for top individual earners, and also increased the corporate tax rate to 40 percent while adding a flat 90 percent corporate tax for "excess profits." It further reduced the personal exemption deduction for individual taxpayers. Companies slammed by higher corporate and excess profit taxes quite naturally began to explore and exploit any loopholes they could find to reduce their tax burden.

And they quickly found one. One of the few new tax deductions created by the Revenue Act was a deduction for medical and dental expenses. The combination of the Stabilization Act and the Revenue Act resulted in the ability to shift employment-related costs by moving salary and wages into larger employee benefit packages, the costs of which could then be deducted from both corporate and employee income taxes.

As described above, previously commercial insurers had been more heavily focused on disability, illness, and life insurance to replace wages for those too sick or injured to work. But now, with these changes to the law, they began aggressively marketing health insurance to companies looking to hire workers.

The hiring companies would purchase the insurance to cover all of their employees, funding the costs via payroll deductions. Thus, the insurance was funded via salary and wage contributions from both the employer and workers, both of which then received tax deductions. That is why we continue to this day to fund health insurance for individual people by partial payment from the employer and partial payment from the employee.

Workers covered by these employer-sponsored health insurance mechanisms increased more than eightfold within four years. Within another decade, workers covered by employer-sponsored health insurance had increased by a further tenfold, to 90 million. The US healthcare system had been established.

The change in American business culture was profound and long-lasting. Long after the War Labor Board was disbanded at the end of World War II, employee benefits had come to be viewed as an expected component of employee hiring packages. They became baked into the culture of American business. Such that in 2020, more than 150 million Americans receive health insurance from their employer, funded by a combination of employer and employee contributions to the insurance premium, and employee payments for deductibles, co-pays, and other gaps in coverage. And, as a result, as we have seen, the US spends far more private dollars than any other country in the world to pay for health insurance.

When you step back from it all and look at the big picture, you have to wonder. The healthcare system in the US is an accidental outgrowth of a series of unrelated phenomena from nearly a century ago that had nothing to do with healthcare. It had to do with getting ready to go to war, preventing economic inflation, changes to tax codes, and expected resulting business opportunism. Our healthcare system is an accidental byproduct of history, not a rationally planned enterprise designed to deliver the services we need delivered and at a cost we find acceptable.

So here's the question I think we need to ask. How is it possible that a system that came into being as a result of an accident of history, deriving from policy events related to war preparations and economics could possibly function in an optimal way to deliver the best healthcare possible at the most affordable price?

The structural deficits of the US healthcare system are the result of a series of accidents in history. These design elements cause us to spend hugely more private money on healthcare than any other country on Earth, including multiple countries which rely heavily on private companies to actually provide health insurance.

But these historical, structural deficits are not the only reason why costs in the US are much higher than in other countries. There are cultural issues we must acknowledge, if not confront, in a quest to understand how we could do things better. There are two broad categories of cultural issues that greatly affect our ability to design a rational healthcare system: 1) historical, cultural themes dating back deep in American history, and 2) modern, maximal consumerism.

US CULTURAL CATEGORY #1: HISTORICAL, CULTURAL THEMES

"Don't Tread on Me."

It's one of the most iconic slogans in American history, dating back to the American Revolution. It evokes images of flags with coiled rattlesnakes ready to strike. It evokes a sense of individualism and a dogged determination to resist against "big brother." Culture matters in our discussion of healthcare. It matters a lot.[8]

Guess what? Americans don't like to be told what to do. Especially not by government. Americans are in it for the individual. The entire ethos of the way the US constitution is set up is to guarantee freedoms of the individual, and to preclude groups of people, such as government, from forcing their beliefs on others.[8]

The flipside is another slogan, "United We Stand, Divided We Fall." That one is also from the Revolutionary War period of US history. A related saying is on US currency to this day, admittedly in Latin, *E pluribus unum*.

So we have these two core components, which are in many ways in opposition, deeply interwoven into US culture. There is a constant tension in American history about doing what is best for the collective versus what is best for the individual. For example, states' rights versus federal authority, individual civil liberties versus public health benefits, etc. There are no easy answers in cases where "Don't Tread on Me" comes up against "United We Stand, Divided We Fall."

Healthcare is one area where they come up somewhat frequently.[8] We do find resolution on some of these matters. For example, when someone has a contagious, dangerous disease and refuses to stay away from other people, public health officials can petition a court to place the individual in custody so they can be quarantined—forcibly if necessary—and the public can be kept safe. Very few people would disagree that that is the right thing to do.

Perhaps what makes this example so simple to agree with is that the action is taken one person at a time, and that one person who is quarantined has put everyone else in society at risk. Thus, the scope of the inhibition of civil liberty is small relative to the great harm that individual could cause to the public at large. There is a comforting asymmetry of the scope of imposition of restraints on civil liberties for only one person, weighed against the risk to many in society that one person created. But things become more complicated, and perhaps more difficult to resolve, when everyone is in the same boat, all at equal risk, and all creating similar risk for each other. Unfortunately, that's the situation we find ourselves in when considering how to insure a large population of people. Then "Don't Tread on Me" runs up against "United We Stand, Divided We Fall," and there are no easy answers.

Yet, the financial feasibility of maintaining insurance for a large population of people depends very much on resolving these two integral and opposing components of American culture. For health insurance to work, it must pool together funds from a large number of people, most of whom will remain relatively healthy over a given period of time, but some of whom may become sick or develop injuries during that time. The pooling of funds allows the unlucky few who become sick or injured to have their expensive healthcare costs covered by the collective insurance fund. And most of the money in that fund was furnished by people lucky enough not to have become the sick or injured. That's why insurance works for the population—the United We Stand ideal.

On the flip side, insurance works for the individual customer—the Don't Tread on Me ideal—because the individual can pay a relatively low amount up front as an "insurance" (pun intended) against bad luck illness or injury in the future. When we participate in health insurance, we're basically all rolling the dice and hoping our number isn't called for illness or injury. We pay monthly premiums just in case we become one of the unlucky ones in the future. If we do become one of the unlucky ones, the money from all the lucky ones is pooled together to help pay for our care. But if we didn't participate in the pool, and we became one of the unlucky ones, we would never be able to pay our healthcare bills. We'd have to forgo care and suffer severe health consequences, or accept care and go bankrupt.

This system depends on retaining in the insurance pool many people who are likely to remain healthy and have only a low probability of becoming sick or injured in the future. As long as that is true, the system works great. In this case, the benefit of the individual and the benefit of the collective are aligned;

the Don't Tread on Me and United We Stand creeds both lead to the same desire to join together in an insured pool.

But, if more and more people in the pool become sick or injured, or more and more healthy people drop out of the pool, the benefit of pooling the funds is lost. This can happen, for example, if the cost of insurance premiums rises for the healthy, so they choose not to participate in the pool, and instead just take their chances on their own without insurance. It can also happen if more and more sick patients increasingly flock to one specific pool. In either case, the result is that the entire pool becomes destabilized.

To prevent this destabilization, all of our peer nations enforce means to ensure that everyone participates in their health plans. In single-payer countries, everyone is taxed to fund the public insurance plan. Countries with multi-payer health plans have individual mandates requiring that their residents purchase into the health insurance system. These countries understand that if healthy people choose to drop out of the pool, the fund becomes destabilized, and stops working for everyone. United We Stand is felt in these countries to be more important than Don't Tread on Me.

And that's what brings us back to where we started, with the deeply imbued US culture of, "Don't Tread on Me." We don't have universal health insurance in the US because of the deep, cultural resistance to mandates. That is a major cause of our inferior health system compared to peer nations that have effective and much less expensive universal healthcare systems. Logically, the Affordable Care Act individual mandate shouldn't have been so controversial, because all it said was, if you don't sign up for health insurance, you would have to pay an extra tax, which would then help fund the insurance pool. There's nothing cutting edge or disruptive about this idea; it is used all over the world. It made eminent sense from a logical standpoint.

But society doesn't live on logic alone. Culture must be contended with.[8] The Affordable Care Act individual mandate was controversial because of the deep strain of Don't Tread on Me in the US. It underwent numerous court challenges, with charges that it was unconstitutional. Since it was judged to be a tax rather than a behavioral modification instrument, it survived its initial round of court challenges. But as I mentioned already, the ultimate reflection of this US culture of Don't Tread on Me was that the individual mandate was then rescinded by Congress, effective the beginning of 2019 (which did not prevent yet another lawsuit against it).

Thus far, we have not seen a big exodus of healthy people from the rolls of Medicaid insurance after the revocation of the individual mandate. If that happens, the stability of the system will be in doubt. However, storm clouds appear to be gathering. Because, unfortunately, in 2019, disenrollments from Medicaid increased and the uninsured rate in the US rose for the first time since the Affordable Care Act was implemented. Thus, there are stark warning signs on the horizon. Absent an individual mandate, the Affordable Care Act may become unsustainable, even if the law itself survives the latest of the seemingly endless court challenges to it.

As we consider how to redesign our healthcare system, we have to contend with this tension between the individual and society. Should we force everyone to participate in an insurance pool to stabilize it and make it work for everyone—the United We Stand model? Or should we allow cantankerous individuals who don't want to be forced to do things to not participate, at the risk of destabilizing the insurance pool for everyone else— the Don't Tread on Me model?

There isn't a correct answer here. This is about choices and priorities. It's not like one side is all right and the other is all wrong. Both sides have valid points of view. How we bridge the divide between these viewpoints becomes central to any effort to redesign our system to provide more comprehensive healthcare. We will further discuss this conundrum and potential solutions in the penultimate chapter 8.

⚕ ⚕ ⚕ ⚕ ⚕

US healthcare reform has another historical, cultural theme to contend with, aside from Don't Tread on Me and United We Stand. This third, deeply imbued cultural theme is the profit motive in a capitalistic society. Capitalists find ways to make money. That is what they do. Capitalists are supposed to try to make money, and we must anticipate that for any system we put in place, capitalists will attempt to make money in it. So, if we're going to create and operate a healthcare system, we must expect that for-profit participants in that system are going to do everything they can to figure out how to make the most money they can from participating.

So, if you're a private insurer, how do you maximize the money you make? How about by selectively insuring only healthy patients, and trying to screen out people who are sick or likely to become sick? Insurers make money from healthy patients because they collect their premiums but don't pay out any claims. Insurers lose money on sick people because the claims paid out exceed the premiums collected. So private insurance companies have a potent motive to try to reduce the number of people who are sick or who are likely to become sick or injured from their insurance rolls.

And if private insurance does act in this way to increase their profits, it leaves the rest of society in the lurch. Then someone in society has to figure out how the heck we are going to pay for the care for those sick patients who lost their health insurance. You know what happens, right? You and I end up paying for them with our taxes, as these patients receive emergency care. And we spend much more to do this than if the sick individuals had been retained on the insurance rolls, receiving regular, primary care to prevent the progression of their diseases.

As we will discuss at length in chapter 6, taxpayers and businesses actually underwrite *all* of the costs of healthcare in the US. Insurance companies are merely pass-throughs for the funds. So, if private insurance companies force sick people from their rolls and dump them into the hands of the taxpayers, the taxpayers are both paying for the insurance companies' profits (by paying our insurance premiums), and then further subsidizing those profits by agreeing to take the costs of the sick off of the insurance companies' rolls. It's not dissimilar from farm subsidies. Only instead of being paid to farmers, who grow food and materials we use to live, these taxpayer-funded subsidies take the costs of the sick off of the backs of health insurance companies.

Not to mention the dangerous precedence that is set by dropping sick people from insurance rolls. For the healthy people who are left, what happens if and when they eventually do become sick or injured? Will they too be dropped? More fundamentally, the only reason to have insurance is to be safe in the knowledge that if we do become the unlucky ones who become sick or injured, the insurance will be there to help us pay our bills. What would be the point of paying the premiums month after month for the insurance when we are well if we know that as soon as we become sick, the insurance company will deny our claim and drop us from its rolls.

Countries mandate insurance for all residents *both* to ensure that healthy people will sign up to defray the costs of people who become sick or injured in the future and also to prevent private insurance companies from dropping sick people from their rolls. Again, we must contend with this cultural complexity as we consider options to modifying the US healthcare system in the penultimate chapter.

We must expect that companies participating in health insurance in the US will have a for-profit motive. We must anticipate the behaviors of those companies in light of this fact. The profit motive will naturally tend to drive companies to want to limit their exposure to sick people, or people who are likely to become sick or injured. Any change to our healthcare system must contend with this reality.

One way to do so is to institute a mandate that not only requires all residents to participate, ensuring a large pool of healthy people to offset the costs of the sick and injured, but also prevents companies from being allowed to refuse to insure patients. But the fate of the Affordable Care Act individual mandate serves as a stark warning. Americans appear unready to tolerate such a mandate. That could make implementing a stable, multi-payer insurance system infeasible.

A potential alternative strategy is to create desirable options in lieu of mandates. People who don't like to be told what to do may well choose to do the right thing if options are presented to them that make clear that the right thing is desirable. As we will see, there may be ways to "have our cake and eat it too" here. Specifically, we are looking for ways to ensure that all residents pay into a national health insurance system while still giving people choices about what specific insurance they want for themselves and their family. We will return to this concept at the end of this chapter, and again in chapter 8.

US CULTURAL CATEGORY #2: MODERN, MAXIMAL CONSUMERISM

We've discussed historical, cultural "themes" that must be contended with if we are to fix the US healthcare system. Now let's consider a modern, cultural category that distinguishes the US from other countries.

This more modern, cultural experience was perhaps best delineated by a former chair of the Department of Health Policy and Management at Harvard University. In a roundtable discussion, he was quoted as saying, "The US is the one country in the world where [people] think death is optional."[9]

The ethos of healthcare in the US is that all patients should get all treatments at all times, almost irrespective of prognosis or actual, meaningful benefit. We will come back to this point in chapter 5 when we look in greater depth at wasteful healthcare.

This cultural ethos runs through so many aspects of our healthcare system. It can cause patients to want and doctors to order expensive tests that don't really help care for the patients. It also causes patients to demand, and doctors to conduct, expensive procedures when simpler ones would have sufficed. It leads to demands to spend unlimited amounts of money on new treatments and technologies irrespective of the magnitude of benefit to one patient. And without considering how the massive amount of money spent on one patient will reduce money available to care for many other people. It also leads people to pursue aggressive and uncomfortable life-sustaining therapy at the very end of life, even when it will make no substantial difference.

In the US, we seem to be looking for a quick fix for all problems, and we seem to refuse to accept that there are problems that cannot be fixed by throwing money at them. We seem to be willing to spend any amount of money, even when the outcome can't be changed. Other countries are much more conservative in their approach to offering such medical care.

One of the most striking examples of expensive overutilization of healthcare is the price we are willing to pay in the US for drugs.[1,10,11] The US is the only industrialized nation that does not have any mechanism for governmental negotiation to reduce drug pricing at the federal level. So we pay hugely more for drugs than peer nations. Just as one example, last year at my hospital, we treated three patients who had a specific form of leukemia with a drug that cost $2 million for the three patients. These kinds of outrageous drug costs come up on a weekly basis.

In fact, just as I was putting the finishing touches on this book, I was asked to approve the use of a non-formulary new drug to treat low blood platelet counts. The drug would cost $50,000 for one week of inpatient use, and then several hundred thousand more dollars as an outpatient over the ensuing months. That was to treat one patient. The doctors requesting permission to use this drug cited a clinical trial in which the drug shortened the time to raising the platelet count to normal levels.

I read the study. It was true. The drug shortened the time it takes to normalize blood platelet counts. By how much, you ask? From 2.88 days to 2.69 days. Yes. That's right. The drug that would cost hundreds of thousands of dollars for one patient shortened the time to normalize the blood platelet count by an average of 0.19 days in its pivotal clinical trial. And the doctors requesting to use the drug were indignant that they couldn't just prescribe the drug without an approval process because they felt that they wanted to do everything they could for their patient.

Now, all patients deserve the best care possible, for sure. Stepping back to take a global view, the healthcare system must care as best as we can for as many people as possible with the money we have. If more money is spent to pay for one patient's expensive drug, that means less money is available for other patients and other services. Resources are not unlimited—they are finite. Is the benefit of that very expensive drug to that one patient more important than all the good those funds could do for many other patients? It is very difficult in individual circumstances to make these judgments.

Do we, as a society, want to make a choice that purchasing such drugs is the best way to spend $2 million or $200,000? For a drug for three patients that isn't curative but prolongs life by months to a year or two? Or a drug for one patient that shortens time to normalizing the platelet count by about five hours, at the cost of several hundred thousand dollars? Or would that money be better spent providing care for many dozens of other people with many other diseases? What if we must limit care to those many other patients to free up the funds to pay for that $2 million? Because, I'll tell you, that is something that hospitals actually do face in the US. Doesn't it seem *not* in the best interest of our patients, or of society, to ration care to the many in order to free up funds for catastrophically expensive drugs for one patient?

More fundamentally, wouldn't it be better to have a more effective means of negotiating down drug pricing, so we don't have to make these very difficult triage decisions about how we are going to spend our limited healthcare resources?

People in the US have not come to grips with the realities that money is finite, our costs are soaring, and our debt is mounting. We simply can no longer afford to offer every treatment for every condition for every patient every time, irrespective of the magnitude of the benefit, or how much resource the treatment requires us to spend. The impacts of these cultural norms are real and are palpable. As we will see next, they contribute to markedly increasing our healthcare costs in the US relative to peer nations.

☤ ☤ ☤ ☤ ☤

As I alluded to earlier in this chapter, in 2018, a remarkable study comparing the US to international healthcare systems was published in *JAMA*, the *Journal of the American Medical Association*. The authors were Dr. Irene Papanicolas, PhD, Liana Woskie, MSc, and Ashish Jha, MD, MPH, from the London School of Economics and Harvard University.[1] They searched through the OECD database, as well as a variety of other individual national databases, to compare various aspects of healthcare delivery in the US versus other peer nations. They specifically evaluated ninety-eight individual aspects of these healthcare systems to try to discern what distinguished the US from other countries.

The investigators also evaluated outcomes. We'll start there, before talking about spending. As expected, they found that the US had the shortest life span of all peer nations, and also had the highest infant and maternal mortality rate. The maternal mortality rate in the US was particularly egregious, at twenty-six deaths per 100,000 live births. That number is shockingly higher than in other peer nations, the latter of which collectively averaged eight deaths per 100,000 live births. But lest you think that the reason overall life spans are shorter in the US is because we lose so many young moms and babies at birth, the investigators confirmed that even adults live shorter lives in the US. The US came in dead last on this measure, also. Specifically, the average remaining life span in the US for adults already forty years old was between one and five years shorter than adults living in peer nations.

To achieve these bad outcomes, the investigators again confirmed that the US spends far more on healthcare than any of our peer nations. And they reported, as we have seen, that this was not because the US spent more public dollars—indeed we spent the seventh most out of eleven nations on public money. But we were by far the most expensive spenders of private money on healthcare.

The investigators next asked a very interesting question, which I had not ever seen systematically asked before. "Which overall type of care do we spend more on than everyone else: in-hospital care, outpatient care (i.e., in a doctor's office or clinic), long-term care (i.e., in a skilled nursing facility), healthcare administration, home care, or preventative care?"

To my shock, while the US spent more money than every other country, it did not spend more on in-hospital care, dealing with the sickest patients. I had always assumed that our in-hospital care was what separated us on cost from other nations. But that is not what the authors of this study found. Indeed, the US spent only 19 percent of our healthcare dollars on in-hospital care, causing us to be ranked tenth out of eleven (i.e., lower spending) in this category. Only Canada spent less. The Netherlands led the world, with 32 percent of its healthcare expenditures being for in-hospital costs. All other countries ranged from 21 to 31 percent.

So where is our overspending problem concentrated then? The difference really all boils down to two categories of spending. Not surprisingly, based on everything we've discussed thus far, one of those categories was administrative costs. The US spent 8 percent of its healthcare dollars on administrative costs. That compares to 1 percent in Japan and France (the least expensive in this category), 2 percent in the United Kingdom, Sweden, and Denmark, and 3 percent in Australia and Canada. The remaining countries spent between 4 and 5 percent of their healthcare costs on administration. If we reduced our administrative costs to the median level, 3 percent, that would result in at least $160 billion in savings per year, in line with projections previously stated by other investigators in other studies.

The second category in which we led the world in spending was a surprise to me. It was outpatient care (that is, in a doctor's office, clinic, pharmacy, etc., rather than in the hospital). People generally want to blame in-hospital care for our excessive expenditures. But the data show that where we actually overspend relative to our peer nations is in overspending on healthcare delivery in outpatient settings. Now, keep in mind, outpatient settings include urgent care, emergency room care, and outpatient or same-day surgeries and procedures. It also includes not just primary care with your regular physician, but seeing expensive subspecialists in their office or clinic. The latter is an important point we'll come back to, because specialists are paid much higher salaries than primary care doctors. And finally, and maybe most importantly, outpatient care includes the cost of outpatient prescription drugs.

Outpatient care accounted for a surprising 42 percent of US healthcare expenditures, compared to 22 percent for the least expensive country, the Netherlands. Other countries ranged between 23 percent and 39 percent. Where did all this outpatient expense go?

Well, the US led the world in utilization of expensive radiographic, diagnostic imaging studies (like CT scans and MRIs). The US also led the world or were near the top in expensive outpatient surgical procedures. These included total knee replacements, hysterectomies, C-sections for deliveries, cataract surgeries, and heart catheterizations to diagnose and treat heart disease.

In contrast, for key inpatient measures, the US did well. The US performed at least in the middle, and for many measures in the better third of the pack, on inpatient care. The US did not overutilize, and did better than many peer nations on the number of hospitalizations for common diseases such as pneumonia, heart attacks, COPD, and mental healthcare. We used the third-fewest number of hospital bed days per admission to the hospital, meaning we kept our lengths of stay in the hospital shorter than most of our peer nations. And we had the fourth-fewest number of total hospital admissions per 1,000 patients.

So despite our huge cost excess in the US, it is not being driven by overutilization of hospital beds or inpatient care. Rather, it is being driven by overutilization of outpatient care and expensive diagnostic testing, elective procedures, and high administrative costs (nearly all of which, as we have previously seen, are in the private health insurance side of things).

And then there's the last component of outpatient spending, which was where we demonstrated the biggest dominance over all of our other competition. This last item is where we really showed how the US can differentiate ourselves from the rest of the pack on overconsumption. I'm talking, of course, about pharmaceutical spending.

In the US in 2016, we spent $1,443 per American on drugs. Just mull that fact over for a moment. We spent more than $1,400 per living person in our country on drugs in one year. That is an astronomical amount. The vast majority of that spending occurred in outpatient, retail settings. Of the $1,443 per person, we spent $1,026 per person in outpatient retail settings. The next most expensive was Switzerland at $776 per person. The cheapest was the Netherlands, at $292 per person. The US spent nearly 700 percent more on outpatient drugs than the Netherlands did. And we spent 30 percent more than Switzerland, the second most expensive country. The median spend across the other ten peer nations was $501 per person, less than half what the US spent.

Now here's where it gets really interesting. The investigators then asked, of all that drug spending, what proportion in each country was funded via public dollars versus private insurance? Surprisingly to me, while the US led the world by far on overall drug spending, we spent the lowest proportion of public dollars on drugs, from among all peer nations. Only 34 percent of US drug costs were attributed to spending covered by public dollars. That compares to 36 percent for the next lowest country, Canada, and 80 percent for France, which was the highest percentage (with the remainder between 36 and 75 percent). So if we led the world in overall drug spending, but spent the least on drugs from public funding, obviously where we spent the most on for drugs was from private funding/insurance.

Indeed. Thirty-six percent of drug costs in the US were spent by private health insurance plans. That compares to 0 percent in Australia, the UK, and Sweden, 1 percent in Japan and France, and 2 percent in the Netherlands. Let me just underscore that. The US spent infinity more private insurance money on drugs than Australia, the UK, and Sweden did (because these countries spent no private insurance money on drugs). And the US spent 3,600 percent more private insurance money on drugs than Japan and France, and 1,800 percent more than the Netherlands. Canada was the second highest behind the US at 30 percent, but the remaining countries were at 7 to 8 percent, or fivefold lower than the US.

The remainder of spending on drug costs were from private, out-of-pocket funds, meaning that they were spent on co-pays for patients who had gaps in their private insurance, or from money spent by people who had no insurance. The US was in the middle of the pack in this category.

So the reason why the US leads the world in healthcare costs is because we spend more than other countries on outpatient care—especially expensive diagnostics, surgical procedures, and specialty care—administrative costs, and drugs (mostly outpatient, and mostly covered by private insurance and out-of-pocket spending). Before we wrap up and draw overall conclusions from what we've learned, there is one more category of spending to consider: the costs of physicians and nurses.

⚕ ⚕ ⚕ ⚕ ⚕

I separate out the category of spending on physician and nursing salaries because I have a conflict of interest, in that, of course, I am a physician who works in the US. So commenting on how much money physicians make puts me in an awkward position.

I've decided to deal with this conflict by disclosing it to you, in case it wasn't already apparent. I'm a physician in the US. I have a conflict. I am going to present the data the investigators in this *JAMA* paper found, and then offer you the thoughts and interpretation of a leading healthcare economist (who is also a physician, mind you) on those data. I will then leave it to you to draw your own conclusions about how much doctors' and nurses' salaries contribute overall to high US healthcare costs.

The investigators in the *JAMA* paper found that, not surprisingly, both doctors and nurses in the US made more money than the median income of all workers in the US. Duh.

In 2016, general physicians in the US made an average of $218,173 per year. Specialists, on average, made much more at $316,000 per year. Nurses made $74,160 per year. All of those numbers were the highest among all peer nations.

At first glance, this may make it seem like physicians' and nurses' salaries contribute to excess healthcare costs in the US. Certainly on an individual basis, they make more money than peers in other countries. But here I need to point out one other bit of information. Dr. Ezekiel Emanuel, a widely respected healthcare economist at the University of Pennsylvania, wrote an accompanying editorial to this *JAMA* study. In his editorial, Dr. Emanuel pointed out that if we want to understand the impact of the cost of physicians on the overall healthcare system, we have to know more than just the average salary of the physicians.[11] The total cost to the system is going to be equal to the average cost per physician multiplied by the number of physicians—total cost = cost per physician × number of physicians.

And that's where things may take a bit of a right turn. Because the *JAMA* paper also reported the number of physicians per 1,000 population in each country. And it turns out, in the US, we have fewer physicians than in most countries. We had the third least physicians across the eleven countries, with 2.6 physicians per 1,000 population. Only Japan at 2.4 per 1,000 and the United Kingdom at 2.1 per 1,000 had fewer. Most countries had 50 percent more physicians than the US per population, and Switzerland had 4.3 per 1,000, or 65 percent more physicians per population.

I will point out that it has long been somewhat intentional that the number of physicians trained per year is relatively low in the US, specifically because it creates a supply-demand phenomenon that maintains physician salaries at a relatively high level. So, in a sense, physician salaries in the US are higher than in other countries in no small part because there are fewer of us than in other countries.

I'll now defer to Dr. Emanuel about the overall impact of physician salaries on US healthcare costs. Considering the highest average salary per person, but low number of those physicians relative to peer nations, Dr. Emanuel wrote, "The number (i.e., "volume") of physicians in the United States is comparatively low, thereby offsetting the effect of high salaries. In the United States, there are 2.6 physicians per 1000 citizens, whereas in Germany the ratio is 4.1/1000 and in Sweden 4.2/1000. Thus, even though US physician salaries are high, the per capita costs attributable to paying physicians is almost identical to that in Germany and $176 per capita higher than in the Netherlands, accounting for just 4 percent of the difference in per capita total health care costs."[11]

In other words, per Dr. Emanuel's analysis, US physicians' salaries are high because there are not very many of them. And if you multiply a high salary times not very many of them, the overall cost to the system becomes similar to most of the other countries, which pay each individual physician less but have many more of them to pay.

So, we have seen that the US leads the world in healthcare costs while delivering bad outcomes. We have seen that the specific healthcare costs that are higher in the US than other countries are *not* in-hospital costs, surprisingly, but rather outpatient costs. These excess costs seem to be driven by expensive specialty care, including expensive radiographic testing, surgical and invasive procedures, inefficient and expensive administrative costs, drug costs, and possibly to some extent, due to the salaries of expensive specialist physicians. We have also seen that the biggest cost differences from other countries are due to much higher expenditures of private money (from employer-sponsored health insurance and out-of-pocket costs) and *not* due to higher spending of public funds.

These are the precise conclusions that Dr. Emanuel came to from reviewing the data in the *JAMA* paper. He wrote,

"Drug prices are a major factor [in the cost difference between US and peer nation healthcare expenditures]...These differences are almost all a result of price—not volume. No other category of spending accounts for as much of the cost difference as pharmaceuticals.

A second major driver of cost differences between the United States and other high-income countries is high-margin, high-volume procedures. The cost difference in these procedures between countries is a combination of high prices and high volumes—not just high prices...

A third area of difference is imaging, which accounts for about 7 percent of the cost difference between the United States and the Netherlands, and again is the result of both high prices and high volumes."[11]

And finally, he added, "Administrative costs contribute significantly to the cost difference between the United States and other countries."[11]

So with these conclusions in mind, let's go back to the premise at the beginning of this chapter. We have a culture in the US of Don't Tread on Me, which makes it difficult to enforce universal mandates for coverage, which is necessary to ensure that healthy people offset the costs of insurance for sick people. We also have a culture in the US of offering maximal care at all times to everyone no matter what, even when that care may not be of clear benefit, and irrespective of its cost. The result is that we overutilize testing, overutilize expensive procedures, overutilize specialty care, and are willing to overconsume drugs, including accepting drug pricing that other countries simply will not pay.

And, perhaps most importantly, the biggest driver of the difference in cost, which underwrites all of the above costs, is the spending of private health insurance dollars, not public dollars. Those high amounts of private expenditures are due to the reliance in the US on a system of voluntary, employer-funded health insurance, which is not universal and leaves unfunded gaps in coverage requiring employees and the unemployed to pick up their own tabs. We are the only country among peer nations that uses such a system. And we use this system because of a series of accidents of history, none of which had anything to do with planning or implementing a healthcare system.

The fact that the US overspends on healthcare because of private expenditures, and that private insurance has much higher overhead than current public options, suggests a path forward. Maybe we can deal with the Don't Tread on Me cultural issue that doomed the Affordable Care Act's individual mandate by creating intelligent options. If private insurance is more expensive and does not deliver a better product than public insurance, people might simply choose to enroll in public insurance on their own. Perhaps rather than banning private insurance, as some have advocated for, an alternative option is to simply expand public insurance and let public and private compete, so that the customer can pick the winner. We will return to this discussion in chapter 8.

Now that we have a deeper understanding of where the US healthcare system has come from, and where it is in 2020, we are getting close to being ready to consider our options for how we can do better. But before we do that, we need to consider one more very important factor. The next discussion we need to have is around the sheer amount of wasteful care we provide in the US.

If you really want to be convinced about how bad healthcare is in the US, consider how much of the money we spend on healthcare is squandered on unnecessary care, or is pure waste that has nothing to do with care. That is the subject of chapter 5. If we want to redesign our healthcare system, we should set a clear priority to identify and eliminate that waste. Wasteful healthcare doesn't just burn cash for no reason; it hurts people physically and emotionally. Indeed, as we will see, sadly, the American system of healthcare explicitly encourages and seeks to increase such waste.

CHAPTER 5

‖‖‖‖‖‖‖‖‖‖‖‖‖‖‖‖‖

A PATIENT- AND SYSTEM-LEVEL VIEW OF WASTEFUL US HEALTHCARE

Ms. G was a successful business executive from out of town. She came to California to participate in a corporate retreat. While she was in California and attending her meetings, she began to notice an uncomfortable swelling on her face, between her nose and her upper lip. She didn't feel particularly ill and thought it might be a pimple coming on. So that night in her hotel, she washed her face to try to clean the area and went to sleep.

But the swelling grew overnight, and she awoke with a golf ball-sized lump on her face that appeared red, was very hot to the touch, and was extremely tender. She was quite understandably unnerved by this and she quickly made her way to a nearby local hospital to get care.

She was, of course, out of network for her insurance because she was out of state. On the other hand, this did seem like an emergency. So she did not think twice about going to the emergency room. It never occurred to her that she might have to pay for the care, since she had good insurance through her employer.

The hospital staff was impressed by the scary appearance of the swelling on Ms. G's face, and right away took her to the back for treatment. There an emergency medicine physician diagnosed her with a skin abscess, likely caused by the common bacterium, staph.

Her vital signs were normal. Nevertheless, the lesion being on her face, the doctors chose to admit her to the hospital for intravenous antibiotics. The emergency medicine physician also consulted a plastic surgeon to deal with the abscess, since the lesion was on the patient's face, and would need to be drained via an incision.

The plastic surgeon reached the patient while she was still in the emergency room before she was moved upstairs into an inpatient bed. The surgeon carefully numbed the skin around the lesion. He then made a small incision into the abscess and quickly drained out the pus. Ms. G was then moved to an inpatient bed. Over three days in the hospital, she received antibiotics administered intravenously, was seen by her inpatient hospitalist physician and an infectious diseases specialist, and had a number of blood tests run.

The good news is that Ms. G responded well to treatment and eventually was released from the hospital so she could go back to the hotel, pack her bags, and fly home. She had missed the end of the conference, and she had missed her original flight and had to rebook it, but she got home safe and sound.

Now, I had no role in Ms. G's care, and she was not cared for at any hospital I have ever worked at. I became aware of Ms. G's case through a mutual acquaintance. But one of the things that struck me about her case was her hospital bill. Ms. G's hospital bill captured more than fifty individual line items. For example, each day of the generic antibiotics she had received was billed at a rate of about $500 per day, compared to wholesale acquisition costs of the drugs that were likely around $20. On top of the cost of procuring the drugs, the patient (or rather her insurance company) was billed for $2,000 per day for hospital fees related to the infusion of the antibiotics. Presumably those charges covered the cost of the IV tubing (likely less than $20 per day wholesale) and pharmacist time to prepare the drug and nursing time to hang the drug, although this was not further delineated in the bill.

There were also professional fees to the insurance company from the plastic surgeon totaling multiple thousands of dollars for what amounted to a five-minute procedure. Other specialist costs were included as well, as were $2,000 per day for laboratory tests of the blood.

The overall bill for the three-day stay was approximately $50,000. Yes, seriously. Now, as I mentioned, this patient had excellent private insurance based in her home state. Ms. G was out of network, which could have put her at risk for the entire bill. Fortunately, the insurance company was not able to put the whole bill on her because they were forced to acknowledge that there was an urgent condition that needed treatment. So they did agree to cover most of the expenses.

But via a combination of deductibles, co-pays, and other gaps, the insurance company managed to only cover $45,000 of the bill. For three days of hospitalization and despite having excellent insurance from her employer, the patient was stuck with a $5,000 bill that she had to pay out of pocket. How many of you reading this book could comfortably absorb an out of the blue $5,000 cost for an infection that came on suddenly and that you neither caused to happen nor had any ability to prevent?

Now, here's the really interesting part. My review of the medical records found absolutely nothing "wrong" with the care Ms. G received. She received the needed incision and drainage of the abscess. She received effective antibiotics. Her infection responded well to therapy. The care she received was consistent with the community standard. Which, to me, is the problem. Because if I had been the treating physician—or even more importantly, if I had been the patient—I would have handled things very differently.

Ms. G had no evidence that the infection had spread from her skin to deeper tissues or her blood. Her vital signs were normal. She did not even have a fever. The level of white blood cells in her blood was normal, again indicating no spread of infection. She was not dehydrated, and so I'm not sure I understood why she needed intravenous fluids, or a battery of tests. And I could've predicted with about 99 percent accuracy that the bacteria causing the infection would be staph. And I have antibiotics that could have been used with great reliability to treat the staph infection that could have been administered orally and work just as well as any intravenous therapy.

So here's my question. Why couldn't Ms. G have undergone a minor incision and drainage procedure in the emergency department and been sent home from there with oral antibiotics without ever being admitted to the hospital? She could have been given instructions to return to the emergency department in the unlikely event that she felt worse the next day. And she could have called her primary care physician in her home state to get an appointment for follow-up within the week. That's what I would've done had I been the treating physician. And that's what I would've insisted on had I been the patient.

As a matter of fact, a little more than ten years ago, something very similar happened to me. I went to sleep feeling fine and woke up early in the morning with a golf ball-sized, tender lump near my jaw. I drove myself into my research laboratory where I lanced the lesion myself using a small scalpel, drained a bunch of pus out of the lesion, and then phoned in a prescription for myself. I took oral antibiotics that cost me $50 (that's with the retail markup—wholesale the price would have been like $10). The entire thing cost me $50 out of pocket, and I never went to the hospital.

So as you can tell, I see no need for Ms. G to have spent three days in the hospital. I see no need for multiple infusions of intravenous antibiotics and fluids or daily blood tests. Frankly, I don't even see why a plastic surgeon was needed to make a small incision to drain pus. And I certainly don't see a need for a $50,000 hospital bill to do something that I did for myself at the cost of $50.

Had I been the treating physician in the hospital, the bill for this patient's care may have been more like $5,000, which includes the cost of the incision and drainage of the abscess, time spent by the emergency medicine physician and emergency nursing, a much more limited and precise set of blood tests sent just once, and perhaps $50 for antibiotic therapy.

Why didn't this happen?

It's not possible to say for sure, of course. But one has to wonder if the way medicine is paid for in the US played a role. Did the fact that doctors make money by referring cases to one another contribute? Or the fact that hospitals make money by admitting patients to the hospital to rack up individual line items of various expenses to charge the insurance company?

Our healthcare system financially rewards doing as many invasive things as possible to people. Nothing pays better than complex surgeries done in seriously ill patients. The more complex and invasive the procedure, the more lucrative the pay. Even for Ms. G's relatively straightforward case, involving a patient who was certainly not critically ill and needing only a minor procedure, the costs add up. With my treatment plan, the hospital would have been paid at least $40,000 less than they ended up getting. The doctors would've been paid less, too. And the pharmaceutical companies? Well, my oral generic medication wasn't going to help them drive up shareholder value, let's just put it that way.

I'm not saying that doctors and hospitals are sitting there dreaming up ways to bilk money from payers, patients, and insurance companies. I'm merely pointing out that the way reimbursement is set up in our healthcare system encourages rather than dissuades this kind of treatment plan. In fact, this is precisely what is meant by the term "overtreating" when describing wasteful healthcare.

I remember back in the late 1990s, when I was a third-year medical student rotating through a major teaching hospital, the hospital was just entering the era of itemized billing. They installed specialized barcoded vending machines. Before that, if nurses or doctors needed to use anything to care for a patient, they would walk into the supply room, get what they needed, and go take care of the patient. They might pick up a gauze pad, or forceps, or scissors, or various IV tubing or lines, all of which were stocked in the supply rooms. But those vending machines replaced the supply rooms. You had to punch the patient's medical record number into the vending machine and then select what you needed. The machine would release what you needed, and in so doing, it would automatically add its cost to the patient's line-item bill. Down to the level of a gauze pad!

US healthcare has increasingly moved to nickel-and-diming every single individual possible expense to rack up costs, continuously adding to line-itemed bills. Every line item is scrutinized, and games are played among the hospital, doctors, and the insurance company to try to squeeze more money out of the system. And when the payer refuses to pay, the cost ends up in the lap of the patient.

Unfortunately, the person who loses the most in all this is indeed the patient. How did Ms. G benefit by staying in the hospital for three days? It's dangerous to be in the hospital. You only want to be there when you have to be. Hospitals are where the most dangerous bacteria concentrate, since hospitals are full of sick people, receiving broad-spectrum antibiotics, with immune systems that are often compromised. People lying in bed all day in a hospital get deconditioned and lose muscle mass. Due to this deconditioning, they become at risk for falling, causing injury when they try to stand. They are at risk for bed sores. They are at risk for all kinds of medication errors, etc.

You need to be in a hospital if the care you require can only be delivered in the hospital. But given the incontrovertible evidence of the frequency of being harmed in the hospital, it is wrong to think that the care is better in the hospital if it can be safely given out of the hospital. If we can deliver the needed care safely out of the hospital, we should. As soon as you can safely be discharged home, you should be.

Aside from the dangers of an unnecessary stay in the hospital, Ms. G also missed out on her work conference and had to reschedule her flight back home at her own expense. Would she not have been much better off going home from the emergency room with a simple prescription of cheap, generic, highly effective, oral antibiotics?

Again, let me reiterate, the care Ms. G received met the community standard of care. The care she received worked, and many hospitals likely would have treated her similarly. But my point is that it was highly inefficient and wasteful care. It was burdensome to the patient, to the insurance company, and to the taxpayers. More importantly, putting someone in the hospital who does not necessarily need to be there is potentially dangerous for the patient.

What I'm describing is an inherent tension among those providing healthcare about how best to treat our patients. The prevailing model in the US is to put people in the hospital and do as many procedures and tests as necessary to provide 100 percent reassurance. That model is encouraged by the obsession to create line-itemed bills to allow billing of insurance companies. That model, in my mind, is not only inefficient, but unsafe for patients.

It is also terribly inconvenient for patients and burdensome for those who have lives to get back to, family to care for, etc. But it is undeniably more lucrative than the model of care that

I prefer, which is to only put people in hospitals when they absolutely have to be there, only do invasive procedures when they absolutely must be done, only give intravenous therapy when orals cannot be given, etc.

The "less is more" ideal of medical practice is out of sync with how healthcare is paid for in the US. That's a big part of the problem. If we want to change how healthcare is delivered and how expensive it is, we must align the financial incentives to drive towards a more global, holistic model of care. The current incentives encourage invasive, expensive testing and treatments. And I have to believe the care Ms. G received was at least influenced by those incentives, which the US healthcare system continues to choose to have in place.

A different payer system, which offers global budgeting—the way we fund firehouses, for example—makes much more sense to incentivize the healthcare system to not overtreat and not overdiagnose. As we discussed briefly in chapter 1 and will discuss again in this chapter and in chapter 6, such models are effective at reining in costs while maintaining high quality and efficiency of healthcare. These international experiences demonstrate the potential that moving to global budgeting can greatly improve healthcare outcomes while reducing costs in the US.[1,2] But given how deeply entrenched the itemized billing movement is, I fear that only a major, forced transformation of our healthcare system will help us move away from it.

Is it worth it? I think so, yes. The way we financially incentivize our healthcare system isn't just bad for finances. It's dangerous for patients. And it's bad for the very foundations of the doctor-patient relationship. Let's look briefly at why.

✝ ✝ ✝ ✝ ✝

In the classic '90s sitcom, *Seinfeld*, there is an episode where Jerry's car needs servicing. Unfortunately, he has irritated his friend Puddy, who is the one, honest auto mechanic in town that he trusts to care for the car ["The Fusilli Jerry," Season 6, episode 21]. Jerry drops the car off with another mechanic, who then calls the house to discuss the estimate.

Jerry picks up the phone and shouts, "What? Twenty-eight hundred dollars!? That's the estimate on my car? No, don't even do anything. I'm gonna think about it." He hangs up.

"What's to think about?" George asks. "If Puddy says it's what it is, it's what it is. He's not gonna cheat you."

"Except that it's not Puddy," Jerry says.

"What happened to Puddy?"

"Eh, we had a little fight about the move. I took the car to this other place. I think they might be trying to screw me," Jerry says.

"Well of course they're trying to screw you!" George replies. "What do you think? That's what they do. They can make up anything. Nobody knows." George puts on a mocking tone and goes through a rhetorical dialogue between a shifty mechanic and a car owner.

"By the way, you need a new Johnson rod in there."

"Oh, a Johnson rod. Yeah, well, you better put one of those on."

So, here's the thing. When I'm talking to a patient, I don't want them worried that I'm "trying to put a new Johnson rod in there" for no reason. And I don't want them to ever reply, "Oh, a Johnson rod, of course, yeah I guess you better put one of those on."

I want my patients to trust that I'm there to offer tests and treatments only when they are needed, that I will only put a patient in the hospital when necessary, and that we will not make healthcare decisions driven by the desire to drive up itemized billing. And I can tell you this: that is what I expect from any physician who tries to take care of me.

Remember the Maryland hospital executive from chapter 1 that reporter Tara Golshan quoted in her *Vox* article?[3] The executive expressed discomfort with his former, fee-for-service existence, prior to Maryland implementing global budgeting for its hospitals. In that prior world, the hospital benefitted from patients getting sick enough to fill its beds, as more patients in more beds meant more revenue. Global budgeting completely changed his and his hospital's worldview. Now the incentive is to keep people healthy rather than find as many ways as possible to insert "Johnson rods" into patients for billing purposes.

The trust between doctor and patient is at the very core of the Hippocratic oath. It should never be jeopardized by a fear that the doctor is acting out of an interest to drive up a reimbursable bill. Nor should trust in the hospital and its staff (e.g., nursing) ever similarly be put at risk. That would corrupt the very essence of patient care.

I mentioned Dr. Don Berwick's review of waste in the US healthcare system in chapter 2. He and his colleague estimated that in 2012, the US healthcare system spent more than $900 billion (inflation-adjusted to more than $1 trillion in 2018 dollars) on pure waste.[4] Waste in healthcare has been the subject of a number of other studies since then, all of which have agreed with their general conclusions.

The most recent analysis was published in 2019 in the leading medical journal *JAMA*. The study was authored by Drs. William Shrank, Teresa Rogstad, and Dr. Natasha Parekh. The latter two authors were academics based at the University of Pittsburgh Medical Center. Interestingly, the first author, Dr. Shrank, worked for the for-profit, health insurance industry giant, Humana.

Just for context, Humana earned $60 billion in revenue from July of 2018 to June of 2019, which was a 14 percent increase versus the year before.[5] However, like many companies in the healthcare industry, Humana has been under cost pressure. As costs of healthcare have risen, their profit margin has fallen. While Humana's revenue rose 14 percent in 2018, their costs rose by more than 14 percent. As a result, in 2019, Humana reported that its annual profit for 2018 fell below analysts' expectations due to higher costs, causing the stock price to dip.[6]

Before you become concerned that Humana may end up in the poorhouse, their net profit fell to "only" $1.7 billion.[7] So…they're still doing okay. But since their costs are rising, putting pressure on their profits and therefore stock price, do you think that may be why even a health insurance industry giant like Humana is now interested in eliminating medical waste?

The study by Shrank and colleagues reviewed more than fifty separate peer-reviewed publications on waste in healthcare.

From this review, they gleaned an estimate that waste costs the US healthcare system between $760 and $935 billion per year. In an accompanying editorial, Don Berwick pointed out that some additional types of waste were not evaluated, and adding in those additional wastes would likely push these numbers over a trillion dollars in waste per year, accounting for a third or so of total healthcare spending in the US.[8] So, nothing changed between 2012 and 2019. We haven't advanced. We haven't gotten better. We're still as wasteful and unnecessarily expensive as ever.

It is rather remarkable how many employees in the US health-care system we must have in order to do all of the work around detailed financial screening and clearance, authorization or denial to treat, and billing. Our system is so complex that at least 10 percent of a hospital's staff, and maybe even more like 20 percent, are engaged in these activities. None of that work, or the costs associated with that work, have anything to do with actually providing medical care.

When patients come to the hospital, they are rapidly met by some-one who takes down all their relevant information, such as date of birth, social security number, health plan number if the patient has it, etc. They then run the information through computer systems to confirm what type of insurance coverage the patient has. Then they must contact that health plan to determine if the health-care being sought is authorized or not. Discussion and debate ensue. Hours or days can go by, with back and forth between the local hospital financial screeners and the health insurance payer financial screeners. In the meantime, the care team is somewhat paralyzed by the final decision regarding what they are allowed to do for the patient. Waste, waste, and more waste.

The financial workers have multiple layers of supervision above them, and a large reporting structure within a hospital's organizational chart and budget. And we absolutely have to have these folks, because without them, we wouldn't know who we are allowed to treat, and what aspects of care we are allowed to provide.

For example, once we've stabilized the patient's emergency, must we transfer this patient to an in-network facility, or is our hospital in-network for this patient? If we don't transfer them, but they are out of network, how will their follow-up care be arranged at discharge from the hospital? Can we do outpatient specialty care (like surgical or cardiology or infectious diseases follow-up care) even if we are not authorized to do outpatient primary care? Can we do nonemergency surgery for this patient? If so, are we allowed to have a postoperative outpatient visit to ensure the wound is healing and the patient is recovering? And how will home care, or physical therapy, or social worker support be managed?

I'm just giving you examples, but the reality is there are innumerable such questions that come up constantly, for nearly every patient admitted to the hospital. All of this activity soaks up a huge amount of time the physicians are caring for patients, not to mention time spent by the hospital administrators trying to keep the hospital ship afloat.

In 2014, a rather eye-opening exposé was published comparing the administrative costs in the US healthcare system to the administrative costs in seven other wealthy countries (Canada, England, Scotland, Wales, France, Germany, and the Netherlands).[2] The study was conducted by an international consortium of healthcare scientists. Note that each of these countries (with England, Scotland, and Wales all considered as the United Kingdom) has universal healthcare. Two of them (Canada and the combination of England, Scotland, and Wales as the United Kingdom) are single-payer, and three are multi-payer systems. Furthermore, three of the nations (Canada, Scotland, and Wales) use up-front, global budgeting rather than fee-for-service reimbursement to fund hospitals. So, how did the administrative costs in the US compare to these other nations? I don't think you need to be Nostradamus to predict where this is going.

The US dominated in administrative costs. An astounding 25.3 percent of US hospitals' total costs were soaked up by administrative costs. US hospitals are being bled dry by administrative burdens placed on them by the payer complexity of our healthcare system. That rate was more than twice the administrative costs seen in hospitals in the two least expensive countries. Guess which countries those were? Could it be the countries that use up-front, global budgeting for hospitals?

Indeed it could be. Scotland and Canada had the lowest fraction of healthcare costs spent on administration at 11.6 percent and 12.4 percent, respectively. Wales was the third least expensive at 14.2 percent. So, the three countries with the lowest percentage of hospital costs spent on administration were the three countries that use global budgeting to fund their hospitals. Interesting coincidence, eh? Or to put it another way...duh.

Furthermore, when the total costs were adjusted by the GDP of each country, to account for wealth-adjusted spending as we did in chapter 2, the differences were even more dramatic. Total national hospital administrative costs in the US reached a remarkable 1.43 percent of GDP. That number is more than triple (i.e., more than 300 percent higher) the cost per GDP of hospital administration in Canada, which was 0.41 percent.

Alternatively, we might hypothesize that the reduced administrative costs in the three least expensive countries are due to use of single-payer healthcare systems, rather than specifically being due to global budgeting. Yet, England also has a single-payer healthcare system and does not use global budgeting. Its hospitals spent 15.5 percent on administration, which was well below the US rate, but well above the rates of the three countries that use global budgeting. England had higher administrative costs than Wales and Scotland, even though all three countries (England, Wales, Scotland) collectively operate under the UK's National Health Service. Thus, of the three component nations of the UK that were evaluated, the lowest hospital administrative costs were seen in Scotland and Wales, both of which use global budgeting for their hospitals.

One more interesting point about administrative costs in the US. I work in a public hospital in the US. As I have alluded to, I am continually amazed at how much resource, energy, and time we must spend on dealing with the administrative complexity of the US healthcare system. You might predict that public hospitals would be less efficient than private hospitals. After all, public hospital budgets are floated by the government, and private hospitals not only need to stay within budget, but for-profit hospitals are trying to make money for shareholders. So you might expect that public hospitals would spend the most on administrative costs and private, for-profit hospitals would spend the least, in their continual capitalistic efforts to cut costs and increase profits.

Not so. In fact, quite the opposite. The study found that for-profit hospitals in the US spent the most on administrative costs (27 percent of their costs), private, nonprofits were in the middle (25 percent of costs), and public hospitals spent the least on administrative costs (23 percent).

Why do you suppose this might be? It is safe to assume that for-profit hospitals would not be spending these costs if the expenditures did not bring in more money in the long run. Public hospitals are not in it to make money. We regularly eat the cost of care for uninsured patients (remember, we are funded by the taxpayers). That's our job. And we not infrequently eat the cost of out-of-network care for patients who really need the care, but their insurance company won't authorize it (as described in several of the patient stories I've told you). So, while the pressure is always on us to accurately identify who is in- versus out-of-network, we have some flexibility managerially to decide who truly needs treatment.

For-profit hospitals are different. They're in it to make money. Every dollar they invest in such administrative effort to identify who is in- versus out-of-network likely pays off by avoiding the unfunded care they would have to eat if they didn't have staff to find ways to avoid it. Also, by ensuring that paying patients stay in their hospitals, they maximize their ability to rack up comprehensive line-item bills for funded patients.

Remember Ms. C from chapter 1? The administrators at her in-network, private hospital worked hard to not authorize us to transfer her to their hospital as an inpatient. They asked for and received reams of forms and paperwork and had multiple phone conversations with our case managers and utilization review people. But in the end, they did not authorize the transfer. Ms. C would have been an expensive inpatient admission. Aside from the fact that she had been repeatedly readmitted because her social situation made stable outpatient care difficult to maintain, she also needed housing. She had complex psychosocial needs beyond the provision of traditional medical care. She might end up in the hospital for a long time, and the insurance would not pay for more than a few days of hospitalization. By keeping her out of their hospital, those administrators at Ms. C's in-network hospital likely saved their organization a lot of money.

What I am telling you is that the reason for-profit companies have higher administrative costs is because those administrative costs are an investment that helps the for-profit hospital make more money. Isn't there something wrong with a system that encourages more administrative costs, spent on activities having nothing to do with providing healthcare, as a means to make more money?

At the beginning of 2020, the prodigiously productive Drs. Himmelstein and Woolhandler (multiple studies by whom we have already reviewed in this book), along with author Terry Campbell published a new study in the *Annals of Internal Medicine* revisiting concerns about administrative costs in the US. Overall the study found that in 2017, the US healthcare system spent a truly astounding $812 billion on administrative costs.[9] That breaks down to $2,497 per person in the US for healthcare administrative costs, compared to $551 per person spent in Canada.[9] Canada spent nearly *80 percent less* on administrative overhead than the US did. Isn't that embarrassing?

Insurance overhead costs were 8 percent overall in the US, compared to 3 percent in Canada.[9] Administration ate up 27 percent of hospital costs in the US, compared to 13 percent in Canada. Administration ate up 27 percent of nursing home costs in the US, compared to 16 percent in Canada. Private physicians' overhead ate up 22 percent of their costs, compared to 11 percent in Canada. Are you detecting the subtle pattern here?

Clearly our administrative and overhead costs continue to worsen in the US, even as our outcomes also worsen (i.e., life spans shorten). Something is very wrong with this picture. If we reduced administrative overhead in the US to levels similar to that in Canada, we would spend $600 billion less per year on healthcare. Americans like to poke fun at the "efficiency" of Canadian healthcare. Maybe we need to rethink that, eh?

As further evidence for the power of single-payer systems to keep administrative costs down, we can look to Taiwan. Taiwan is in many ways instructive for the US, because it used to have a healthcare system somewhat similar to the US, with disjointed, fragmented care and a high proportion of uninsured patients. However, in the 1990s, Taiwan explicitly, intentionally, and thoughtfully redesigned its healthcare system into a single-payer system. We will discuss this transformation further in chapter 6.

The point for the current discussion is that Taiwan's single-payer system uses global budgeting for its hospitals. As a result, its administrative costs for their healthcare system are astoundingly low, less than 1 percent.[10,11] That compares to 23 percent overall for the US, including both public and private payers.[11] Of note, in the US, the largest public insurance plan (Medicare) spends only 1.3 percent on administrative costs,[12,13] similar to the rate paid in Taiwan for their single-payer system.

If we just step back from things for a moment, it is obvious that a global budgeting system would reduce healthcare complexity and cost. In a fee-for-service system, a complex bill must be generated for each individual patient encounter. My hospital admits and discharges around 32,000 patients per year. We see 160,000 emergency department and urgent care visits. We see more than a half million other outpatient visits per year. A bill must be generated for each of these encounters.

As you can imagine, generating a hospital bill is very complicated, requires the input from numerous salaried employees, and takes a lot of work. That's quite literally tens of thousands of person-hours per year just to drop bills for patient encounters, not even counting the time spent dealing with outside health plans, getting authorization to treat, coordinating transfers, etc. If we were instead paid an up-front, global budget, almost all of that time, energy, and money spent would vanish.

It is disheartening to think that the uncoordinated, complex maze of a healthcare system in the US is funded principally by doing things to people, and that the more invasive the things, the better the system gets paid. And it is disappointing to think that the US healthcare system has devolved to an obsessive need to catalog every bit of money spent on a patient, down to the gauze pad and tongue depressor, all to enable us to crank out as expensive a bill as possible for each episode of care. All of this only encourages more care to be delivered, and more intensive and invasive care to be delivered, which ultimately creates an incentive to let people get sick in the first place, so they need all of that care.

And all of this creates a need to have many administrators to do the complex financial screening, health plan authorizations and denials, and transfers of patient care responsibility. The goal of these efforts is to maximize revenue and decrease the costs of providing unfunded care.

Instead of all of this activity unrelated to patient care, the goal should be to keep people healthy in the first place, so they don't need dangerous, invasive things, and don't need to be in the hospital, and don't need to inquire about authorization from their health plan.

Both Mr. E and Ms. G show us that people who are perfectly healthy and doing all the right things can have sudden medical illnesses come upon them. We definitely need the ability to do inpatient, sophisticated, invasive, and expensive care when it is required. We have to maintain that capacity because people like the nine patients I've introduced you to will always need it. People will always get into car accidents. And fall off ladders. And there will always be infections, heart attacks, cancer, strokes, diabetes, high blood pressure, and other diseases no matter how healthy we live. But we can at least change the way we operate our healthcare system, so the goal becomes to minimize those illnesses and to incentivize giving more efficient care to patients when they have such illnesses.

Paying hospitals and doctors for each episode of care they provide, for each test ordered, for each invasive catheter placed, and each intravenous infusion infused, and each surgery performed, only encourages us to let people get sick enough to need all of this in the first place. It also encourages us to choose more aggressive interventions over equally effective, less invasive care, and over more efficient and safer preventative measures.

This fee-for-service model of care is at the very heart of the disjointed, complex web of insurance carrier-based care we have in the US. In contrast, if we reformed healthcare so that there was a streamlined payer and simplified coverage, it would be much easier to implement changes such as global budgeting to better align the financial incentives with patient and societal interests. And that would absolutely cut down on waste, improve efficiency, improve patient care, and decrease cost.

☤ ☤ ☤ ☤ ☤

Let me make it clear at this point that I am not intrinsically opposed to the insurance industry. Just as for the hospital industry, the purpose of this book is neither to bash the insurance industry nor declare them moot. Not at all. Indeed, as you will see in later chapters, not only am I not opposed to the industry generally, I think the private insurance industry needs to have a place in the future healthcare system for a variety of reasons.

I believe in investments, and I believe capitalism has the power to create capital with which to do good. The flip side of this is that I clearly understand that the purpose of for-profit industry is to make money, and its purpose is *not* to "do good." It's not that the purpose of for-profit businesses is to do bad. Again, not at all. Their purpose is, very simply, to make money. That's actually the explicit charge of for-profit businesses.

Indeed, courts have ruled in the US that corporate officers have a fiduciary responsibility to the shareholders to make money for them, and that choosing to make less money in order to "do good" is not consistent with that fiduciary responsibility. The Dodge brothers proved that in 1919 when they successfully sued the Ford Motor Company for trying to cut dividends to shareholders so the company could hire more workers to help them build communities around the company.

The judge in the case ruled, "A business corporation is organized and carried on primarily for the profit of the stockholders. The powers of the directors are to be employed for that end. The discretion of directors is to be exercised in the choice of means to attain that end, and does not extend to a change in the end itself, to the reduction of profits, or to the nondistribution of profits among stockholders in order to devote them to other purposes."[14]

It's pretty simple, really. Companies exist to make money for their shareholders. And we should expect that is what they will do.

So, when I raise issues about the extent of profitability of the health insurance industry—as I am about to do—it is not out of any disrespect or disdain for capitalism. It is done in the context of a healthcare system that is buckling at the knees due to massive cost while delivering a poor product.

It makes no sense to blame insurance companies for the fact that they make lots of money. That's what they're supposed to do. You might as well blame a shark for eating other creatures. That's what sharks do. Sharks have an important role in the ocean ecosystem, holding in check, for example, populations of animals that would grow out of control without some form of predation. Nevertheless, we can recognize that while it is important to have sharks in the ocean and allow them to feed, we do not need to offer to serve ourselves up as their next meal.

Similarly, it makes no sense to blame insurance companies for providing products in the US healthcare marketplace. As we saw in chapter 4, they started doing this in the 1940s because of legal changes the US government implemented to its tax code as part of its war effort. Insurance companies provided a service that Americans found very useful at the time. So the health insurance industry is no more to blame for the dysfunctional US healthcare system than are patients, doctors, or hospitals. They emerged into it organically as it was being accidentally created. And they are all trapped in the same broken system along with the rest of us.

But that doesn't mean we should be willing to accept the *status quo*, where huge amounts of money are spent unwisely, and care is inefficient and ineffective. It means we should redesign the system of care so that the pieces that are important play a role well-suited for them and aligned with their purpose, and all in support of optimal patient care at a reasonable price.

Rather than blaming individual entities, I take the same view I espoused earlier, that the problem is the healthcare system itself. As Paul Batalden said, "Every system is perfectly designed to produce the results it gets."[15] So the question is not, are insurance companies bad or evil for making lots of money—they are neither. The question is, do we want to redesign the overall healthcare system in such a way as to decrease cost while improving care and outcomes and improving corporate competitiveness? And if so, what role should insurance companies play in such a redesigned system? We will get to the list of options, which absolutely does include multiple options in which private insurance companies play important roles, in the penultimate chapter.

In the meantime, I will discuss concerns about insurance

company profitability and overall revenue. The purpose of this discussion is to point out that there is a huge amount of capital in our healthcare system that could be redeployed to fund a much more intelligently functioning system. The fact is, insurance companies are very good at figuring out how to make money from the complexity of US healthcare. And every dollar in profit they earn is a dollar not spent on delivering care.

There are lots of ways to illustrate a disconnect between profitability and the product being provided. One of the more dramatic may be the profits that were made in California when the Affordable Care Act resulted in expanded state Medicaid. Medicaid is a federal program that funds healthcare for poor and disabled people. The working poor comprise the large majority of people on Medicaid rolls. For example, these include minimum wage workers, people who are independent contractors, or people who work for small businesses that do not have their own insurance benefits.

California's Medicaid program is called MediCal. When it expanded under the Affordable Care Act, an additional 5 million residents in California signed up for MediCal, dramatically cutting the rates of the uninsured in the state. At my large public hospital, the rate of uninsured patients fell from 45 percent to 5 percent. Seriously. That is a really good thing for all the reasons discussed earlier in the book.

Most of those who signed up for expanded MediCal were poor or had relatively low income. They could never have afforded healthcare out of pocket (who can?). So they signed up for MediCal, and now they can afford to get healthcare. They have access. The other positive side effect of this expansion of insurance is that our patients now have choices. So our public hospital has had to work hard to become competitive with the private sector because if patients don't like the care they get, they can simply pick up and go to another hospital (usually they have to change their provider network first). That competition is a healthy, underreported, underappreciated, positive side effect of the Affordable Care Act.

As MediCal expanded in California, insurance companies eagerly participated in the private exchanges the state set up to facilitate residents signing up for coverage. MediCal contracted with various private insurers as carriers for those insurance plans. And those private insurers figured out very quickly how to make money from the arrangement.

In 2017, an *LA Times* exposé found that from 2014 to 2016, private insurance companies collectively made $5.4 billion in net profit while insuring those poor people who purchased MediCal health plans under the Affordable Care Act expansion.[16] That's not total revenue. That's pure, net profit. Let me repeat, private insurance companies made more than $5 billion in pure profit to provide health insurance to poor people. That just has a bad feel about it, doesn't it?

Overall, the healthcare insurance industry makes a ton of money. In just the last calendar quarter (that is, three months) in 2017, the eight largest health insurance companies in the US made $7 billion in profit on an astounding $132 billion in revenue.[17] Again, they made that in just three months.

According to the National Association of Insurance Commissioners, in total in 2017, the US health insurance industry made $16.1 billion in profit on $671 billion in revenues.[18] Those astronomical numbers further increased in 2018 to a whopping $23.4

billion in net profit on $709 billion in revenues. That revenue number was equal to about 20 percent of all expenditures for healthcare in the US. Put another way, about one in every five dollars spent on healthcare in the US goes to pay companies that provide no care, but rather serve as middle agents in an exchange of money (from employers, workers, taxpayers, and patients) for services (provided by physicians, nurses, physical therapists, etc.). That money includes insurance industry profits, insurance overhead and administrative costs, and the exchange of money for those services.

Note that like hospitals, health insurance companies don't have high profit margins (the profit margin is net income divided by total revenue). The 2018 health industry sector profit margin was only 3.3 percent, which, as you may remember, is akin to nonprofit hospital operating margins, which average even lower at around 1.7 percent.[19,20] So it's not like insurance companies are making pharmaceutical-level profit margins (10-20 percent).[21] Nevertheless, their profits did increase from $16 to $23 billion from 2017 to 2018, and that happened despite their costs going up 5 percent. How does an industry increase net profit while its costs go up? By bringing in even more revenue, of course. They did this, at least in part, due to price increases, passed along to their policyholders—that would be you and me, folks.

Furthermore, health insurance company administrative costs were $92.4 billion—that is 13 percent of their total costs. So if you add together profits and administrative costs, neither of which participate in the exchange of money for healthcare service delivery, 16.6 percent of insurance company revenue had nothing to do with providing healthcare. That amounts to $115.8 billion in one year that did not contribute to healthcare delivery at all.

To foreshadow a coming conversation, by contrast, Medicare reports that it spent $740.6 billion on healthcare in 2017, of which only $9.9 billion, or 1.3 percent, went to administrative expenses (which includes salaries, overhead, and fraud detection and recovery programs).[12,13] And of course Medicare makes no profit and thus has no profit margin. That means if there were to be a switch from private insurers to a government-funded, universal healthcare program, one could anticipate a reduction in cumulative administrative and profit margin costs from around 16 percent to around the 1-2 percent range.

It is premature to entertain a discussion about whether there *should* be such a switch, as that is the subject of coming chapters. For now, we're just considering the potential dollars that could be saved. Several published analyses from distinct experts have estimated that if the US were to change from a system based on voluntary, employer-sponsored, private insurance to a single-payer system, the savings from administrative costs alone would be more than $200 billion, and possibly as much as $600 billion, per year.[2,4,8,9,22,23]

The point is, there is lots of money in our system that is not used to provide care. That money creates a buffer zone from which funds could be repurposed to help implement a more intelligently designed healthcare system in the US.

With all of this in mind, the question becomes, how should we redesign our system? It is time to take a look at the healthcare systems in our peer nations. Maybe we can learn from how they do things, to see if there are lessons that we can adopt in a redesign of the US system.

CHAPTER 6

||||||||||||||||||||||||

OTHER MODELS OF HEALTHCARE AMONG PEER NATIONS

Ms. H had breast cancer, insurance, and a private oncologist who was treating her with outpatient chemotherapy. One day, she began gasping for breath and collapsed at home. Her family called 911 and the ambulance rushed her to our hospital, where she was diagnosed with a pulmonary embolus. A pulmonary embolus is a blood clot that formed in her leg, likely as a complication of her cancer, and then traveled to her lung, reducing the oxygen level in her blood. Ms. H was admitted to the Intensive Care Unit and treated with an aggressive blood thinner. After a couple of days, she stabilized and was transferred to my internal medicine team.

When I went to meet her, I found Ms. H feeling much better. Her body had begun to break down the clot in her lung. So she was breathing more comfortably and requiring minimal oxygen.

Ms. H was a small, sweet, gray-haired dumpling of a grandma. She was lying in bed with her family gathered around her when

I walked into the room. After I introduced myself, I asked how she was feeling.

"Oh much better, thank you. I'm breathing better."

"Good! So, have you been up and walking around at all?"

"Yes, I was able to walk to the bathroom on my own today."

"You didn't get too short of breath when you walked?" I asked.

"Just a little. I'm feeling better."

"That's great. You're close to being able to go home."

"Oh good. I would like to go home as soon as I can."

"I don't blame you. It's no fun being in the hospital. Do you think you can get an appointment with your cancer doctor for this coming week?" I asked. "The blood clot you had could be a complication of your cancer, and you will need to take a blood thinner daily, in addition to your chemotherapy. Your doctor will need to be involved in managing all that."

She looked at me for a few moments. "Well, I'm not sure I'm going to be continuing to see him," she finally said.

"What do you mean? You're not happy with your oncologist?"

"It's not that," her son spoke up. "It's that the pills are very expensive."

"The pills she is already taking?" I asked. "The chemotherapy?"

"Yes," her son replied.

"But doesn't your insurance cover it?"

"Only part of it," her daughter answered. "We have to pay every time we pick up the medications. It's too expensive for us."

"Oh boy," I replied. "Well, the blood thinner is kind of expensive also. I'm not sure if you will have to pay more for that one, too. It depends on your insurance."

"When Mom leaves, we're going to take her to Mexico," her daughter said. "We can get much cheaper medicines there."

"Are you sure?" I asked.

They all nodded. "We just can't afford her treatment here," her son reiterated. "The insurance doesn't make it affordable. We were already considering moving Mom before this happened. Now we're going to for sure. She has relatives she can live with there."

I shook my head in amazed dismay. Our discharge plan was to help Ms. H move to Mexico so she could afford chemotherapy for breast cancer and a blood thinner for her potentially lethal blood clot.

⚕ ⚕ ⚕ ⚕ ⚕

That people need to leave the US to travel to another country to afford healthcare is disheartening. And to be sure, Mexico is not the only destination. As I was finishing up this book, one of my colleagues told me that one of her friends had developed cancer and had chosen to have it treated in South Korea instead of the US. This man was a US citizen, and owned a small business in the US. But the cost of treating the cancer was so outrageous in the US, compared to South Korea, he turned his business over to his relatives and moved to Korea for two years to complete his chemotherapy. He then moved back to the US to resume his life. Can you imagine? That seems Kafkaesque, doesn't it?

Stories among my colleagues abound about situations like this. People from the rest of the developed world are astounded that Americans tolerate paying the prices we pay for healthcare. The same week I learned about my colleague's friend going to Korea to take care of his chemotherapy, an article on the Taiwanese healthcare system was published on Vox.com. This article was part of the "Everybody Covered" project that I briefly discussed in chapter 1, and will discuss again at length at the end of this chapter.[1] At the end of the article, the reporter, Mr. Dylan Scott, wrote about a Taiwanese man who stopped him on the side of the road in rural Taiwan to ask him what he was doing in those parts.

Mr. Scott writes, "When I said I was an American reporting on healthcare, [the man] told me a story. He had a [Taiwanese] friend in Los Angeles who broke his arm…Rather than get it fixed in the United States, his friend decided to fly back to Taiwan and have it mended there because he said it would be cheaper."[2]

I've heard and read stories like this from countless people, and I'm betting you have as well. They involve trips to Canada, Latin America, and Asia, all to avoid the crushing costs of US healthcare. What is it that makes care so much more affordable in those countries?

⚕ ⚕ ⚕ ⚕ ⚕

Before we take a deep dive into exploring the various structures and workings of the healthcare systems from other countries, we need to clarify, distinguish, and define a few terms.

For example, what is a single-payer healthcare system, and how does it differ from or relate to universal healthcare? I find this to be a source of constant confusion, caused in part by the blurring of the terms in recent proposals made by prominent politicians regarding how to fix healthcare. Also, what is the difference between a national health service and single-payer? And what is the difference between government-provided healthcare and government-funded healthcare? Or between privately funded health insurance and privately operated health insurance?

CLARIFYING THE COMPONENTS OF THE HEALTHCARE SYSTEM

Let's start with the basics. We can broadly divide all healthcare systems into three participatory groups. When we use the term "healthcare system," we really mean all three of these groups.

THE PATIENT (I.E., THE HEALTHCARE RECIPIENT)

The first and most important component of the healthcare system is the patient who is in need of and/or receiving care. They are the people to whom healthcare services are being provided.

THE HEALTHCARE PROVIDER

The second component of the healthcare system is the healthcare provider, which in aggregate will provide medical and health services to the patient. Doctors tend to hate being called "providers," as they feel that the term cheapens the sacred fiduciary trust that doctors must have with their patients. We like to be called doctors or physicians, not providers. So, if you're a doc, I mean no disrespect when I use the term *provider*. In fact, when I use the term *provider*, I'm actually not referring to doctors, or indeed to any individual person. Rather, here and in the following sections, I use the term *provider* to refer to an entire organization comprised of many individuals who provide healthcare to many people (e.g., hospital, clinic, health maintenance organization, etc.). The term *provider*, as I use it, therefore includes both people who directly provide patient care, as well as the myriad and innumerable support staff that work collectively to enable care to be provided. So, just as the patient is the one who is receiving care, the provider is where they go to receive that care.

THE HEALTHCARE PAYER

The third component of the healthcare system is the payer. The payer is the source of money that pays for the care provided to the patient. As we have seen, in some ways, this is the most complex aspect of the US healthcare system. In other countries, as we will see, things are not so complex. But in the US, it can be hard to figure out in any one instance who the payers are or should be.

Before we name the various types of healthcare payers, I want to underscore a very important concept. There are actually two levels of healthcare payers—an obvious level that actually pays the immediate bill, and then a silent, but critical, deeper payer level. The obvious level of healthcare payers directly pays the healthcare providers for the actual episode of care. So when the hospital, pharmacy, or doctor's office drops a bill for healthcare rendered, the obvious level payer is the entity that actually pays that bill for services rendered.

But that obvious payer level is often simply a pass-through to a deeper payer, whose name is never on the actual check or wire transfer used to cover the bill, but who actually underwrites the money used by the obvious level payer to pay the bill. As we consider international models of healthcare in this chapter, and how we might change the US healthcare system going forward, it is critically important to remember these hidden payers who actually establish the financial bedrock on top of which the entire US healthcare system is funded.

With respect to the obvious level payers, we've got four types of participants in the US. First, we've got straight government insurance, such as Medicare and Medicaid, or the Veterans Affairs (VA) system. Government insurance is the obvious level payer for patients enrolled in those programs.

Second, we've got private insurers. These are private insurance companies that sign up individuals as customers. Customers pay insurance premiums to these companies to purchase and maintain health insurance. In turn, the companies are supposed to pay healthcare bills, as obvious level payers, when their customers become unlucky enough to have become patients who incur medical costs.

And then third we've got the patients themselves, who are not only the "customers" of the healthcare industry, but turn out to be participants as obvious level payers as well. We've described the many ways patients end up being obvious level payers. Uninsured patients are obvious level payers, as they pay their bills, or at least the amount they can afford, out of pocket. Insured patients pay deductibles, co-pays, and coinsurance, and a variety of other fees and add-on costs (e.g., per diem hospital rates, etc.), that go directly to the healthcare provider. So these payments also reflect obvious level payments. In contrast, the health insurance premiums patients pay go to private insurance companies, rather than directly to healthcare providers for care. So insurance premiums don't count as obvious level payments. We'll discuss premium payments further below.

Finally, we've got the American taxpayer, distinct from the patient who is paying for their own healthcare. We're going to discuss the all-important, deeper, hidden payer level next, and you can expect to see taxpayers come up again there. But for now, we should remember that the American taxpayer is also an obvious level payer. Why? Because someone has to pay for emergency care for patients who have no insurance and cannot afford their healthcare bills. The American taxpayer gets stuck with the bulk of that cost, paid directly to healthcare providers, funded by local, state, and federal taxes and fees.

Now let's turn our attention to the final participant in the healthcare system. Those elusive, hidden, nearly anonymous and invisible payers I mentioned. They provide the real funding that makes the entire healthcare system work. Who are we talking about? There are two groups in the US who serve in this foundational role. The first is you and me of course. It's the taxpayers of America. The second group is comprised of the businesses and employers of America.

Why do I refer to you, me, and corporate America as hidden, invisible payers? Let's stop and think about the obvious healthcare payers I listed above. Government insurance is funded entirely by American taxpayers, including individuals and corporations. Medicare, Medicaid, the VA, and other government/public health insurance programs may be the obvious level payers, but they don't have money trees in their backyards that they go pluck trillion-dollar bills from to pay healthcare bills. They are, rather, essentially intermediary pass-throughs funded by us and our taxes. So when we discuss these public insurance programs, we need to remember that the taxpayers of the US control and fund them, and we have a heckuva lot more influence over them than we do over private payers. Or at least we should, because we fund them with our taxes, and these programs answer to our elected officials, and we get to choose who we elect into office.

What about the second obvious level payer I mentioned before, the private insurance companies? How does the hidden, deeper, anonymous payer underwrite their costs? It's very simple. As alluded to earlier, we, the people, pay health insurance premiums. And those premiums are what fund the private health insurance industry. That is so important to remember. Like Medicare and Medicaid, private insurers are no more than pass-throughs for Americans and their employers who pay health insurance premiums.

We have seen in prior chapters how health insurance premiums are paid by a hidden, internal corporate "tax" (i.e., employer-funded benefit) combined with taking money out of workers' paychecks. For those who do not have employer-sponsored health insurance, the individual subscriber pays for the premium out of pocket, with or without a subsidy provided by the federal government (which, of course, is funded by other, fellow taxpayers).

Here's the fundamental, critical point. All healthcare costs in the US are ultimately born by the American people and businesses, who pay for healthcare directly out of pocket (personal or corporate). These payments are made via local, state, and federal taxes, and/or via reductions in worker pay to free up money for insurance premiums. To pretend otherwise is to be disingenuous.

Why is this so fundamentally important? Because people entrenched in the current model may attempt to mislead you. They may disingenuously claim that changing from an employer-sponsored health insurance system to one funded entirely by federal taxes will cause a massive tax increase on the American people. But Americans are already paying for healthcare via "employee benefits." The reality is those benefits are nothing more than a hidden tax on employees and their employers. It is a farce to pretend that American businesses and workers are not already underwriting current healthcare costs via taxes (including employee benefits), one way or another.

Switching the system from an employer-sponsored insurance system to a national, public sponsored health plan changes the direction of the flow of money, but does not inherently change the amount of money required to fund our system. Anyone who tells you otherwise either does not understand how our system works or has an agenda to maintain the status quo and is trying to scare you away from meaningful reform.

Since employers and taxpayers ultimately underwrite all healthcare costs in the US anyway, changing who the obvious level payers are will not change our healthcare costs. The obvious level payers are just pass-throughs for money spent by taxpayers and employers. If all we did was move from public insurance to private insurance or private insurance to public insurance, we would just be rerouting the money, not changing the amount spent.

At the end of the day, there are only three ways the cost of our healthcare will go down. First, people could live healthier lives so we could have fewer sick people. We should work on that, but let's not hold our breath—especially with the existing fee-for-service US healthcare system that thrives financially off sick people. Second, we can change the type of healthcare coverage our society offers (e.g., cover fewer people, or conversely cover everyone in society rather than just 90 percent as in the US currently). Covering everyone might, at first glance, appear to be more expensive. But that ignores the discussion we've already had that leaving people uninsured saves money up front, but costs much more later as the patient's illnesses become emergencies that cannot be ignored. So refusing to insure up front to save money may be being penny-wise and pound-foolish.

Third, we can fundamentally change the healthcare system to allow reform, shifting away from a fee-for-service model and towards global budgeting, eliminating unnecessary administrative overhead, negotiating better pricing, eliminating waste, and focusing on cheaper preventative care rather than expensive emergency care. Only by truly changing our healthcare system can we meaningfully reduce our costs. We'll talk more about this in the next two chapters.

CLARIFYING TERMINOLOGY

Now that I've clarified the basic components of our healthcare system in the US, let's define some very specific and confusing terms.

SINGLE-PAYER

A "single-payer" healthcare system is one in which the primary payer for a basic, comprehensive health plan available to all residents in the country is the government, funded by taxes. In this model, private insurance companies do not offer the national health insurance plan for the general public (which is not to say that there is no role for private insurance companies, a point I'll come back to in a moment). Rather, the government payer pays all the primary costs to deliver basic healthcare for all residents of the country. When healthcare bills are dropped by doctors, pharmacists, hospitals, clinics, etc., they bill the government as the payer. Period. It's simple, easy, and everyone is covered, essentially by definition. You don't really need an individual mandate per se, in a single-payer country, because the country just taxes everyone, and uses the funds to give everyone insurance.

As I mentioned, there can be a role for private insurance companies in single-payer countries. The single-payer exists for the mandatory care for which everyone is eligible. But private insurance companies can be allowed to exist to provide supplemental coverage or to provide access to private healthcare facilities to get expedited care. You can almost think of this like FasTrak or express toll lanes that exist alongside crowded freeways. The freeway exists for everyone's use and everyone pays taxes to maintain the freeway. But you can allow private industry to exist alongside the public freeway for people who choose voluntarily to spend their own money to buy expedited service.

People who choose to voluntarily spend extra to go into the Fas-Trak or express toll lanes still pay their share of taxes to support the public access portion of the freeway. This is a very important point that will come up again several times in coming chapters.

This concept has the potential to offer a compromise solution that bridges the divide between private insurance advocates and public insurance advocates.

To reiterate, individuals who choose to pay for the deluxe service in the FasTrak or express toll lanes are not exempted from paying their basic taxes that are used to support the public portion of the freeway. They simply choose to pay extra on top of that public cost for their expedited service. Similarly, as we will see, expedited healthcare is typically optionally available via private insurance, for extra cost, in essentially all countries that use a single-payer system.

What then is the difference between a single-payer system and a nationalized healthcare system? There is a big difference. A single-payer system only describes how healthcare is *paid* for, not how healthcare is *provided*. Remember the three components of our healthcare system, described above: patient, provider, and payer. Single-payer is the payer. That does not mean that government is the provider. The single-payer government plan can pay private and nonprofit groups and individuals to actually provide the care.

This is how Medicare and Medicaid work in the US. There are no Medicare or Medicaid hospitals in the US. Rather, private hospitals bill Medicare and Medicaid for the care the hospitals provide. Even county- or state-operated public hospitals bill federal Medicare and Medicaid for care. Thus, the federal government is the payer, but the private (or locally owned public) hospitals are the providers.

Alternatively, the single-payer system could own and operate its own healthcare provider delivery system. That is how the VA system works in the US. The VA system does own and operate its own federal hospitals. In the VA model, the federal government is both the payer and the provider.

Thus, single-payer systems can coexist with either a nationalized healthcare provider model (a la the VA), or a private healthcare provider model (a la Medicare/Medicaid). As we will see in a moment, international examples of both models exist.

UNIVERSAL HEALTHCARE

Some people use the term single-payer and universal healthcare synonymously. But they are not synonymous. Universal healthcare simply means that everyone is covered by healthcare. That's it.

As we've just described, single-payer means that the basic, mandatory universal coverage is only provided by a single government payer. But universal coverage can be achieved many ways. All single-payer systems are universal healthcare systems. But not all universal healthcare systems are single-payer. Indeed, universal coverage can be achieved via a blend of public and private insurance payers, or via multiple private payers. International models of both exist, which we will review.

So universal healthcare simply means that all permanent residents of a country are covered via health insurance, with no implication necessarily about how that insurance is funded, or who provides it. In order to achieve universal coverage, obviously everyone has to participate in the insurance plan. For single-payer systems, this is very straightforward. The government just taxes everybody and offers everybody insurance. Even if you choose not to use your government health insurance, it's still there for you, because in a single-payer model, you're still paying for it via taxes.

But without a single-payer, not everyone is taxed to pay for the public plan. People have a choice about where to buy their insurance from and they could choose simply not to spend any money on insurance. So in non-single-payer countries that have universal coverage, there is always an individual mandate that requires participation in one form of insurance or another. If people can simply choose not to participate, it destabilizes the insurance market, as we discussed at length in chapter 4.

AN OVERVIEW OF INTERNATIONAL HEALTHCARE MODELS

Having defined common healthcare terms, let's look at how healthcare is delivered in other countries. We will focus primarily on the same eleven, wealthy, peer nations we've discussed repeatedly throughout the book thus far. Lessons can certainly be learned from other countries, too. But the advantage we have with these eleven nations is that we have objective performance rankings for them from the Commonwealth Fund, so we can use those rankings to try to sort out which models of care perform better than others.

First, we will take a brief look at each individual nation's healthcare system, how it's financed, who provides the insurance, and who provides the care. We will then compare and contrast the healthcare systems in these countries, and hope to be able to draw some conclusions about the strengths and weaknesses of the various models.

The following healthcare system descriptions are amalgamated from a variety of sources, including multiple insightful Commonwealth Fund articles, as well as other academic and scholarly works.[3-9]

BRIEF DESCRIPTION OF INDIVIDUAL NATIONS' SYSTEMS

The United Kingdom

The British provide universal healthcare for all legal residents through a national healthcare organization called the National Health Service. The National Health Service is the largest single-payer healthcare system in the world. It is funded primarily by payroll taxes, which cover about 80 percent of its budget. Another 19 percent or so is covered by a so-called National Insurance contribution from employers and employees. Less than one percent of the single-payer system is funded by patient charges. Most care covered by the single-payer insurance system is completely free for the patient at the point of care.

The National Health Service is not only the payer, but is the provider of healthcare as well. The British national government owns and operates hospitals, clinics, and other care services components. Physicians and staff who work in the hospitals are employed by the government. Thus, the UK system is a universal, single-payer, and national healthcare provider healthcare system all in one.

All basic medical services are covered under the UK's single-payer plan, including inpatient and outpatient care, drugs, surgeries, and even ambulance transport and emergency care in the field. There are no deductibles or coinsurance payments for residents. There are some co-pays for drug prescriptions and dental services, but no other co-pays. These co-pays tend to be of relatively small amounts (e.g., under $20 for prescriptions). Thus, there is minimal out-of-pocket expense, no surprise bills for patients or their families, and thus no resulting bankruptcies or stress/trauma due to medical bills.

Despite having a universal, single-payer, government-run provider system, private health insurance does exist in the UK. As mentioned above, private insurance can be purchased by private citizens who want expedited service or a deluxe healthcare option, akin to using the FasTrak or express toll lane on a freeway. Those who pay extra have greater choice over who their specialist physician will be and likely shorter wait times for procedures.

Australia

Australia has universal healthcare provided through a federal government-run insurance program that, like the US's, is called "Medicare." Australian Medicare is funded by federal taxes on its citizens and provides insurance coverage for all citizens and permanent residents. Because Australia's government Medicare insurance program covers all permanent residents, it is a single-payer system.

Like the UK, Australia has an expansive network of public hospitals and outpatient facilities to provide care to all permanent residents. However, these facilities are owned and operated at the local or state/territory level of government rather than at the federal/national level. Hence, these facilities are more akin to public hospitals in the US, which are typically county-, district-, or state-operated. The Australian federal government insurance program, Medicare, covers full costs of care at these public facilities.

Outpatient primary care is fully covered with no out-of-pocket costs, while outpatient specialty care is mostly covered, except that there are co-pays for these visits. Similarly, the public Medicare insurance covers the cost of pharmaceuticals that are listed on the national formulary (list of approved drugs, with negotiated prices to keep costs under control), except that there is an out-of-pocket co-pay. In contrast, drugs not on the national formulary are not covered at all and must be paid for out of pocket entirely.

Australia also has a robust network of private physicians and facilities. Australians can access care at these facilities by voluntarily paying for private insurance, on top of the taxes they pay for federal Medicare. In addition to full coverage of costs of care at public hospitals, Medicare covers 75 percent of in-hospital fees for specific services at private hospitals.

Despite having a robust public system, the Australian government actually financially incentivizes high earners to obtain private insurance in order to off-load overcrowding at the public hospital and clinic networks. People making over a specific income threshold are levied an additional tax if they choose to not obtain private insurance, but that tax is waived if the individual purchases private insurance. Encouraged by this tax system, nearly half of Australians subscribe to some form of private insurance on top of the universal public coverage they have.

In addition to providing public insurance through Medicare, the Australian federal government also maintains a separate, "private" but publicly sponsored insurance plan that competes with for-profit health insurance plans. The purpose of this government-sponsored, nonprofit firm is to create competition with the private sector, seeking to counter the natural tendency to increase prices to raise profits.

The Netherlands

While the Netherlands also has universal healthcare coverage, its payer source is completely different from the UK and Australia. It is not a single-payer system. Rather it is a multi-payer system that relies on competing private insurance companies to pay for healthcare. Health insurance is mandatory for all residents in the Netherlands.

The Dutch purchase their insurance from private companies. However, much of the funding that ultimately goes to the private companies is paid by residents via taxes directly to the government. The government takes the centrally collected taxes and then distributes the funds as subsidies to the private health insurance companies. So the private companies that manage the insurance plans act sort of as fiscal intermediaries for the public money.

In addition to the bulk of payment to the health plans being provided by centrally collected taxes, insurance premiums are also paid out of pocket by the insured individuals to the plans. This then represents a third variation on the theme of government-funded universal healthcare, and on the theme of cooperation between government-mandated universal healthcare and private health insurance companies.

A complicated system of government oversight keeps close control over the private insurance companies. The government sets minimum standards for the basic insurance package with which all privately managed plans must comply. The insurance plans cover all basic medical care. For expensive treatment, there may also be out-of-pocket, add-on costs, akin to co-pays or coinsurance.

Insurers that pay out fewer claims receive less funding from the oversight regulator, and insurers that pay out more claims receive more funding. Also, all premiums for a given level of service are at a flat rate, so insurers cannot charge higher premiums for patients who have preexisting conditions. This system is intended to try to prevent private companies from gaming the system to increase profits.

In addition to paying into the universal (but multi-payer) health coverage, many Dutch residents choose to purchase supplemental, private insurance, as described for the UK and Australia. These plans cover the cost of co-pays for drugs and other expenses that may not be covered by the universal plan (e.g., dental care, eye care). In contrast to universal coverage, private, supplemental insurance isn't regulated by the government, allowing the companies providing them to compete.

The Netherlands has state-run public hospitals, but most healthcare is delivered by private, nonprofit hospitals and clinics.

New Zealand

The fourth-ranked healthcare system on the Commonwealth Fund list is that of New Zealand, which also has universal, single-payer healthcare. Like Australia, New Zealand has an extensive network of public hospitals and clinics that are operated by district health boards. These public healthcare entities provide care to permanent residents at no cost, including for any hospitalization or specialty care referred by a primary care physician.

Visits to primary care physicians and prescription drugs on the national formulary do require co-pays, but are otherwise free—as for the other countries above, drugs not on the national formulary are not covered at all and must be paid for entirely out of pocket. There is also a public corporation, the Accident Compensation Corporation, which covers cost of care related to traumatic injury due to accidents, even for tourists.

The public, universal aspects of the healthcare system are funded by income taxes and payroll tax contributions from both employers and employees, as well as other taxes (e.g., on vehicle registration). Low-income residents can qualify for government subsidies to defray much of these costs.

As in Australia, the public health provider network seeks to off-load care by encouraging individuals to purchase private insurance. Private insurance is used as described above for the UK and Australia, to enable expedited care compared to the potential waits in the public system. Nevertheless, individuals who purchase private insurance may still use the public system.

Norway

Norway operates a universal, single-payer healthcare system more akin to the National Health Service in the UK. All legal residents are covered and may receive free care in public hospitals operated by the government. The national health insurance budget is funded by taxes, as well as an annual "deductible," of around $250 per year for all adults, which functions like a fixed tax payment to the government. This annual expense enables adults to receive most types of healthcare for free, with the exception of co-pays for most outpatient visits, elective surgery, medical equipment, and for some pharmaceuticals.

As for the other countries mentioned, pharmaceutical costs are only covered for specific drugs that are listed on a national formulary; non-formulary drug costs are not covered by the national public insurance plan and must be paid for out of pocket, although government subsidies may be available for expensive drugs.

Private health clinics also function for outpatient care for those who pay extra. However, in Norway, the vast majority of healthcare costs are spent and care provided in the public system. There are no private hospitals for inpatient care. Hence, as mentioned, Norway functions somewhat akin to the UK, as a universal, single-payer, government healthcare provider.

As for each of the countries thus far discussed, private insurance is primarily used to receive deluxe, expedited outpatient and surgical care. Less than 10 percent of Norwegians purchase private health insurance.

Sweden

Sweden has universal, single-payer healthcare, funded primarily (>95 percent) by taxes, with small contributions of out-of-pocket expenses from individuals. The public health insurance system covers all legal residents. In contrast to the other countries thus far discussed, the primary taxing authority to fund the healthcare system is local and state, rather than the national government. The providers of healthcare are primarily employed by the local district authority, and the local districts operate the hospitals, clinics, and medical facilities. In that sense, the public hospital system may be more akin to those found in Australia and New Zealand.

Residents of Sweden pay co-pays for outpatient visits and also a daily co-pay for inpatient stays. However, there is an annual maximum out-of-pocket expense Swedes pay, after which the national health insurance takes over payment. In contrast to the other countries thus far discussed, the national health insurance does not cover prescription drug costs, although if annual prescription drug costs for a patient exceed a maximum, government subsidies defray the costs.

Private insurance exists in Sweden, but it covers 1 percent or less of the population. However, private physicians, who are not employed by the district or regional health facilities, can accept patients and payments from the public insurance system.

Switzerland

The Swiss system is different from most of the countries thus far discussed. It is most similar to the Netherlands. It has universal healthcare, but it is multi-payer, not single-payer, and it does not have a public option. Rather, Switzerland requires all residents to purchase insurance through a private health exchange. Insured individuals have annual deductibles and also coinsurance that requires the individual to pay 10 percent of the costs of healthcare above a specific threshold.

The deductible and coinsurance model is different than the other countries mentioned, and as a result, places a larger burden on out-of-pocket spending. As for the Netherlands, private insurers are required to offer the same basic healthcare package to everyone, irrespective of underlying illness or other factors. They are not allowed to profit off the basic package. Private insurance company profits derive from supplemental plans purchased by individuals. For residents whose annual premium costs exceed 8 percent of their income, there is a government subsidy to offset the balance.

The basic Swiss universal health insurance package covers most costs of primary and specialty care services, as well as drug costs. Hospital costs are also covered, but are further subsidized by local taxes, which support the infrastructure of healthcare provision.

Germany

Like the Swiss system, German universal care is not single-payer. Instead, Germany relies heavily on private, nonprofit insurance entities, which are called "sickness funds" to universally cover its residents. As for each of the other countries on the list— except for the US—Germany has an individual mandate. All German adults must purchase participation in a public sickness fund or private insurance.

The sickness funds are paid for via a combination of employer benefit payments and employed and unemployed individuals' out-of-pocket contributions. The government subsidizes these contributions for low-income earners. The public, nonprofit insurance funds offer comprehensive coverage for inpatient and outpatient care and drugs. However, there are co-pays for each of these services. As mentioned, residents can also choose to purchase private insurance in lieu of the public option, a choice obviously more commonly made by high-income earners. The healthcare providers are private physicians who receive pay from public or private insurance sources. However, the state does own and operate large teaching hospitals as well.

Canada

The US's neighbor to the north has one of the more famous single-payer systems. Residents are automatically eligible for the universal, single-payer health insurance. However, the insurance is operated at the level of the state/province, rather than the national level, somewhat akin to Australia and New Zealand. The insurance is funded by income, sales, and corporate taxes, and individual provinces can levy additional funds via other means if they choose.

There is a substantial amount of insurance coverage offered via private, often for-profit insurance companies, to supplement the public system. Most Canadians (e.g., 75 percent) choose to pay for supplementary private insurance, which covers 25 percent to 30 percent of Canadian healthcare costs. The private insurance enables deluxe, accelerated care for some specialty care and surgeries for which there may be waits in the public system. Much of the costs of the private health insurance premiums are covered by employers as components of benefit packages.

Healthcare providers, such as physicians and hospitals, are not employed by the government—this is not a national healthcare service like in the UK. Indeed, Canada is the only country on our list that has a single-payer system but where the government does not own and operate a large network of hospitals or clinics that provide the majority of care for its residents. Private physicians and hospitals bill the public insurance system directly to get paid for care.

The public insurance covers outpatient and inpatient care, and there are no deductibles and very limited co-pays for basic healthcare. However, the public insurance does not cover prescription drugs, which is one reason so many Canadians choose to purchase private insurance.

France

The French healthcare system is very similar to the German system. It is a universal healthcare system in which participation is compulsory, and the insurance is handled by private, nonprofit health funds. The insurance is purchased from the funds by deductions from employee's pay or out-of-pocket costs. The payments are proportionate to income level. The funds also receive money from national tax sources, such as income tax.

The funds work by reimbursing healthcare costs after they have been spent (rather than up front), with reimbursement rates ranging between 80 to 100 percent depending on the cost. As for the German system, people can also purchase supplemental private insurance to help fill in coverage gaps and expedite care.

Most physicians are privately employed. However, the majority of French hospitals are publicly operated.

⚕ ⚕ ⚕ ⚕ ⚕

As you can tell, there are myriad ways to deliver healthcare among these eleven peer nations. Thus, we need not think rigidly in black-and-white terms about how healthcare systems must be designed. If there is one rule we can take away from looking at these eleven countries, it seems to be that there is no specific rule about how healthcare must be designed, paid for, or delivered.

But which systems work better? To try to answer this question, we can analyze the relationship between the various design elements of these healthcare systems and how they perform relative to one another in Commonwealth Fund rankings.

WHICH MODELS PERFORM BETTER?

UNIVERSAL HEALTHCARE SYSTEMS

As mentioned, the US is the only one of the eleven countries that does not operate a universal healthcare system. If we plot the Commonwealth Fund Overall rankings for these countries, separated by whether they have universal healthcare coverage or not, we find that the average Overall ranking for the ten countries that have universal healthcare is 5.5, versus eleven for the one that does not (Figure 6-1).

The same is true for Healthcare Outcomes rankings. Thus not having universal healthcare results in poor overall performance and poor performance on healthcare outcomes, as well. Since not having health insurance is an independent predictor of death for patients, it makes sense that countries that provide health insurance to all residents have better outcomes than a country that does not.

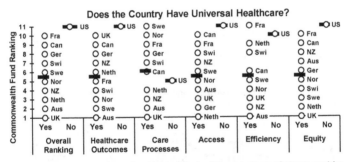

Figure 6-1. Commonwealth Fund rankings of the healthcare systems of eleven wealthy, peer nations, separated by whether or not they have universal healthcare coverage. Yes or No indicates whether the country has universal healthcare or not—only the US does not. The category of ranking is indicated on the bottom row. The black lines indicate the average rankings. Data are adapted and reproduced with permission from the Commonwealth Fund, https://www.commonwealthfund.org/chart/2017/health-care-system-performance-rankings.[8]

Universal healthcare also appears to be associated with better

Access to Care (duh), Equity of Care (double duh), and Administrative Efficiency.

The one category that does not appear to be affected by having universal healthcare coverage or not is Care Processes. Recall from chapter 1 that this category ranks the healthcare system based on preventative care measures and safety of care. It may seem somewhat surprising that having universal healthcare does not intrinsically bring advantages to preventative measures and care safety. Clearly, how one implements the universal system must have an impact.

SINGLE-PAYER COVERAGE

In contrast to universal coverage, which had a dramatic impact on most categories, Figure 6-2 shows a much more even mix of outcomes across countries with vs. without single-payer coverage. The overall rankings trend better for countries with single-payer coverage; the Netherlands is the outlier, as the only high ranking multi-payer country. The Netherlands, as an outlier, is a theme we will come back to at the end of this chapter.

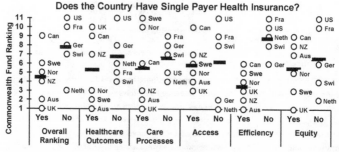

Figure 6-2. Commonwealth Fund rankings of the healthcare systems of eleven wealthy, peer nations, separated by whether or not they have single-payer insurance. Yes or No indicates whether the country has single-payer coverage or not. The category of ranking is indicated on the bottom row. The black lines indicate the average rankings. Data are adapted and reproduced with permission from the Commonwealth Fund, https://www.commonwealthfund.org/chart/2017/health-care-system-performance-rankings.[8]

The three countries with the best Healthcare Outcomes are single-payer, but behind those three countries, things become blurred, so single-payer is not reliably associated with better outcomes. Single-payer systems also do not appear to have better Access or Equity of Care, which makes sense, since access and equity are assured by having a universal system, whether single-payer or not.

But the one category that is clearly affected by single-payer status is Administrative Efficiency. This makes complete sense. If there is only one payer, far fewer administrators, paperwork, and bureaucracy are needed to assess financial status, eligibility and authorization for services, billing, and collections. Thus, single-payer should be, and is, more efficient than a multi-payer system.

NATIONAL/GOVERNMENT-OPERATED HEALTHCARE PROVIDERS

We can also consider the impact of having government-owned-and-operated hospitals and clinics serving as the healthcare provider for the majority of a country's residents (Figure 6-3). The UK is the most extreme example of this. However, all the single-payer countries, with the exception of Canada, maintain a comprehensive network of public hospitals to provide such care to most of their residents.

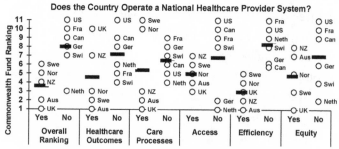

Figure 6-3. Commonwealth Fund rankings of the healthcare systems of eleven wealthy, peer nations, separated by whether or not they operate a national healthcare provider system. Yes or No indicates whether the country operates such a system or not. The category of ranking is indicated on the bottom row. The black lines indicate the average rankings. Data are adapted and reproduced with permission from the Commonwealth Fund, https://www.commonwealthfund.org/chart/2017/health-care-system-performance-rankings.[8]

Thus, there is great overlap between the impact of single-payer and national/governmental healthcare provision on the rankings. The only difference between the two is that Canada flips to a "No" in the National Healthcare Provision category. Nevertheless, Canada ranks fairly low on many categories, so this does clarify several rankings. There is a clear trend to better overall rankings for countries that operate a public system of care providers, with the Netherlands again the primary outlier. Healthcare Outcomes, Care Processes, Access to, and Equity of Care are more mixed. However, countries operating their own network of public care providers are clearly more efficient.

PRIMARY RELIANCE ON PRIVATE INSURANCE

Finally, we can ask what the impact is of relying primarily on public insurance versus private insurance as payers for healthcare (Figure 6-4). Countries that rely on private insurance generally had worse overall rankings, with the Netherlands once again being an outlier. Administrative Efficiency was also substantially worse for countries relying on private insurance.

Most of the other rankings were similar for private vs. public payer countries.

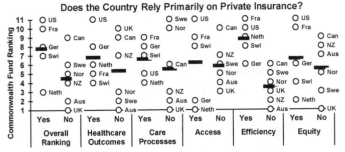

Figure 6-4. Commonwealth Fund rankings of the healthcare systems of eleven wealthy, peer nations, separated by whether they rely primarily on private or public insurance to cover their residents. Yes or No indicates whether the country operates such a system or not. The category is indicated on the bottom row. The black lines indicate the average rankings. Data are reproduced with permission from the Commonwealth Fund, https://www.commonwealthfund.org/chart/2017/health-care-system-performance-rankings.[8]

SUMMARY OF RANKINGS BY SYSTEM CHARACTERISTICS

In aggregate, these rankings plotted against healthcare system characteristics tell a series of compelling stories. In general, nations with single-payer insurance have better rankings overall and on Administrative Efficiency, and trend better on Healthcare Outcomes. In contrast, countries that predominantly rely on private health insurance tend to have worse overall rankings, as well as worse rankings on Healthcare Outcomes and Administrative Efficiency.

Most impressively, the countries that use private, multi-payer health insurance systems all have the worst Administrative Efficiency ratings, and also have higher overall healthcare costs per GDP. For example, the US, Germany, Switzerland, the Netherlands, and France have the worst Administrative Efficiency ratings and are also among the most expensive countries, whether assessed by cost per person or cost per GDP (Figures 2-3 and 2-4). It seems intuitive that being administratively inefficient would be associated with greater cost to the system.

Now there are major caveats to these patterns and trends. For example, there are not that many countries analyzed. As a result, we can't draw definitive conclusions from these comparisons. But we don't need statistical precision here. We are looking for trends and patterns as a guide to how we might redesign a US healthcare system that is convincingly inferior to all of its peer nations, and many nations that are economically not its peers.

We have choices to make. Those choices should be informed to some extent by the experiences of others. The international models of care that exist do give us some signposts as to which paths we might consider taking on our own journey in the US. We will extensively consider these paths, and the implications of the above international patterns, in chapter 8.

THE EVERYBODY COVERED PROJECT

In chapter 1 and earlier in this chapter, I briefly mentioned the "Everybody Covered" project, published in January of 2020 by the news website Vox.com.[1] The project was funded by a grant from the ubiquitous and prolific Commonwealth Fund.[1] The "Everybody Covered" articles, written by reporters Dylan Scott, Ezra Klein, and Tara Golshan, provide an incredibly insightful, contemporary look at key aspects of the healthcare debate, framed against existing systems in several countries. In chapter 1, we reviewed Ms. Golshan's article on the Maryland effort to implement hospital global budgeting. Now let's review the other articles covering international healthcare systems.

TAIWAN

Taiwan is not included in the Commonwealth Fund rankings of international healthcare systems. So its healthcare system has not been discussed as robustly as other nations to this point in the book. Nevertheless, the history and experience of healthcare in Taiwan is highly informative to the US healthcare situation. Perhaps that is why the first story released by reporter Dylan Scott as part of the "Everybody Covered" series was a fascinating look at the healthcare system in Taiwan.[2]

As described by Mr. Scott in his *Vox* article, Taiwanese have excellent access to care, with short wait times for procedures.[2] Taiwan has also managed to greatly rein in healthcare costs. In the early 1990s, immediately before switching from their prior, multi-payer system to their current single-payer system, costs had been growing at a staggering 10-17 percent per year. Within five years of single-payer implementation, cost increases were down to 4 percent per year, and have continued at that level or lower for the ensuing fifteen years.[10,11] Taiwan's current healthcare costs run around 6 percent of its GDP, placing its costs at about one-third of the costs of the US system.[10,11]

Taiwan has used two key strategies to rein in its costs. The first is unleashing the power of national/federal negotiations regarding pricing. Taiwanese residents pay 50 to 75 percent less than Americans do for drugs, surgical procedures, and radiographic imaging.[11] The second mechanism employed by Taiwan to keep its costs under control is global budgeting. In fact, as alluded to in chapter 2, Taiwan instituted a hospital global budgeting system similar to that used by the state of Maryland to effectively keep costs down.[11]

As mentioned in chapter 5, Taiwan's single-payer, globally budgeted system keeps administrative costs to a remarkably low proportion of overall healthcare costs, akin to the rate in the US Medicare program.[2] In fact, in 2019, Taiwan's administrative costs were less than 1 percent of its overall healthcare costs.[11] Thus, the Taiwanese experience supports the greatly streamlined efficiency of single-payer systems compared to multi-payer systems, consistent with the data we've seen in this chapter.

Despite having a much less expensive healthcare system, Taiwan's healthcare outcomes are better than those in the US. Taiwanese have longer life spans than Americans, and Taiwan markedly improved its mortality rate amenable to healthcare, even while the US has done worse.[2,10]

In 2015, Dr. Tsung-Mei Cheng, professor at Princeton University, who, with her husband, helped to design the Taiwanese system in the mid-1990s, published a twenty-year retrospective on the system.[10] She noted that in the late 1980s, fully 40 percent of Taiwanese residents had no health insurance. Exploration into changing the system began in the late 1980s, and by 1995, the single-payer system was in place. In 2020, more than 99.9 percent of Taiwanese people have full health insurance coverage.[10,11] The uninsured primarily consist of Taiwanese ex-patriots living overseas.

As to the concern about choice in the US, Dr. Cheng has pointed out that we may have set up a false dichotomy between having a single-payer system and having choice. In the conclusion of her retrospective, she wrote, "Taiwan's experience also might induce

Americans to think more deeply about the term freedom of choice...For Taiwan's citizens, freedom of choice among providers of health care trumped freedom of choice among insurance carriers and contracts...By contrast, in the United States, freedom of choice among insurance carriers and products ranks above freedom of choice among health care providers, which often is limited to narrow networks of providers."[10]

What Dr. Cheng was pointing out was that picking your health insurance carrier does not mean you have a choice as to who your doctor is, because insurance carriers set up networks of physicians and hospitals. As we've repeatedly discussed, these networks actually limit your choice of where you get your care. And if you get care out of network, you are facing a crushing financial consequence.

Dr. Cheng more recently added, "Patients in Taiwan can choose their doctors and hospitals freely, in sharp contrast to the US, where patients often have limited choice of both insurers and providers. There is no such thing as in- or out-of-network providers, a distinction which in the US not only restricts patients' access but also subjects them to vastly different charges. Patients in Taiwan do not receive the "surprise medical bills" that many Americans do after their inpatient or outpatient treatment... [and] co-payments and coinsurance are low, and generous ceilings and exemptions safeguard access to needed care."[11]

In short, Taiwan serves as an example of a country that was able to successfully and fairly rapidly switch its healthcare system from a disjointed, expensive multi-payer system, to a much more efficient single-payer system. Costs have been held in check, in contrast to the US. And outcomes have improved, again in contrast to the US. Thus, Taiwan provides additional supporting evidence regarding the Commonwealth Fund data showing the relationship between efficiency, outcomes, and single-payer status.

MORE THOUGHTS ON AUSTRALIA

The second story published by Mr. Scott as part of the "Everybody Covered" project focused on the Australian healthcare system.[12] As we reviewed in this chapter, the Australian system of healthcare is one of the most successful in the world. It seems to have achieved a remarkable balance between single-payer, universal coverage while still retaining a vibrant, multi-payer private health insurance system that affords choice to its residents. And indeed, that is what Mr. Scott found when he went to Australia to take a closer look at the system.

However, Mr. Scott wrote about one very important additional aspect of the Australian system: the decades-long pendulum swinging back and forth between government alternatively emphasizing support for the public or the private system. The current state appears to be one in which private healthcare costs are rising above those in the public system, and Australians are increasingly asking why they should spend so much to subsidize a private, multi-payer system.

In his article, Mr. Scott asked the question: is the private health insurance system intended to serve as an alternate, equivalent system to the public plan? Or is it rather intended to serve as a supplement to the public plan for those who are willing to pay extra for deluxe or premium service? If the former, it makes sense for the government (and hence the public, who pay taxes) to subsidize the private enterprise. If the latter, it doesn't make so much sense to do this.

Mr. Scott described concerns in Australia about a potential death spiral of costs in Australian private health insurance. The private system has been less effective than the public system at restraining costs. As private health insurance premiums and costs spike, Australian residents are increasingly favoring use of the public system. Over time, this may make the private system increasingly unstable, requiring many billions of dollars per year of government subsidies to keep it afloat. And if you have to heavily subsidize the private marketplace with public dollars, why even have it? Why not fold it into the public system?

It is important for us to remember that no system will ever be perfect. Any system will have growing pains and will need to adjust and accommodate to changing realities in the country over time. So, we should not think of any country as having an "ultimate" or permanent solution.

Nevertheless, given the dysfunctional state of the US healthcare system, I think Americans would all *love* to be in a place where we are having a philosophical debate about how to further optimize a system that is already one of the best, most effective, and most cost-effective systems in the world. Instead, in the US we are considering how to completely turn around a failed system that has resulted in by far the most expensive healthcare in the world, leaving people broken, bankrupt, and dying.

In the coming years, Australians will make choices about how to optimize their already incredibly high-performing system. Meanwhile, Americans have been struggling to figure out a way to make their system bearable. In which country would you rather receive *your* healthcare?

A SECOND LOOK AT THE NETHERLANDS

The third story run by Dylan Scott for Vox.com as part of the "Everybody Covered" project was about the Netherlands. The Netherlands is a particularly interesting focus because, as I alluded to several times throughout this chapter, it seemed to be an outlier in the Commonwealth Fund rankings. Is there an explanation for the fact that the Netherlands was the only non-single-payer country using private insurance that performed very well on these rankings (Figures 6-1 to 6-4)?

The first observation I'll make in exploring this interesting question is that the overall #3 ranking for the Netherlands is driven by Access to Care (for which they ranked #1), Equity of Care (for which they ranked #2), and Care Processes (for which they ranked #4). The Netherlands was in the middle of the rankings on Healthcare Outcomes (#6), and they performed relatively poorly on Administrative Efficiency (#9).

What this suggests to me, personally, is that the individuals who manage healthcare in the Netherlands really know how to run a healthcare system, despite the efficiency obstacles intrinsically created by having a complex web of private insurance. For this healthcare system to achieve excellent equitability and accessibility ratings, the managers must be sufficiently skilled to maintain access to appointments and hospital beds despite the inherent inefficiency of the multi-payer system. Thus, my first potential explanation is that unusually good management may be at play here, accounting for these rankings, and overcoming the potential limitations of a multi-payer, private, insurance-based system.

A second set of hypotheses was raised to me in a Twitter exchange I had with two healthcare systems experts in October of 2019. Lisa Bari, a consultant on value-based healthcare, and Herko Coomans, a Dutch expert on health information technology, were gracious enough to engage in a fascinating discussion around this issue. They felt that part of the explanation for the Netherlands' excellent performance in healthcare was due to the homogeneity of the population and the small size of the Netherlands relative to the US. And the Netherlands is indeed smaller than some of the other European nations that use private, multi-payer insurance, such as Germany and France. Perhaps the size and scope of the coverage, and the relative homogeneity of the population, makes it easier for strong managers to ensure the system works well.

But Mr. Coomans offered another explanation, which feels equally, if not more likely to be correct. He suggested that the relative healthcare successes in the Netherlands versus the US may relate more to culture than to actual operations or schematics of the system. In the Netherlands and in other European countries, he tweeted, healthcare is seen as a social responsibility. He indicated that private insurers in the Netherlands behave in a way aligned with this sense of social responsibility, as much or more as being driven by economic and profit concerns.

In contrast, as I have alluded to earlier in this book, the US is deeply imbued with a culture of capitalism (which is no doubt responsible for much of the US's economic success over the centuries—so again, this is not a pejorative). That culture may potentially make the focus of private insurance companies in the US different than in other countries, like the Netherlands.

This cultural explanation is supported by the investigative reporting by Mr. Scott on Vox.com.[13] After studying their system and visiting the Netherlands to get a firsthand look, Mr. Scott likened the system in the Netherlands to the Affordable Care Act, but expanded to cover everyone. As Mr. Scott relates, what makes this system work in the Netherlands are: 1) the enactment of an enforced individual mandate, which requires that everyone participate in health insurance; and 2) the acceptance of a greater degree of government regulation over private, capital markets. Thus, Mr. Coomans appears to have been onto something in his Twitter responses to me. Culture may be the predominant factor here.

The individual mandate in the Netherlands is rather austere. According to Mr. Scott, people who do not sign up for healthcare not only pay a fine, but they are also then automatically enrolled in a health plan (whether or not they want it) and they are charged 20 percent more for their premiums than had they voluntarily enrolled in a plan. Can you imagine Americans standing for this? The much more benign individual mandate in the US was an abject failure, beaten into submission, and ultimately into nonexistence, by endless, partisan bickering. Would those same partisan forces somehow mellow and tolerate a much more austere individual mandate like the one used to make the Netherlands' system work?

Furthermore, we could seriously question whether American businesses and the public would tolerate the degree of government regulation over private enterprise that is culturally acceptable in the Netherlands. Without strict government controls to set premium pricing and preclude nudging sick patients off of private insurance rolls to maximize profit, a private multi-payer system that had no public backstop would quickly devolve. For these reasons, it is not clear that a system like the one in the Netherlands could work in the US.

And there are storm clouds on the horizon for the Netherlands' private, multi-payer system. Specifically, Mr. Scott highlighted rising costs in the private system,[13] similar to those experienced in Australia. Furthermore, he described increasing difficulties of patients being able to pay rising out-of-pocket costs for their healthcare in the Netherlands, raising concerns about people increasingly voluntarily foregoing care, as they do in the US.

As in Taiwan, the Netherlands' current healthcare system is new (less than twenty years old in its current form). The fact that costs are rising more rapidly than before and that patients have substantially larger gaps in coverage and out-of-pocket costs than before raises concerns about the sustainability of the system in the long run.

The Netherlands' multi-payer system is working for now. But whether it is sustainably cost-effective over the long run and can maintain current healthcare access for patients even as prices rise and out-of-pocket costs go up remains to be seen. The Australian system appears to be inherently more stable because even if prices drove people out of the private insurance market, everyone is already paying into, and therefore has access to, the public system that has remained stable. There is no such backstop for insurance in the Netherlands.

In any event, two major take-home points are worth noting. First, any system can be made to work if it is managed properly and it fits within the overall, global, cultural framework of the nation it serves. Second, just because one country can make such a system work does not mean another country, which has different sociodemographics, population, and culture will be able to do so.

It is nearly time for us to take a deep dive on potential options to redesign the US healthcare system to move away from its accidental origins and to move towards a rationally planned system of care. But before we do, there is one more potentially instructive comparator to look at: an effort to design a single-payer system in the most populous and wealthiest state in the US.

CHAPTER 7

‖‖‖‖‖‖‖‖‖‖‖‖‖‖‖‖‖‖

CALIFORNIA (SINGLE-PAYER), HERE I COME!

Ms. I was a delightful, middle-aged lady who had been admitted to my internal medicine team with heart failure. As we have discussed before with several prior patients, heart failure is one of the most common reasons patients are admitted to the hospital. One of the problems is that patients with heart failure need to take diuretic medications to help them urinate out all the excess water that builds up in their bodies because their hearts aren't pumping blood well to the kidneys. When patients run out of medications, or their heart failure worsens and the dose of medication they are taking is no longer adequate and needs to be adjusted higher, they typically end up back in the hospital. That's what happened to Ms. I.

We put Ms. I on strong medication administered intravenously to help her get rid of her excess fluid. We controlled her blood pressure to help her heart pump blood more effectively. And, as expected, Ms. I responded well to treatment over a several-day period. As she got substantially better, we began to consider what our discharge plan was going to be. So, I went with our residents to chat with Ms. I, to sort out her follow-up plan, and to figure out where she was going to get her medications from in the future.

After we walked into the room and exchanged greetings, I asked, "Tell me, where do you live?"

"Oh my, I live far away from here. I live all the way out in the desert area."

"The desert area?" I asked. "That's like an hour and a half away from here. How did you end up with us, here?"

"Sweetie, it's hard to find a place to go with my insurance. I've got MediCal, and lots of places out there don't want to take it. This is where I come, because I know you guys will take care of me."

"But how do you get down here?"

"I drive. I drive. Swollen legs and all."

"So your car is here, parked somewhere?"

"Mm-hmm."

"Jeesh! We can't find a place closer for you?"

"Like I said, this is where I come, because I know you'll take care of me. I haven't had good experiences out by where I live. I get turned away. They don't want to take the MediCal."

"But it seems ridiculous that you should have to drive all the way over here when you get sick."

"You're preaching to the choir, Doctor. Amen to that."

⚕ ⚕ ⚕ ⚕ ⚕

Imagine if you were Ms. I. You have heart failure. Your legs swell up like giant, boggy sponges. You put on ten pounds of water weight in a few days. Your medications aren't working. You can't walk. You can't breathe well. You can't lie flat without gasping for breath, so you sleep bolt upright at night. You need to go to the hospital. But the hospitals in the area aren't thrilled with your insurance. So you pile into your car, with your boggy, swollen, heavy legs, and drive ninety minutes to reach a public hospital.

Does that seem right to you? Does that seem like something that would happen in a first-world, developed country? Not to mention the richest country on Earth?

What's wrong with this picture? Why is this okay? We know this doesn't happen in our peer nations. They have universal healthcare. Ms. I would have been able to go to any hospital to get care. Why can't that happen where we live? If not in the US, what about in the state of California? That is the subject of this chapter. And the lessons we learn from evaluating this question will be directly applicable to our penultimate chapter 8, when we consider the feasibility of revamping healthcare in the US to make it universal, effective, and affordable.

⚕ ⚕ ⚕ ⚕ ⚕

In 2017, a serious effort was initiated to pass legislation in the California State Assembly to implement a statewide, single-payer healthcare system. Ultimately the bill, The Healthy California Act, also known as Senate Bill 562, was sent to committee, where it died. But while the bill was under consideration, an extensive dialogue occurred around the possibility of successfully establishing a single-payer system in the nation's most populous state.

Critics vehemently denounced the financial infeasibility and the crushing tax debt that a single-payer system would impose on the public. Proponents advocated for it based on considerations we've repeated throughout this book: the US healthcare system is broken, outrageously expensive, leaves many people uninsured and even more underinsured, leads to bad care and poor outcomes, and leaves ordinary citizens at risk for sudden, catastrophic medical debt.

The single-payer concept was not a crazy or irresponsible idea. As we have seen in prior chapters, universal healthcare delivers better results internationally than the US achieves without it. Single-payer countries tend to operate less expensive, more efficient systems of care. It seems intuitive that it should be workable to implement. But, of course, the devil is always in the details.

The learning that occurred during dialogue around the California SB 562 legislation is very applicable to considerations for implementing a universal healthcare system across the US. It uncovered the primary economic, regulatory, legal, and political barriers to enacting such a system. Let's delve into the history of this bill. This analysis will help us understand how a giant healthcare system can be switched from a voluntary, multi-payer, nonuniversal system heavily reliant on private insurers, to a single-payer system.

To underscore why this exercise is relevant to considerations for a national health plan, let's start with a brief background on the scale of California relative to the US as a whole. California is the most populous state in the US, with 39.6 million residents—the next most populous state is Texas, which has nearly 11 million fewer residents.[1] California's population comprises more than 10 percent of the entire US population. California's population is actually larger than the population of either Canada or Australia, both of which, of course, have successful single-payer healthcare systems.[2] California's population is, however, smaller than the UK, which, as we have seen, also has a successful single-payer program. Thus, we know it is possible to scale single-payer to a population the size of California's.

With respect to economic productivity, in 2018, California's GDP was an astounding $3 trillion per year, which was 15 percent of the entire US GDP.[3,4] The next most economically productive state was Texas with a GDP of $1.8 trillion, or 8.7 percent of the country's GDP. Indeed, if California was an independent country, it would have had the fifth biggest economy in the world, running just ahead of India, France, and the UK, which were in the sixth through eighth positions.[3,5]

Finally, California also has an incredible diversity of economy and jobs, ranging from the tech sector, to manufacturing, to entertainment, to finances, to being one of the largest agricultural producers in the US and the world.[4] Thus, it may be the ideal experimental lab to test concepts of implementing a single-payer program that is relevant to an eventual national effort.

In short, if single-payer healthcare could be implemented in California, it would blaze the trail and show the way for how the same process could be done nationally. That's what makes this example so compelling as a lead-in to our next chapter, which will consider how to reform healthcare within the larger US healthcare system.

☤ ☤ ☤ ☤ ☤

As I mentioned at the very beginning of the book, from 2017 to 2018, I was one of the Leshner Fellows in Public Engagement run by the American Association for the Advancement of Science.[6] I chose to focus that fellowship experience on learning about the problems with the US healthcare system and how to communicate to the public about it. The year I spent in that fellowship program coincided with the timing of the debate over California SB 562, the single-payer initiative that was being considered in the State Assembly. I followed the bill's progress closely and even got to meet some of the powerbrokers pushing the bill.

While the bill was under political pressure and heading towards committee consideration, the California Nurses Association commissioned an economic feasibility study for implementation of a single-payer system in California. To complete the study, they hired Dr. Robert Pollin, PhD, an expert in healthcare economics from the University of Massachusetts-Amherst. Dr. Pollin is a distinguished professor of economics and co-director of the Political Economy Research Institute (PERI) at UMASS. He and his team completed the analysis and released it shortly before I started my Public Engagement Fellowship. When I saw the analysis, I decided to reach out to Dr. Pollin and begin a dialogue.

What I learned from talking to Dr. Pollin was that he had come to the table with some initial skepticism as to whether it would be feasible to fund and implement a single-payer system in a state the size of California. Before he began his analysis, he actually flew to California to meet with the team that had commissioned him, led by Michael Lighty, who was at the time the director of public policy at the California Nurses Association. During that trip, Dr. Pollin also arranged to meet with the then governor of California, Jerry Brown. They had interacted previously over the years and knew each other reasonably well.

Governor Brown was a very savvy leader. As governor, he oversaw a complete fiscal turnaround in the California state budget. Governor Brown inherited a staggering $27 billion budget deficit, and in eight years, turned it around so that he left office with a nearly $15 billion surplus, not including more than $14 billion in additional money that he had squirreled away in a rainy-day fund.

Now, there is no doubt that Governor Brown benefitted from the economic recovery that happened on his watch. But there is also no doubt that he greatly reined in California's spending during the darkest depths of the recession, and then he very effectively resisted efforts by his own party to pressure him into increasing spending as the economy recovered. The point is, Governor Brown was a deficit hawk. And as Dr. Pollin learned, the governor was worried about the fiscal impact of a move to single-payer. The governor wanted an honest economic assessment of the fiscal cost, not a Pollyannish one. And Dr. Pollin agreed to give it to him.

One of the first things that happened after Dr. Pollin's team released their report was that the media pounced on it and began to misquote it. We're going to walk through the analysis in a few moments. But the bottom line is that the analysis found that switching to a single-payer system would not only *not* be more expensive than the current healthcare system in California, it would actually reduce costs by billions of dollars per year.

Unfortunately, that's not how the media reported it. Either due to confusion, duplicity with an agenda, or both, most news stories repeated the same talking point: that the analysis had found California would have to come up with $400 billion in new taxes in order to pay for the plan. That media circus likely helped doom the assembly bill. These inaccurate news reports gave erroneous but very effective talking points to the opposition. Unfortunately, accuracy was sacrificed for sensationalism.

In the meantime, I needed to complete a capstone project for my Public Engagement Fellowship, so I decided to hold an all-day symposium on healthcare, with a focus on the single-payer initiative in California. I invited Dr. Pollin to come out to LA to be the keynote speaker. He graciously agreed, on the condition that the California Nurses Association approve, since they had commissioned his study. Not only did the California Nurses Association approve, but Michael Lighty decided to attend the meeting too, and even helped sponsor Dr. Pollin's trip to Los Angeles.

So it was that on December 8, 2017, a large healthcare symposium was held in the main conference room at the LAC+USC Medical Center focusing on the economic, political, and procedural feasibility, or not, of converting California to a single-payer system. We learned very interesting things.

The report Dr. Pollin's team generated for their economic analysis of SB 562 is eighty-five pages long and is publicly available.[7] I would encourage people who are interested to read through it. In the white paper, methods of data collection and analysis are described. For the sake of brevity, I am only going to summarize the results of the report here, and I'm going to do so by walking through the slide presentation that Dr. Pollin gave at the symposium.

Dr. Pollin began by summarizing the state of California's healthcare spending at baseline, with the existing system. In 2017, California spent $368.5 billion on healthcare, reflecting 14 percent of the state's GDP (remember, by comparison, the US spends about 18 percent of GDP on healthcare). That number was comprised of $328 billion (89 percent of total costs) on actual healthcare delivery, $31.3 billion (9 percent of total costs) on a combination of administrative costs and private corporate profits, and $9 billion (2 percent of costs) on public health activities.

Just for scale, the $368.5 billion in healthcare costs for California exceeded the entire amount of France's ($323 billion), India's ($285 billion), and the UK's ($274 billion) annual healthcare expenditures.[8] Indeed, that massive number exceeded the entire healthcare spending for every country graphed in Figure 2-1 from France on down. It was exceeded internationally only by the healthcare costs of the US, China, Japan, and Germany. Indeed, just California's annual healthcare administrative and insurance profit costs alone exceeded the national total health-care spending of Norway, Denmark, and New Zealand, and indeed every country graphed in Figure 2-1 from Norway down. I'll reiterate, California is an excellent test subject to determine financial feasibility of rolling out single-payer coverage for the country as a whole.

For this gargantuan amount of healthcare expenditures, California was able to cover 33.4 million residents, or 92.5 percent of the state's permanent resident population. That compares to 91.2 percent insurance coverage for the US as a whole, again a fair comparator. Of note, California's uninsured number of 7.5 percent had declined dramatically from a peak of more than 20 percent before the Affordable Care Act expanded Medicaid in the state, which certainly made it easier fiscally to approach achieving final, universal coverage.

However, the team's analysis did not stop at just the uninsured. The goal of universal healthcare is to fully ensure everyone and to close as many out-of-pocket gaps as possible. So Dr. Pollin's team also considered how many underinsured people there are in California. Underinsurance was defined as choosing to forego medical care due to cost. This number was known from prior research to be a dismaying 36 percent of the population.

The team then calculated the average annual cost to fully insure (including closing coverage gaps) the 33.4 million currently insured individuals in California. The team's estimate for the cost per year to fully insure each individual was $11,629 (that compares to the current total healthcare spend per person in the US of $11,212). Multiplying that number by the number of insured individuals generated an estimate of $388 billion to fully insure all currently insured Californians.

The team next considered the costs of the uninsured. Data regarding out-of-pocket and public expenditures to cover healthcare for the uninsured suggested that it would cost $16 billion to insure them. Adding together the costs to fully insure people who are already insured plus people who are currently uninsured ($388 billion + $16 billion) generated a total annual cost estimate for implementing single-payer, universal health-care in California of $404 billion.

That $404 billion was the source of all of the media attention, confusion, and disinformation about the feasibility study. It was reported over and over again by numerous different reporters that California would need to come up with another $404 billion to pay for single-payer healthcare.

That, of course, is absurd. The $404 billion would be the total cost per year to expand coverage to everybody in the state, assuming no change in cost structure was realized by changing to a streamlined, single-payer system. Furthermore, California is already spending $368 billion per year on healthcare. So Dr. Pollin's actual conclusion was, if all we do is take the existing healthcare system (without changing to single-payer) and spread it to fully insure all residents of California, the state would have to find another $36 billion in funds ($368 billion currently spent + $36 billion new = $404 billion total).

Dr. Pollin then walked us through the many ways that changing to a single-payer system would save costs. You've gotten a taste of this already in the prior chapters. First of all, there would be marked reductions in administrative costs and elimination of profit from private insurers as part of funding the universal coverage. Medicare spends 1.2 percent of its costs on administration, a number commensurate with all of our peer nations with single-payer models. By comparison, as we said, California is spending 9 percent of its total costs on healthcare administration and insurance company profits.

Single-payer systems also have the authority and ability to aggressively negotiate for better prices for pharmaceuticals, whereas the US does not currently do this at all. Since the US spends twice as much as single-payer, peer nations do on pharmaceuticals, there is substantial savings potential there. The single-payer system also would be more effective at negotiating payment rates for other healthcare services. Finally, by shifting from a fee-for-service, line-itemed reimbursement model to a model where global payments are made (like a firehouse, for example), there would be huge potential savings from a realignment of financial incentives.

The team used published data from a variety of studies to estimate how much cost savings would result from each of these activities. They estimated administrative costs would be reduced by 50 percent by moving to a single-payer system—that is conservative since we know that single-payer countries spend 75 percent less than California on healthcare administration (and 80 percent less than the US). They estimated pharmaceutical spending would decline by 30 percent—again that is conservative given that the US spending is closer to two to three times the average cost in peer nations with a single-payer healthcare system. Including other savings resulting from negotiated pricing and shifting care models away from fee-for-service, they estimated a move to a single-payer system would result in an 18 percent overall cost reduction from current spending.

Just to emphasize the conservative nature of this cost-reduction estimate, let us remember that California, at baseline, was spending 14 percent of its GDP on healthcare. If California were to reduce its spending by 18 percent, that would result in spending 11.5 percent of its GDP on healthcare (reducing spending by 18 percent would bring us down to 82 percent of current levels; 82 percent of 14 percent = 11.5 percent).

Remember that all of our peer nations with universal healthcare systems spend 8 to 12 percent of their GDP on healthcare. Thus, cost reductions actually achieved from single-payer would likely be better than the conservative estimate used by Dr. Pollin and his colleagues. If California were to reach the midpoint of the average cost of healthcare per GDP among peer nations (10 percent of GDP), we would have to reduce our spending by 30 percent, nearly twice the estimate that Dr. Pollin used (reducing spending by 30 percent would bring us down to 70 percent of current levels; 70 percent of 14 percent = 9.8 percent of GDP).

How realistic is it that we could achieve a 30 percent reduction from the current 14 percent of GDP to reach 10 percent of GDP? In chapter 6, we found that existing, international single-payer systems tend to be more efficient and less expensive than multi-payer universal models. Healthcare cost per GDP in these single-payer countries include: 10 percent (UK), 9 percent (Australia), 9 percent (New Zealand), 8 percent (Norway), 10 percent (Sweden), and 11 percent (Canada), for an average of 9.5 percent of GDP. In contrast, multi-payer systems' cost per GDP were higher: 10 percent (Netherlands), 9 percent (Switzerland), 12 percent (Germany), and 12 percent (France), for an average of 11 percent of GDP. So single-payer systems tend to be less expensive. Indeed, four of the five international, single-payer models achieved 10 percent of GDP or lower spending on healthcare. So achieving a 30 percent cost reduction, down to a cost of 10 percent of GDP, seems very feasible in a single-payer model.

Nevertheless, for the sake of Dr. Pollin's analysis, let us stick with his team's much more conservative estimate of 18 percent cost reduction achieved by switching to single-payer. Remember that would bring California down from 14 percent to 11.5 percent of GDP. Now let's go back to the $404 billion total cost number. You'll recall that number is the team's estimate of how much it would cost to fully insure every permanent resident of California if all we did was to expand the existing healthcare system with all of its current costs and operations to cover them. If California achieved only an 18 percent cost savings by switching to single-payer, the $404 billion annual cost would be reduced to $331 billion (18 percent cost savings means you're spending 82 percent of the original amount of money, 82 percent of $404 billion = $331 billion). This number, $331 billion, is the total amount of money that Dr. Pollin's team *actually* calculated it would cost California per year to fully insure all permanent residents using a single-payer system. Not the $404 billion the media erroneously reported over and over.

Now, a critical point here is that this does *not* mean California would have to raise $331 billion in new taxes. Remember, California currently spends $368 billion in total costs per year for healthcare. In other words, and here comes the denouement… drumroll please…wait for it…wait for it…

If California switched to a single-payer system, it could fully insure every permanent resident at a cost that is $37 billion *less than it currently spends*!

You talk about fake news. Not only was it not true that California would have to come up with $404 billion to switch to a single-payer system, but the actual finding was that California would insure everyone and still spend $37 billion less per year! Holy cow! I was blown away when I saw him walk through the numbers.

Please digest this reality for a moment before proceeding.

Dr. Pollin's team demonstrated that there is absolutely no financial or fiscal barrier to switching to a single-payer system in California. A conservative estimate of cost savings resulting from a switch to a single-payer system would allow a complete expansion of coverage to universal levels while actually still reducing annual expenditures by billions of dollars per year.

So here's the thing. We don't have a financial problem to go to a single-payer system in California. More than enough money is there already. Indeed, conservatively estimated, we have $37 billion more than is needed right now to switch to a single-payer system in California. What we have instead is three other problems. First, we have a problem of procedural execution to redirect money in a seamless way from the way it is currently being spent to instead fund the single-payer system. Second, we have some prickly legal problems that we would have to overcome. And third, and perhaps most problematic, we have a problem of political will. Let's start by looking at the first problem (we will discuss the second and third problems later in the chapter).

To switch California to a single-payer health system, we would have to find a way to switch the flow of money from its current multi-payer streams into a single stream managed by the state. What do I mean? Government currently funds 71 percent of California's $368 billion per year of healthcare expenditures. Of this 71 percent, 3 percent is comprised of state and local tax subsidies that would be eliminated under the single-payer plan and thus would disappear. That means 68 percent of healthcare expenditures in California are already being spent by the government and could be hypothetically redirected into this new single-payer plan. We will address the issue of how to redirect those funds later in the chapter. For now, just remember that about two-thirds of current California healthcare expenditures are from public money.

Where can that remaining one-third of funds be redirected from? The remaining, nongovernmental expenditures in the current system, of course, come from private, employer-sponsored insurance. That is where we need to find the missing one-third of funds to pay for the single-payer system. We need to "redirect" those private funds into the public system. How would this work?

First, we would stop paying those private, employer-sponsored insurance premiums, because private insurance would stop functioning to provide the core component of insurance for universal, basic coverage. That is a very important point. It means that businesses and people would get back their money from the "hidden" tax that employee benefits cost them. Employers and employees would, in essence, keep the approximately 10 percent of employee's salaries they jointly are forced to spend today on healthcare benefits for the employee. Businesses would retain more money to reinvest in growth and also be able to pay a wage increase to current workers.

With those private health insurance costs no longer being spent by businesses and their employers, the state government would create a new tax to fund the balance of the single-payer program. Dr. Pollin's team proposed multiple ways this could be done. They proposed about a 2 percent sales tax and 2 percent gross receipts tax to raise the needed funds. Alternatively, a 3.3 percent payroll tax would work.

Remember, we are *not* adding taxes. What we are doing is shifting the tax from the existing, hidden, current benefit "tax" on employers and employees, to a centralized tax. We are eliminating one form of hidden tax (employee health insurance benefits), and replacing it with a different type of central, government tax. In other words, we are cost-shifting—moving money around—not taking more money.

In fact, due to the cost savings enabled by the single-payer system, we are actually overall *lowering* the tax burden on people and their employers. Remember, even if we only conservatively reduce costs by 18 percent from current (half of what we should shoot for), we would reduce the annual tax bill on California residents by $37 billion per year, which is nearly $1,000 per person less in taxes per year.

The financial analysis by Dr. Pollin is very illuminating for a number of reasons. Most importantly, it dispels the notion that tax increases have to occur in order to switch to a single-payer healthcare system. Cost savings would result from: 1) reducing administrative costs and profit from the existing multi-payer system; 2) negotiating lower prices and instituting better pricing for pharmaceuticals, devices, and other healthcare costs; and 3) implementing rational financial payment structures that align healthcare providers' interests with reducing unnecessary and wasteful diagnostics and therapeutics. Those cost savings would more than compensate for the additional costs necessary to expand coverage to the uninsured and fill in the gaps in coverage for the underinsured.

I will reiterate the point that Dr. Pollin's team incorporated conservative estimates of cost savings that would be achievable with a single-payer system. Achieving their cost savings estimate would still leave California at the top end of healthcare cost per GDP when compared to international healthcare systems. If instead, California achieved sufficient cost savings to reach the midpoint in international, single-payer costs (10 percent of GDP), that would save an additional $48.5 billion per year. In that case, the total cost of fully insuring all Californians would be only $283 billion, which is $121 billion per year less than we would spend if we expanded the current system to cover everyone. That would mean a reduction in tax expenditures amounting to more than $2,200 per Californian per year from current, while enabling the state to achieve universal healthcare.

☤ ☤ ☤ ☤ ☤

About a year after the California effort to pass a single-payer bill, New York State came up with the same cause. The New York bill was named The New York State Health Act. And the RAND Corporation was commissioned by the New York State Health Foundation to do a study of the financial feasibility of the New York State effort.[9] Guess what they found?

Yes, they found the same thing that Dr. Pollin's team found regarding the California single-payer effort. Not only could New York afford to expand coverage to all residents via single-payer, but they would actually lower their statewide healthcare costs in so doing. Their analysis was remarkably similar in method, character, content, and conclusions to Pollin's team analysis of the California single-payer effort.

The analyses by Dr. Pollin's team and the New York team show us that we do not have a financial or fiscal problem converting giant healthcare systems to single-payer. As we mentioned above, rather than financial, the real problems to moving to a single-payer system are procedural, legal/regulatory, and ultimately, political.

Procedurally, we have to figure out how to shift costs from the private, employer-sponsored health insurance benefit tax currently funding 32 percent of California's healthcare to a central, governmental tax. Remember, this is not a tax increase, it is a tax shift. It is moving money from one place to another. And, with cost savings resulting from shifting to a single-payer system, it would actually amount to a tax reduction. So it would be a shift in where money is taken from and directed to, as well as a reduction in the amount of money taken. In order to do this, politicians would have to agree to create whatever new tax was necessary to fund the shift away from employee benefits.

The reality is, once there is political consensus, we could fairly easily figure out how to establish a payroll tax or general receipts or sales tax to fund the new healthcare system. That could be done via normal governmental procedures once the political will is there. That's not the hard part. The really hard part? Well, we need to cross two huge minefields, alluded to above. One relates to current federal law and regulation, which governs state health expenditures. The other relates to the fallout politically and economically of markedly reducing the revenues of giant, for-profit health insurance companies.

THE LEGAL BARRIERS TO A STATE SINGLE-PAYER SYSTEM

California and New York are not the first states to consider moving to a single-payer system. Erin Brown, Associate Professor of Law at Georgia State University College of Law and Elizabeth McCuskey, Professor of Law at the University of

Massachusetts, recently published an article in the widely read health politics journal, *Health Affairs*, evaluating these efforts.[10] They counted twenty separate states in the US in which legislative bills were introduced between the years 2010 and 2019 to initiate a single-payer system. They point out that all such bills suffer from two legal problems, which could ultimately preclude success at the state level no matter what political conditions exist within the state. These problems would not affect federal single-payer efforts, however.

The first problem relates to the flow of funds from the federal government to the state for Medicare and Medicaid. I alluded to this problem above when I said that it would be necessary for California to shift the 68 percent of government money it currently spends on healthcare to the new single-payer program. Ultimately, states do not have discretionary authority over how they spend federal health dollars.

Medicare and Medicaid dollars flow to the states from the Centers for Medicare and Medicaid Services, or CMS. CMS is an agency within the US Department of Health and Human Services (DHHS). The US DHHS retains authority over how those funds must be disbursed. In practice, DHHS is able to use a program called a "spending waiver," which is built into federal Social Security Code section 1115 (usually pronounced "eleven fifteen"), to allow some creativity around state expenditures. The purpose of section 1115 in the Social Security Code is to allow federal and state governments some latitude to experiment with new healthcare programs that have the potential to improve care delivery or reduce healthcare costs.

This is a wise law. Whoever wrote it realized that healthcare is very complicated. And in order to find the right way forward, it is optimal for there to be some experimentation done at smaller scales to see what works and what doesn't before making a big change at the federal level.

Section 1115 gives the US Secretary of DHHS the authority to grant such flexibility to states one at a time, based on individual program waiver requests from the states. When granted, the waiver effectively waives stringent provisions of how federal dollars must be spent on major health and welfare programs. The explicitly stated purpose in the law is to allow for "experimental, pilot, or demonstration" projects that can improve healthcare delivery. Typically these waivers are only granted if the waiver project will not increase health expenditures (i.e., the project must be cost-neutral to cost-saving).

Only the Secretary of DHHS has the authority under law to grant such a waiver. So, if the current executive branch of government is hostile or in opposition to the concepts in the proposed waiver, it is very unlikely to be granted. And without a waiver, California could not legally shift Medicare and Medicaid funds into any new program, single-payer or otherwise, like it or not. This would preclude switching to a single-payer system by preventing the state from accessing 68 percent of the funds it would need to fund the new system.

Which brings us to the second legal barrier, which is likely even harder to overcome. After all, if there is a hostile executive administration currently in power that is not in favor of single-payer, really you would just need to wait for a new administration to be elected that was more favorable to a single-payer approach (which could happen every four years). Then you could apply to DHHS to get the 1115 waiver you need, allowing Medicare and Medicaid funds to shift into a state single-payer program. It's just a matter of waiting for the right political environment in the executive branch to make the ask.

Unfortunately, the other legal barrier is less subject to the discretion of the executive branch. Meet the big, thorny, second barrier. Its name is ERISA.

The Employment Retirement Income Security Act (ERISA) of 1974 is a tax and labor law that sets US federal standards required for private industry health and retirement plans. Thus all employer-sponsored health insurance programs are governed by ERISA. It is a very complex law, and complex laws make my brain sad. So I'm not even going to try to explain all the ins and outs of this extremely long and convoluted law. Suffice it to say that ERISA clearly puts authority over private health insurance plans squarely within the control of the federal government, and also explicitly removes any state control over such plans.

And that's where the iceberg may be hitting the state single-payer ship.

Remember, even if we can consolidate Medicare and Medicaid funds into a state single-payer program by getting an 1115 waiver approved from the US Secretary of DHHS, that only covers 68 percent of our healthcare costs in California. We have to come up with the rest by altering the flow of funds from private health insurance plans. This would be done by abolishing those private health insurance plans and replacing them with a state tax. Except ERISA explicitly removes from the states any authority to alter employers' private health insurance plans. D'oh!

Brown and McCluskey surveyed states, exploring moving to

single-payer insurance and found that there are some creative ideas out there about how to get around the thorny barrier that is ERISA. These are all work-arounds that attempt to nudge employers, employees, and doctors to do what the state wants them to do.

For example, if the state enacted new payroll taxes on employers and income taxes on employees to fund single-payer insurance, both would then be getting hit with a double-tax—the new single-payer tax plus the cost of the existing employee health insurance benefit they are already paying. Perhaps the employers and employees would come to their senses and voluntarily drop the employee-sponsored health insurance and encourage their employees to enroll in the single-payer plan.

States have also considered trying to prevent doctors from accepting private insurance payments, which could force employers and employees to voluntarily drop their private insurance coverage and switch to the single-payer coverage. It's not at all clear that the latter idea would pass legal muster, and one would suspect there would be a challenge immediately in court on Constitutional grounds. These are fairly thin strategies to rely upon when bankrolling a $331 billion endeavor.

Of course, laws like ERISA can be amended, and political leadership in the White House can choose to set policy to selectively ignore federal enforcement of certain laws. But again, would you bankroll a $331 billion initiative on those hopes? Especially knowing that ignoring federal enforcement of certain laws is also subject to change every four years with a new election?

As I mentioned, neither of these legal barriers affect federal implementation of single-payer insurance for the entire country. They only affect implementation at the state level. That's the irony. You really would prefer to test out something like single-payer on a smaller scale before going live with a big-bang, nationwide program. That indeed is the very purpose of the 1115 waiver program, to allow such smaller-scale demonstration projects to occur before going full scale nationally.

But given the risks inherent in not getting a waiver approved from that very 1115 waiver program, the vicissitudes of political leadership in the executive branch, as well as the ERISA law, it may not be possible to test a single-payer approach at the state level before a federal go-live. If it was possible, it would only happen because of highly motivated and innovative leadership from the executive branch of government, which wanted to try a single-payer approach at the state level as a test case.

POLITICAL BARRIER TO SINGLE-PAYER

As tough as the legal challenges are to overcome, there is possibly even a bigger barrier. What happens to the private insurance industry in the largest state in the nation if California goes single-payer?

Now, we've discussed repeatedly that going to single-payer does not have to completely eliminate private insurance. Indeed, as we saw in chapter 6, there are multiple international models where private insurance not only exists but is integral to an overall healthcare system in single-payer countries. So, it should be possible to carve out a role for private industry to "stay in the game" on health insurance even if California moves to single-payer. But that role would certainly be reduced compared to now, possibly with a reduction in total profit. Reducing profits makes for-profit shareholders sad. And when they get sad, they take it out on the stock. And then the board of directors gets mad, and the C suite gets fired. So, the point is, for-profit insurance companies might not take kindly to this happening.

The implications of this risk to the insurance industry are far-reaching in our society. Pretending they don't exist won't make them go away. The insurance industry brings in hundreds of billions of dollars per year in revenue. They would undoubtedly launch a vigorous and well-funded political and public relations campaign to discredit a single-payer approach should it look like it might be nearing success. Would advocates be able to overcome the intense public messaging that would occur? Not to mention the active lobbying in the state capitol, and on Capitol Hill in Washington, DC.

Perhaps more importantly, what are the implications for layoffs and job losses to an industry that employs tens of thousands of people? What economic impact will that have on the state? And share prices of widely held insurance company stocks could plunge, bringing in pressure from institutional investors, and even individual investors whose retirement plans take a nose-dive during a downward stock market move.

The political, social, and economic upheaval would need to be factored into a plan to launch a single-payer health plan. The damage could be mitigated and potentially even headed off with early and constant messaging from advocates. Early partnership to engage the insurance industry in ways to bring them in on the back end as supplemental private coverage could also help. It would be wise to offer job training and employee support programs to help workers relocate to other industry sectors in anticipation of layoffs.

It also would be wise to help the insurance industry understand how they can continue to make a profit in the space even with a single-payer system in place. For example, remember from chapter 5 that in 2018, the US health insurance industry brought in a massive amount of total profit and revenue ($23.4 billion in net profit on $709 billion total revenue). However, as a percentage of total revenue, their profit margin is actually low (3.3 percent). By comparison, profit margins in the pharmaceutical industry and tech sectors tend to run more like 15 to 30 percent. So the health insurance industry has huge expenses relative to its revenue. That makes it tough to grow, which can make it tough to drive up the stock price.

Part of the reason for this low profit margin is that private insurance is currently providing the bulk of basic coverage, including for lower-income Americans. If the government took over responsibility for providing a basic, universal health insurance package, the for-profit industry could focus on higher-end customers that voluntarily choose to sign up (similar to those choosing to pay FasTrak and toll fees to go faster on the highway). Health insurance industry total revenue and absolute profit may go down, but if they focused on higher-end insurance packages, their profit margin (profit divided by total revenue) may go up. And stock prices may be driven more by increases in profit margin anyway.[11] In other words, this could be an opportunity for the insurance industry to streamline its costs and services to focus away from lower margin, basic packages, and focus on higher-margin, premium packages. That might actually give them greater stock growth potential in the long run. They might be interested in something like this.

Let's not pretend any of this would be simple, either in concept or execution. But if there is one thing the public has taught me, it's that if they mobilize collectively, they can move mountains.

I never would've predicted in my lifetime that McDonald's and dozens of other food companies would have moved to antibiotic-free meat due to rising public concern over antibiotic resistance. When the public is collectively mobilized, they are much more effective at moving politicians and businesses to act than anything else is. That's the very reason I wrote this book.

With this confidence in the American people in the forefront of our thinking, we are now coming into the home stretch. Two more chapters to go. It is now time to ask serious questions about how we could modify our national healthcare system in the US to make it more effective and more cost-sustainable.

CHAPTER 8

||||||||||||||||||||||||||

SO WHERE DOES THE US HEALTHCARE SYSTEM GO FROM HERE?

At this point in the book, it's time to consider what to do about the national healthcare system in the US. It seems as though we need a refresh. The problems with our healthcare system have only become more and more apparent to me over time as I have been in my role as Chief Medical Officer at LAC+USC Medical Center. This role has given me a vantage point as both a physician who still cares for hospitalized patients, and also as a healthcare administrator who has thousands of employees and contractors reporting up through my budget centers.

It was from this vantage point that I decided to focus on healthcare reform for my Leshner Fellowship in Public Engagement through the American Association for the Advancement of Science (AAAS). In the last chapter, I described for you the symposium that we held to discuss healthcare reform as part of that fellowship. Now I would like to tell you about one more, very instructive experience I had during my fellowship.

One day, in late July of 2017, the AAAS Fellowship coordinators took our cohort of Public Engagement Fellows to Capitol Hill to meet with Congressional staffers and policy makers. It was a beautiful, hot and humid summer day in Washington, DC, and the fellows were excited to make the trip. We were all very eager to initiate a dialogue with these federal, legislative powerbrokers as a starting point for our yearlong fellowship experiences. For several hours, we went from office to office, meeting with staffers and committee organizers from both sides of the political aisle.

In several of the offices there were staffers who had worked on various aspects of healthcare, including on the Affordable Care Act and subsequent initiatives. So in each of these meetings, I engaged these policy makers in a discussion on the problems of our healthcare system, and what could be done to resolve them.

And what I heard threw me for a loop. When I began to describe for the staffers what I saw as the dysfunctions of our system, and conversely the merits of a universal model of care, I heard, over and over, variations of the same response.

"Hold on, hold on," they would interrupt. "It makes no sense to dump our employer-based system in the US and go on a wild-goose chase to implement a system that will bankrupt us. Our employer-based system is working for Americans. What we need to do is focus on improving it. Not get rid of it for some fantasy public system."

The first time I heard a variation on this response, I was sort of stunned into speechlessness. For those who know me, that is not a very common thing. I'm rarely speechless. But the response was so far away from what I was expecting to hear, I hardly knew where to begin to respond.

I had prepared a whole elevator speech about the Stabilization Act and the accident of history that created our mess of a system. I was prepared to recite chapter and verse of the data showing that international models deliver more effective, less expensive care. But I never got to it. I got interrupted and derailed. And the next thing I knew, the meeting ended. All I had learned was, this might be harder than I thought.

In the second meeting, when I heard that same response, it was accompanied by what I would call the verbal equivalent of an eye roll and a slightly condescending tone about how it would be kooky to move away from employer-sponsored insurance.

The third time I heard that response, it was more politely put. And I got dismayed. Clearly, things were going to be a lot harder than I imagined. Inertia is a powerful force in human behavior. Barriers to change require a lot of "activation energy" to overcome. I think I had underestimated the inertia.

Let's break down the staffers' argument here. The Congressional staffers made three points bundled together into one argument regarding why we shouldn't and/or couldn't move away from a voluntary, employer-sponsored health insurance model. First, they said that the employer-based system in America is working, so why would we dump it? Second, they said that any other system would be far too expensive to implement. Third, they implied that we don't even know if systems *not* based on employer-sponsored insurance are possible to implement. Let's tackle these points in reverse order.

Is it true that we don't know if universal coverage and coverage based on something other than voluntary, employer-sponsored insurance can work? No. Of course, that's not true. We know with 100 percent certainty that it can work because it's being done. It always amuses me when I hear that something is impossible to do when others are already doing it. It literally cannot be impossible to do something if that thing is already being done. Countries all over the world have figured out how to provide universal healthcare not based on voluntary, employer-sponsored insurance. So if they can do it, but we can't, are we saying the American people and their elected officials are not as capable as people in these other countries? That would be pretty offensive, right?

But on reflection, I think this argument actually boils down to a euphemism. Let me try to translate it from political speak (a language I call "politic-ish") to English. I think what the staffers actually may have been implying was something to the effect of, "The American people aren't ready for such a dramatic change, and I won't stake my boss's political career on a radical idea that isn't popular or supported among the public." Framed in that light, their responses were more understandable. Indeed, they would be correct. The failed history of healthcare reform in the US has demonstrated that even charismatic leaders can't sustainably change things unless the public is ready for it.

What about the second argument, that we can't implement a public, universal healthcare system because it is too expensive? That, too, is obviously incorrect. It is objectively incorrect. It is actually the opposite of correct. It's sort of like attacking the opposition in a debate for the very thing that one is most weak on—the political term for this is "swift-boating," I believe.

The nerve of making such an argument—the sheer audacity, what some might call "chutzpah"—is sort of breathtaking. Can you imagine? The people who run the country that has, by far, the most expensive healthcare system in the world are sitting across a table from me saying, with a straight face, that we can't implement a system similar to what other countries do because it would be too expensive. When all of those other countries' healthcare systems are massively less expensive than ours. Wow. How do you even respond to something like that? That's in part why I was speechless at first.

On reflection, I think this argument is also a euphemism. I translate it from "politic-ish" to English as something to the effect of, "To pay for a public, universal healthcare system, we will need to create new federal taxes. That's the death knell for a politician's career. Not gonna happen." Again, framed in this light, the argument may be more understandable coming from a staffer who works for an elected official. I'm not saying I agree with it, mind you. Just that at least I can understand this rationale after putting the staffers' spoken words through a "politic-ish"-to-English translator. Heck, I wish Google Translate had a politic-ish language option; that would have saved me lots of time.

As we've already discussed in the last chapter, it is true that new taxes would have to be created to fund a public, universal healthcare insurance program. But those taxes would replace the existing "hidden" tax of employee benefit costs. So, it would not be a tax increase. In fact, due to cost savings, it would actually result in a big tax break to both employers and employees.

Remember California, conservatively, could have saved at least $37 billion per year by switching to a single-payer system. If we extrapolate those savings nationwide, the US could be saving, conservatively, $500 billion *per year* in healthcare costs. Which would amount to a sizable net tax reduction on workers, businesses, and the public. But that's nuance. And nuance is not something that politicians, or their staffers, are particularly fond of. On this point, it's really not their fault. Let's be fair, in the twenty-first century with twenty-four-hour-per-day news and social media bombardment, voters don't often respond to nuance.

Finally, the very first component of the counter argument the staffers made to me was that it makes no sense to dump a system that is "working for the American people." That phrase, the system is "working for the American people," is one I heard repeatedly, and it befuddled me each time.

"*Huh,*" I thought to myself. "*Interesting. The healthcare system is 'working for the American people.*'" Okay. Where do you go with that? What does it mean?

I had to think through this one for a while. Finally, my politic-ish language translator converted "is working for the American people," into the English phrase, "the American people are using the existing system." If that is indeed what is meant, then…well, yes, it is obviously true that the American people are paying for and receiving healthcare using the voluntary, employer-based system that is in place. So, if what we mean by "is working for the American people" is that the system is happening, and people are using it, then, yes, it is working.

But if what we mean by "working for the American people" is that the American people are receiving quality healthcare at a reasonable price—or heck, just something other than receiving awful healthcare at an outrageous price—then, no. No, it is not working. Americans have the worst healthcare outcomes and shortest life spans of all peer nations while paying hugely more than everyone else on Earth for our healthcare. We are broken, bankrupt, and dying.

So, after long and careful reflection, here's my response: The US healthcare system is working for the American people in the same way that New Year's resolutions work for the American people. That is to say, we do them. We do them every year, without fail. We just keep doing them. Oh, they don't actually achieve anything (and we kind of know they won't when we do them). They don't actually deliver what they are supposed to deliver. But we keep doing them just the same. It's a cultural thing.

In that same way, we keep using the US healthcare system. It's there, and we don't have an alternative system, so we use it. It doesn't actually deliver what other healthcare systems throughout the world deliver. And we pay way more than residents of those other countries do to have our healthcare system not deliver what we want it to. But we still keep using the system just the same, year after year.

At the time, I felt very discouraged by that trip to Capitol Hill. However, after considerable reflection, I came to view it as a clarifying experience. After long and careful reflection, trying to discern the message below the words, that trip pointed out a clear direction to move forward. I will describe why and how in the final chapter.

In the meantime, it is very clear that one of the primary problems that confronts us regarding how to move forward with changing our healthcare system is cultural. All the facts and figures in the world don't change the reality that there are unique threads that run through American culture. We've alluded to these cultural threads previously. Americans don't like to be told what to do. Americans have a strong sense of individualism and a mistrust of government, perhaps more so than in other countries. The for-profit motive is very strong in the US, perhaps more so than in many European countries. As a result, Americans don't like regulations. The political staffers we met with that day were simply reflecting back on me those realities.

On the other hand, the other thing Americans hate is being ripped-off. And our healthcare system is unquestionably ripping us off. We're getting terrible value for the outrageous costs we're spending. And, of course, Americans, like all other people, are also not overly fond of dying unnecessarily early (duh).

So, where do we go from here? How do we align the desire not to get ripped off, and the desire to not die unnecessarily early, with the strong Don't Tread on Me belief in individualism and capitalism that runs through American culture? With these cultural themes and questions in mind, let's review the healthcare reforms that have been proposed by leading political figures in the US.

PUBLICLY PROPOSED OPTIONS

In the US, multiple healthcare reform plans have been publicly proposed. The name that has become attached to these general proposals is "Medicare for All." But what does Medicare for All mean? The confusing thing is that it can mean different things to different people. People may think that all of these plans are single-payer in nature, but they are not.

Fortunately, in late 2018, the Kaiser Family Foundation released a white paper summarizing many of the versions of healthcare reform that had been proposed at that point in the US.[1] As mentioned, several of these plans have attached themselves to the name Medicare for All. Since then, additional variations have been added which have been referred to as "Medicare for Those Who Want It," or a "Public Option." We will discuss each of these plans below.

SINGLE-PAYER UNIVERSAL PROPOSALS

As we have seen, single-payer systems tend to perform better overall, and with respect to Administrative Efficiency, than other systems in peer nations (Figure 6-2). But of the plans publicly proposed thus far, only two are genuinely single-payer. Both of these plans would essentially do away with private insurance.

The single-payer models would be funded by centrally collected taxes. Both propose to cover all healthcare costs, with no premiums or deductibles. Co-pays would be limited to a capped amount for prescription drugs annually. Both plans would create a national global budget for healthcare, so that total expenditures were predictable and known year to year. Both also propose to establish a published list of fee schedules for hospitals and doctors. So some component of fee-for-service would remain, but with standardized fee rates. Thus, neither implement true global budgeting to the level of individual hospitals or physician groups. That is unfortunate, as the latter would be desirable to align the providers' interest with the patients' interest (keep the patient healthy so they don't need expensive, fee-for-service, "Johnson rod" interventions in the first place).

The proposals differ in that one would explicitly allow patients and providers to enter into direct contracts with each other to provide care outside the national health plan. The second plan has no provision for this. Nevertheless, as mentioned, both plans would essentially eliminate private health insurance. Indeed, one of them would also prohibit any for-profit hospital or healthcare network from receiving money from the national health plan.

There is much to offer in these plans. They would achieve universal coverage. They would allow greatly streamlined administrative efficiency and create a strong organization for negotiating down pricing on drugs, devices, and services. They would also create a platform from which healthcare delivery could be changed, as we have described. In particular, they would enable changes in price transparency and price negotiations. They would also at least start to shift away from fee-for-service healthcare delivery to more of a global budgeting model, which aligns the financial incentives of providers and patients (although, as mentioned, they do not go far enough, in my mind, with respect to global budgeting).

The problem with the plans, from my perspective, is cultural. In a vacuum, either plan could work just fine. In the US, I fear that the elimination of private insurance will run into some of the same problems that we discussed in the last chapter. It will create a huge economic, social, and political upheaval, and trigger enormous back-pressure to resist implementation from a massive industry sector in the US, the private health insurance sector. It will trigger job losses, stock price changes, and huge lobbying efforts to derail implementation.

Furthermore, as we've discussed, the Don't Tread on Me thread of American culture likes options, not mandates. Having Americans choose participation would make implementation of this massive socioeconomic change more palatable to the US public.

I like the ideas behind these Medicare for All proposals. I just worry about how feasible either will be to get done. And I'm not interested in philosophical success with no practical outcome. If we want change implemented, we need to incorporate considerations of culture and broad acceptability into our system redesign.

MULTI-PAYER UNIVERSAL PROPOSALS: MEDICARE FOR THOSE WHO WANT IT

The two most recently proposed variations of Medicare for All are based on creation of a universally available "public option," into which anyone can participate if they want. But those who don't want to participate in the public option could stick with their private plan, and would not financially contribute to the public option. These proposals have been referred to as "Medicare for Those Who Want It," or something to that effect.[2] Of note, because these proposals allow private insurance companies to provide basic health insurance in lieu of the public plan, they are multi-payer, not single-payer, proposals.

While at first glance these proposals may appear to create an ideal balance between mandatory single-payer and optional private health insurance, there may be deep deficiencies that could destabilize such plans. As we discussed in prior chapters, private, for-profit plans have an intense incentive to find ways to keep people who are already sick (e.g., preexisting conditions), or who are already paying premiums but later become sick, off their rolls. People who are sick cost more in claims than they pay in premiums. If the insurance companies can minimize sick people on their rolls, they can maximize profits, which drives up stock prices, makes investors happy, and results in corporate leadership earning financial bonuses. Conversely, the more sick people on private insurance rolls, the lower the profit, the lower the stock price, the more dissatisfied the shareholders are, and the more likely corporate leaders are to be fired.

Companies have multiple mechanisms to try to streamline sick people off of their insurance rolls. Increasing premiums, charging special fees, denying claims, and establishing onerous prior authorization paperwork before treatments can be given, are only some of the ways private insurance companies make it difficult for people who have illnesses to receive their care.[3-5] Maybe the most effective means of attrition is simply being inefficient. Have you ever been frustrated by the numerous hoops and seeming inanity of getting a health cost covered by your insurance? Is that really just unintentional inefficiency? Or is it an intentional means of reducing paying claims and shedding those who need claims paid from their rolls?

Over time, these methods can result in attrition of more expensive members (i.e., those who are sick) from private insurance rolls. Remember my many friends and colleagues in chapter 3 who suffered through bewildering attempts by their insurance companies to deny payment for care that was actually covered? And what about Ms. C from chapter 1 and Mr. D from chapter 2, both of whom ended up in the public hospital for most of their care because their private hospitals wouldn't accept them as transfers?

Remember also Mr. F from chapter 4, who voluntarily gave up posh private insurance to sign up for MediCal because he was tired of the runaround his insurance was causing him? Or Ms.

G from chapter 5, who ended up paying $5,000 out of pocket for an inpatient stay that was of questionable necessity, despite having very good private insurance? Or Ms. H from chapter 6, whose private insurance had such large gaps in coverage for her chemotherapy that she chose to go to Mexico to get her care?

Private insurance can make life miserable for people who are expensive to care for. Eventually some of them will simply give up their private insurance, just as Mr. F did. And where do those sick, expensive individuals end up after giving up their private insurance? Either being covered by the public insurance plan, or uninsured (in which case the taxpayers still bear the burden of their cost).

So the combination of private plans shedding sick patients to increase profits and sick patients concentrating in the public plan can lead to a feed-forward loop. As public plan costs go up, healthy people will increasingly shun the public plan and instead sign up for the private plan (until they get sick and get encouraged to change to the public plan). The sicker patients would increasingly concentrate in the public plan. Public premium costs would go up in excess of private costs. In essence, the taxpayers would increasingly subsidize the private, for-profit plans by taking the costs of the expensive, sick patients off the private insurance rolls, and tacking them on to the taxpayers' backs.[3,4] Eventually, the system would become destabilized.

The purported solution to this problem in Medicare for Those Who Want It is to utilize "retrospective enrollment," which is based on a form of individual mandate akin to that in the Affordable Care Act.[2] The proposal is that individuals who do not purchase either a private or public plan would receive an additional tax penalty that would force them to contribute to the public option even if they didn't want to. This would at least force everyone to obtain health insurance—in other words, it is a backdoor individual mandate.

There are two problems with this approach. First, it puts us right back into the Don't Tread on Me vs. United We Stand tension. The Affordable Care Act individual mandate could not survive the political attacks against it; do we want to go through that politically and socially divisive process again? Why would it work this time when it failed so spectacularly before (and is still undergoing challenge in the courts)?

Second, and more fundamentally, requiring people to pay into the public option if they do not purchase private insurance does not address the death spiral risk to the public plan. Actually, it *exacerbates* the death spiral risk.

As we've just said, those most likely to be removed from private rolls are those who are sick and have substantial healthcare needs. They are most likely to end up not purchasing private insurance. They would then be hit with the retroactive enrollment, mandatory tax, and end up on the public option. In essence, retrospective enrollment would help push sick patients on to the public option.

Thus, retrospective enrollment does nothing to stop the flow of sick patients moving from private plans to the public option—indeed it could accelerate this shift. Therefore, it would not resolve the problem of enriching the public option with expensive sick people, resulting in that public plan death spiral while maximizing private plan profits.

There is a resolution to this conundrum, which we have alluded to already. It requires that everyone pay into the public plan, including those who choose to use private insurance. We will discuss this below.

MULTI-PAYER UNIVERSAL PROPOSAL: AFFORDABLE CARE ACT-BASED

Several other universal, multi-payer proposals have been made in the US, which are more similar in nature to the system in the Netherlands and Switzerland (but would not be as effective as these). They would create an entirely new national health plan and create an option for individuals to voluntarily buy in to that plan. But individuals could also choose to retain their private insurance and their employer-sponsored insurance. Or, they could choose not to participate at all. These plans propose to use the existing healthcare exchanges set up under the Affordable Care Act as the marketplace where individuals and companies can shop for this new form of national health insurance.

Note the key word here is option. In contrast to the Netherlands or Switzerland, there is no individual mandate proposed. Universal coverage would not be achieved. Taxpayers would continue to get stuck with the rising costs of the uninsured, as people are shed from private insurance rolls or just choose not to participate. The death spiral of public costs would not be avoided, and the public would subsidize rising private plan profits.

The strengths of these plans are that they give Americans choices and that they leave room for private insurance, which could diminish the back-pressure from the insurance industry to prevent implementing the change. The limitations are that they leave substantial gaps in coverage in place, and they don't fundamentally reform the way we deliver healthcare, nor alter the financial alignments of those who provide care and those who receive care. They will not rein in costs. In fact, they will increase costs by taking the existing, absurdly inefficient and wasteful system and expanding it. Under them, US health-care costs will increase. People will remain broken, bankrupt, and dying.

Finally, leaving in place employer-sponsored insurance means we continue to burden American businesses with a 10 percent hidden employee benefit tax, affecting their international com-petitiveness. Eliminating that hidden tax, which would both grow American workers' wages and give money back to busi-nesses to reinvest in their growth would be a huge benefit of a true, single-payer system. Keeping the hidden tax retains the "tapeworm," as Warren Buffett put it, of healthcare costs sucking the lifeblood of American businesses.

As mentioned, there is an alternative way to have private and public insurance coexist, which I believe offers the advantages of choice without the risk of a public plan death spiral, and while ridding American businesses of the tapeworm of healthcare costs. We will discuss this alternative possibility below.

EXPANSION OF THE EXISTING SYSTEM

Finally, two other proposals are incremental expansions of existing Medicare and Medicaid, which do not propose to cover everyone in the US. Which of these plans are practical and workable?

I think we can discard as almost unimportant to the conversa-tion to incrementally expand existing Medicare and Medicaid.

Yes, I am sure this could be done. But why? It would fail to achieve the goals we have set forth, to improve healthcare while lowering costs.

As we have discussed repeatedly, the US healthcare system is really badly broken. What sense does it make to take a broken system and use it to cover more people? Look at the California example from the last chapter. If we took the existing healthcare system in California and stretched it to cover the 7.5 percent of residents who are without insurance, and the 36 percent of people who have insurance but are underinsured, it would cost an additional $36 billion per year. And the quality, efficiency, and outcomes of care would be no better. But if we changed the way we fund care, the state could achieve universal coverage while actually reducing its spending, conservatively, by $37 billion per year from what we currently spend. And at the same time, the state could fundamentally shift to true preventative, population-based healthcare to improve outcomes.

The Affordable Care Act successfully insured an additional 18 million Americans, which is great. But it did not prevent medical bankruptcies because of the persistent holes in insurance coverage in the US. And it has not reined in healthcare costs. To the contrary, even after Affordable Care Act implementation, US healthcare costs continue to rise at thrice the rate of inflation, and at least 50 percent higher than worker wage increases. As a result, a half-decade after the go-live for the Affordable Care Act, the average cost to an American family to receive healthcare is an astounding $20,000 per year in health insurance premiums and another $4,000 per year in out-of-pocket costs. The net take-home pay of American workers has *declined* because all of their salary increases have gone to pay for skyrocketing healthcare costs.

US healthcare costs are projected to rise to $6 trillion within the next decade, choking off all other forms of spending in the federal budget, creating a national security risk. Our healthcare outcomes continue to be dead last among peer nations. That is all with the existing system, after Affordable Care Act implementation. How can the plan here possibly be to invest even more money into *this* system, and expand it? Are you really serious about that?

Look, this is a matter of plain common sense. If you have a system that is a huge rip-off in its current state, would your natural inclination be to grow it by investing more money in it? Do you "lean in" to the rip-off? Come on! Who does that? You would have to believe the current system is fine to want to do that. You would have to be someone who would have the chutzpah to say, "The healthcare system is working for Americans, so it makes no sense to change it."

After everything we've discussed, and all the objective data we've reviewed, do you believe everything is fine? If so, yes, it makes sense to just expand the current system by creating a new health plan that is voluntary to pay into, or by incrementally growing Medicare and Medicaid to a slightly larger pool of people who would be eligible.

PUTTING IT ALL TOGETHER

So now we've come to it, the final synthesis of all of the chapters and information to this point. What should we do?

Let us start by making a list of characteristics of a healthcare plan that we would like to see implemented in the US.

First, we want universal coverage.

Second, we want to eliminate as many gaps in coverage (e.g., deductibles, coinsurance), and hence out-of-pocket expenses, as possible. However, we may want to retain some co-pays to discourage overuse of pharmaceuticals and specialty care (a particular problem in the US, as we have seen), and encourage use of primary care instead.

Third, we want everyone to pay into an insurance pool, whether via exchanges or a central pool, to maximize the available funds from the lucky people who remain healthy to offset expensive care for those unlucky individuals who become sick or injured. We want everyone, including all healthy adults, to pay into the public plan. We also want to prevent private insurance plans from disenrolling sick patients, forcing such patients onto a public option or to be without health insurance. Such a system would result in that death spiral referred to above, in which the public plan becomes unsustainable as its costs grow out of control, even as private insurance profits are maximized.

Fourth, we do not want to rely on a government-operated healthcare provider system for political reasons. Switching to a system in which the federal government owns and operates healthcare delivery in the US, employing the majority of doctors, nurses, pharmacists, social workers, and other professionals, is simply not going to fly with Americans. Those systems do perform very well in other countries. But we could not make such a system work politically or culturally in the US.

Fifth, we want to eliminate employer-sponsored coverage to remove the hidden employee benefit tax that saps American corporate competitiveness.

Sixth, and seemingly paradoxically, we want individuals to have a choice about how they participate in the national health plan, rather than shoving care down a person's throat. It is not actually paradoxical to want a choice of participation despite requiring that everyone pay into the plan. We've discussed international models like this in chapter 6, and we will discuss how to achieve balancing these principles below.

Seventh, we would like a meaningful role for private insurance companies to remain in place, both for the choices they offer and to avoid the economic, social, and political tumult that would result from killing a $700 billion dollar per year industry in the US.

Let's consider these criteria in a table that describes the health-care systems of the ten peer nations the Commonwealth Fund ranked. As Figure 8-1 shows, most of our peer nations achieve most of the goals we've laid out. This is because they are all universal systems in which everyone contributes money and participates in a basic health insurance plan (either because they are single-payer or they are multi-payer but with an individual mandate).

Ideal Criteria	UK	Aus	Net	NZ	Nor	Swe	Swi	Ger	Can	Fra
National Ranking:	1	2	3	4	5	6	7	8	9	10
Universal Coverage	X	X	X	X	X	X	X	X	X	X
Minimal Coverage Gaps*	X	X		X	X					
Not National Govt. Provider		X	X	X			X	X	X	X
Mandatory Participation	X	X	X	X	X	X	X	X	X	X
Not Employer Funded	X	X	X	X	X	X	X		X	
Choice to Purchase 2nd Plan	X	X	X	X	X	X	X	X	X	X
Private Insurance Still Exists	X	X	X	X	X	X	X	X	X	X

Figure 8-1. Which peer nations meet the ideal criteria we've laid out for an optimal healthcare system? An "X" indicates the country's healthcare system meets the specified criteria. Overall ranking refers to Commonwealth Fund ranking. UK = United Kingdom, Aus = Australia, Net = the Netherlands, NZ = New Zealand, Nor = Norway, Swe = Sweden, Swi = Switzerland, Ger = Germany, Can = Canada, Fra = France, US = United States. *Minimal coverage gaps means there are no deductibles, coinsurance, or complex inpatient gaps (e.g., per diem gaps as in Sweden) but there can be outpatient co-pays with a maximum limit for prescription drugs and for specialty care outpatient visits.

Furthermore, all of our peer nations allow private insurance to exist, even in the single-payer countries. Thus, all countries allow the individual resident the choice to purchase a supplemental private insurance plan. That last point is key. Choice. Maybe desiring choice isn't such a unique American cultural characteristic, after all.

Our peer nation colleagues seem to have figured out the secret sauce of how you resolve the apparent paradox of having an individual mandate for participation as a payer in the national health plan, while still leaving people a choice. And they have done this in a way that does not allow private insurance to dump the costs of sick patients on to the public coffers or the patients' bank accounts. As mentioned, the multi-payer systems all have individual mandates, requiring people to participate in the universal plan—so no one can "opt-out" of health insurance. Furthermore, in countries where private companies are used as the universal health coverage mechanism, laws set strict standards preventing dropping sick patients from insurance rolls.

The use of central taxes in a single-payer system avoids the need to have an individual mandate in the first place. You just collect taxes from everyone and everyone gets covered with a public plan, whether they choose to use it or not. In the US there are numerous examples of a similar line of thinking that already exist. If you are employed, you pay Medicare taxes, whether or not you use Medicare, or even ever will. Those funds are critical to stabilize the insurance plan for the elderly, who of course tend to have higher healthcare costs than younger workers who are healthy.

With all of this in mind, there are only two countries that meet all of our criteria—Australia and New Zealand. Both are single-payer, in that the national health plan does indeed cover everybody. And everybody pays into the same central pool of funds to pay for that health plan. And all residents are automatically eligible for the insurance benefits under that plan. Yet both still have extensive private insurance marketplaces. Not only that, but Australia actively encourages residents to purchase private insurance by adding a tax penalty to those who don't. So not only does private insurance exist, residents are actually encouraged to buy private insurance. This certainly suggests a path forward for the US.

Now, let's go back to the health plans that have been proposed as healthcare reform in the US, and let's put those plans into the same type of table (Figure 8-2). The Medicare for All plans cover most but not all of the boxes. They are deficient on choice and existence of private insurance options.

The multi-payer plans fail multiple criteria. Most importantly, they do not require payment participation in the national health plan, or necessarily even paying into any plan at all (what happens if someone just feels healthy and lucky and doesn't want to pay for health insurance?). Thus, they do not ensure universal coverage.

Ideal Criteria	Single Payer	Multi-Payer	Incremental
Universal Coverage	X	+/-*	
Minimal Coverage Gaps**	X		
Not National Govt. Provider	X	X	X
Mandatory Participation	X	+/-*	
Not Employer Funded	X		
Choice to Purchase 2nd Plan		X	X
Private Insurance Still Exists		X	X

Figure 8-2. Which of the health plans proposed in the US meet the ideal criteria we've laid out for an optimal healthcare system? The proposed health plans discussed have been distilled into one of three categories. Two Medicare for All proposals are single-payer. Several multi-player plans propose to establish a new public option that coexists with voluntary, employer-sponsored insurance. These include Medicare for Those Who Want It. Several other plans propose to incrementally expand existing Medicare or Medicaid without achieving universal coverage. *The multi-payer options could create the potential to achieve universal coverage, but most do not require that everyone pays into a program, and will leave patients uninsured. Thus, they do not ensure universal coverage (indicated by the +/-). Furthermore, all of these plans (including Medicare for Those Who Want It) will create a risk of sick patients being pushed off of private plans on to the public plan, setting up the unsustainable death spiral of public costs, while maximizing private profits. **Minimal coverage gaps means that the insurance has no deductible, no coinsurance, and only limited co-pays for drug prescriptions and outpatient specialty care. Reliance on private plans for basic coverage retains such gaps.

These multi-payer plans also create a situation in which private plans could push sick patients off of their rolls and onto the competing public option, maximizing private profits and increasingly destabilizing the public plan's financial sustainability. In essence, they force the public plan to compete with both hands tied behind its back. In contrast, in the single-payer, true Medicare for All plans, everyone pays into the central pool of funds for the public plan.

The plans seeking to incrementally expand Medicare and Medicaid are nonstarters for the purpose of this discussion since they don't come close to ensuring universal coverage. They are what we do if we simply couldn't muster the public and political will to make a meaningful change.

The path forward here appears to be a combination of the single-payer plans with multi-payer plans. While this may seem contradictory, the Australian and New Zealand experiences show us that it is not. There is no reason we could not have a single-payer public health plan, into which everyone pays via central taxes, which guarantees insurance coverage for all Americans, while still allowing a private insurance option to supplement or even replace the public plan (after someone has already paid for the public plan). People or companies could choose, on their own, to purchase private insurance if they wanted. But they would do that in addition to contributing to the national health plan. That is precisely how things work in Australia and New Zealand.

Really, this plan is a minor tweak of both Medicare for All and Medicare for Those Who Want It. Indeed, it is essentially a hybrid of both. Rather than a retroactive, individual mandate for those who do not purchase private insurance, everyone would pay a centrally collected federal tax as part of normal taxes. Even people who do choose to purchase private insurance would pay that tax. Thus, there is no need for an individual mandate to participate because the government just collects taxes centrally as usual. We would successfully avoid going through another partisan national nightmare bickering over an individual mandate (Don't Tread on Me vs. United We Stand).

In such a system, even if healthy people increasingly choose to pay for private insurance, they will still help support the costs of care for our sick fellow Americans. This funding of the public plan by everyone would counter the risk of a death spiral caused by having many healthy people choose to stop paying for the public plan. Even if the healthy people selected private insurance, they would have still contributed taxes to the public plan.

In this way, we would achieve a single-payer plan that would have the ability to markedly improve care and cost-efficiency, while still preserving choice for Americans. It would also relieve businesses of a hidden employee benefits tax, and not disintegrate an entire, half-trillion-dollar industry sector in America, with all of the attendant blowback consequences of that move. Furthermore, the model should work for both ardent proponents of publicly funded healthcare and ardent proponents of privately funded healthcare. They would compete, head to head. What could be more American than that?

LEADERSHIP AND VISION: THE AMERICAN COLLEGE OF PHYSICIANS

For years, I have wondered why physician specialty organizations weren't taking a stand on our broken US healthcare system. Physicians are suffering from burnout at record rates in the US. The administrative burdens and excessive documentation requirements to enable fee-for-service, line-item billing are driving all of us nuts. The electronic medical records we all must use are geared to support billing, not efficiency of our work. There are vast pay disparities between expensive proceduralists (who do procedures on patients) and cognitive specialties (whose job it is to think about patients and their environment and try to keep them healthy so they don't need expensive procedures). One would have thought that physician organizations would be up in arms over all of this.

I belong to two physician organizations, reflecting my two board certifications: Internal Medicine specialty, and Infectious Diseases subspecialty. And, just as I was wrapping this book up, the American College of Physicians (ACP), which is the specialty society for internal medicine specialists, came out with a bold vision for healthcare reform.

The ACP is the largest physician specialty society in the US since internal medicine specialists outnumber other specialists. I was delighted and proud of my specialty organization. Because they showed vision and leadership, while other organizations have sat silently watching the degeneration of our healthcare system in the US.

In January of 2020, the ACP released a series of articles describing its vision for healthcare reform.[4-8] The culmination of these articles is a call for either a single-payer system or a system of single-payer with optional private buy-in, very much akin to the conclusions drawn throughout this book, and through the earlier components of this chapter. The rationale laid out by ACP is remarkably similar to that found in this book. They even lay out a thoughtful transition plan regarding how to convert our current system to a single-payer-style system, with or without a complementary private layer (including with job training and support for insurance company employees to transition to other industries).

Never have I been so proud to be a member of a specialty society! The thoughtful and very specific recommendations made in the ACP position statements should serve as an important guidepost to moving the US forward in its efforts to do better for Americans.

IT'S THE CULTURE, STUPID

There's a famous saying in politics about the primary issue that moves most of the electorate to vote. "It's the economy, stupid." Well, in a similar way, for healthcare reform, everything may boil down to culture.

Healthcare is really confusing. It's very complicated. It can be paid for in so many ways. It can be delivered in so many other ways. The ultra-complexity helps account for why coming to consensus on what a new healthcare plan should look like is so hard.

But coming to consensus on the ideal design is actually the easy part. The hard part is ensuring that that design is moderate enough that it will pick up enough advocates and keep from alienating and infuriating enough opposition to avoid being killed outright. Or just as bad, avoid meeting the same fate that the California single-payer bill did. It got sent to committee. Committees are where ideas go to die. In committee, ideas and innovation die in quiet anonymity, suffocated under the artifice of political process and consensus.

As I said before, it does no good for us to come up with the perfect academic or philosophical solution to healthcare reform. We need a solution that appeals to a very large constituency while avoiding triggering a massive backlash and opposition. Political ardency and philosophical purity are the enemy in this process. We must set minimum criteria for acceptability while being flexible enough to accept design elements that will add to the coalition pushing the change forward.

What I think is most likely to succeed is a true universal health-care system with a single-payer backbone, into which everyone pays, but which gives the individual the option to buy their own private insurance if they want. This is akin to people who pay extra for FasTrak or toll lanes, but still pay taxes to support the public lanes.

In point of fact, the FasTrak and public lanes compete for business in a real way. When I'm driving to and from work, I check the toll rate for the morning drive in and afternoon drive home. I also check the travel times. On days where the FasTrak is much faster and the toll is not outrageous, I pay the extra fee. But on days where the value of the extra fee isn't worth the time saved, I use the public lanes.

In the same way, the public and private healthcare plans can compete head to head. Let's not force individuals to use the public option if they would prefer to continue using a self-selected private plan. But if they do choose to purchase private plans, they still contribute funding via taxes towards the universal coverage plan. This is similar to how Australia and New Zealand operate. Hence, there are existing, highly effective healthcare systems that do this, achieving excellent performance scores and at very favorable expense.

The reason I favor this option is because it seems to potentially bridge the divide between the potentially conflicting US core cultural elements we've discussed: Don't Tread on Me; United We Stand, Divided We Fall; capitalism and the profit motive. Any move to any universal system that establishes a national public health plan is already going to trigger opposition, just for the very idea of it. It would be best to defang the opposition as much as possible.

There is no need to intentionally poke constituents in the eye who could potentially be brought around to become supporters to reform. We will need a coalition to make this change happen. For-profit industry, including employers who could save money by eliminating the 10 percent hidden employee benefit tax, and private insurance companies can either be in violent opposition to healthcare reform, or can accept it. Private insurance companies may be attracted by the potential to shed lower margin, basic packages, used to cover everyone, so they could focus on higher-margin, premium or deluxe packages, improving their corporate profit margins. If done carefully, active support could even be garnered from businesses, who could find themselves freed of the crushing, hidden employee benefit tax. And we will need all the support we can get to move forward.

Educating the public and raising awareness about the foibles and flaws of the US healthcare system is a necessary step to building support for healthcare reform. But it isn't enough. The system that moves forward will need to appeal to a broad coalition. That means it must be compatible with American culture.

Whether any one of us is an ardent capitalist or a critic of capitalists or favors an individualistic approach, or a community benefit approach, the only thing that ultimately is going to matter for healthcare reform is what the prevailing, broad culture accepts in America. If we can construct a healthcare system that appeals to that broad culture, we have a shot at getting this done. If we trade broad appeal off for philosophical or academic purity of idea, we will lose. And I do mean lose. Because we will continue to be stuck with this ridiculous system that we have. We will continue to be ripped off to the tune of more than a trillion dollars of unnecessary excess and waste per year. We will continue to be broken, bankrupt, and dying. And that would be just plain dumb.

There is good news, though. There are intrinsic benefits to a new healthcare system that almost automatically appeal to the core culture that is shared with most people. No one likes getting ripped off. No one likes paying more money than they have to for services (not to mention, paying hugely more money). No one wants to die younger than other people. No one wants to be bafflingly confused by their own health plan. No one wants to risk getting hit with massive, surprise medical bills. No one wants to be at risk for declaring personal bankruptcy due to healthcare costs.

I seriously doubt anyone reading this book would disagree with these assertions. If we could implement a system in which you could spend less money to get better healthcare, which doesn't leave gaps in your coverage or leave you at risk for personal bankruptcy, which gives you the potential to live longer, and gives you the option to pick a plan you like, I'm betting you'd be supportive. I'm betting if framed this way, most Americans would be supportive. We just need to avoid needlessly antagonizing them in other ways, by inadvertently triggering cultural foibles.

At the end of the day, whether we get healthcare reform done or not will depend on education, outreach, engagement, coalition building, and advancing a healthcare system design that is ultimately compatible with American culture.

So, what are the next steps? And how can we participate in them? That is the subject of the final chapter.

CHAPTER 9

‖‖‖‖‖‖‖‖‖‖‖‖‖‖‖‖‖‖‖‖‖

A CALL TO ACTION

In the prior eight chapters, I have tried to describe for you some of the many frustrations that our patients, my colleagues, and I experience day after day trying to provide healthcare in our incredibly complex system in the US. It is entirely likely that you or a loved one of yours has encountered similar frustrations on yours or their journey through our healthcare system. It is my hope that we are nearing a tipping point, where the majority of the public in the US is ready to say, enough is enough.

The US healthcare system is confusing, disjointed, has gaps in coverage, and costs far too much, putting us at risk for personal bankruptcy due to sudden health issues that we could not have prevented. Patients don't get the care they need. Doctors burn out. Healthcare providers have to waste huge amounts of time and resources to pay people just to figure out who is allowed to be seen as a patient. The system focuses on racking up as many services and line items for the bill as possible. And then the payers argue with the providers about who is going to pay each fraction of each bill. People and families go bankrupt due to the gaps in payer coverage. They die due to gaps in care.

So yes, it is painful to work in our healthcare system. I've lived this. The dedicated staff who works with me day in and day out have lived with this. The patients who come to see us twenty-four hours per day and seven days per week have lived with this. There surely must be a better way.

The good news is, we have evidence that public opinion has shifted, and is indeed near a tipping point. In 2019, a review of public opinion polls was published in the *New England Journal of Medicine*.[1] The authors found that 69 percent of US adults surveyed said that reducing healthcare costs should be a top priority of the president and Congress. That number placed healthcare costs second on a list of eighteen potential domestic agenda items, just barely behind strengthening the economy (70 percent). In terms of magnitude of domestic problems, out-of-control healthcare costs ranked first out of eighteen, with 70 percent saying that these costs were a "very big problem." More than half of Americans said that healthcare costs were affecting their personal household's financial situation.

The public has begun to understand the drivers of our healthcare problems. A majority of adults surveyed blamed healthcare costs on high pricing at all levels of the healthcare system, from pharmaceuticals to hospital costs to insurance premiums.

But the polls did reveal a public disconnect on one fact. The majority of the public believes the US doesn't spend *enough* on healthcare. That's why we need to educate and spread the word. We need to improve healthcare coverage while reducing, not increasing costs.

There was a partisan divide with respect to which entity would be more likely to be able to control costs effectively. Republicans generally favored using private health insurance and state-run markets, while Democrats generally favored relying on the federal government. This divide underscores the need to find a solution that appeals to both and allows private health insurance to continue participating, while still allowing government to take on a universal healthcare role. Let's put the public and private plans in head-to-head competition, old-school American style.

Now, the issue of competition brings us to a critically important point. As I mentioned in chapter 6, no healthcare system can be perfect and unchanging over time. Life is about change. Competition results in adaptation by the competing parties. If we start with a system competing public vs. private plans, and one side or the other begins to become destabilized, we may need to shift the design in the future. We cannot be paralyzed by fear that we might implement a great system that isn't perfect, and might need to be changed in the future. I got news for you. It won't be perfect, and it will need to be changed. That's just life. Let's not let fear of the reality of life paralyze us. Even if imperfect, great would be better than awful.

At the end of the day, most Americans recognize that the system we have isn't working for them. It's time to change. Let's talk about how to make that change happen.

I hope I've convinced you that the starting point for our discussion on the US healthcare system is *not* that everything is fine and rosy, and that we're asking, "How do we go from good to great?" Not at all. To the contrary, the state of US healthcare is abysmal. In that context, all changes to the system merit consideration, so the best change can be selected.

But of course, healthcare reform is very controversial and also very complicated. That controversy and complexity may have a natural tendency to make people hunker down to their preconceived notions. We may not open our minds to new ideas. And that could cause us to ignore or shoot down ideas that we didn't fully understand, or that are not aligned with our own preconceived notions. An example of this might be the idea that all single-payer systems abolish all private insurance, which would be a nonstarter for many constituents. Rather, if we keep an open mind and consider other views, we might learn from the experiences of others. We might find that a single-payer system is definitely the desirable direction, but we can go that direction completely compatibly with retaining private insurance to play an important role in the new system. In fact, we can make those systems compete.

In considering our healthcare system, we should not ever be anchored to historical precedence. Why would we want to adhere to a historical precedence that has led us to a horribly broken system? When something is completely dysfunctional, paying homage to the history that led to it doesn't make a lot of sense. I don't care how we got where we are. I only care how to make it better from here. The fact that we got into this mess by an accident of history only underscores the point.

As Chief Medical Officer of my hospital, I've learned that there is a dead giveaway to a system that is broken but can be fixed. It is virtually 100 percent accurate and reliable. If I ask, why do we do a process that way, and the answer that comes back is, "Well, we've been doing it that way since 1976," I immediately know I've struck gold. If that's the best answer someone can give me, that process has no actual rationale aside from inertia. That means I've just discovered a broken process that can be fixed and made much better. The same thing is true regarding healthcare reform. The fact that we have been providing healthcare the way we have been for seventy-five years does not mean we need to keep doing it that way. It does not mean that the system works. We are doing it out of habit, not rational justification.

Therefore, we should not be trapped, blinkered, or even influenced by historical precedence. Nor should we be rigidly adherent to "-isms," like liberalism, conservatism, capitalism, or populism. Adherence to -isms distracts us from practical solutions. Let's not rule anything in or out because of a misguided obedience to philosophical purity. Instead, let us work together to build a proposal that appeals to the broadest possible coalition of adherents while minimizing the number of constituents that are alienated.

Finally, let us not take a win-lose approach to our proposal. If we believe we win when the other side loses, it will inherently trigger opposition. Rather, let's look for win-win opportunities. There are multiple examples of win-win in the proposed healthcare system we discussed in chapter 8. For example, we discussed a system designed to benefit both individuals and businesses at the same time. The system decreases costs of healthcare while allowing expanded healthcare coverage. The system maximally stabilizes insurance for everyone, but still gives people choices about their insurance. The system does this by allowing both public and private insurance to coexist and compete.

With this introduction in mind, let's talk about the path forward.

How do we get to the point where we could feasibly implement such a system?

⚕ ⚕ ⚕ ⚕ ⚕

In chapter 7, I described the trip my cohort of Leshner Public Engagement Fellows took to Capitol Hill in 2017. I've reflected a lot on that trip. It was sort of a watershed moment for me because it had striking parallels to my prior experience working on policy issues related to antibiotic-resistant infections.

As I mentioned in the introduction, I spent years working on national policy issues related to antibiotic resistance long before I became a Chief Medical Officer. Back then, I went to Capitol Hill repeatedly. I gave briefings to large groups of both House and Senate staffers about the problem of antibiotic resistance and its solutions. I then testified before Congress at a formal hearing on behalf of the Infectious Diseases Society of America. I did lots of media interviews. What I learned from these collective experiences was that in order to convince political powerbrokers to put legislation forward, or change regulations, we first had to convince the voters. We had to educate the public and make them aware of the problem, its causes, and solutions. That's why I wrote the book *Rising Plague* back in 2009.

Nearly ten years later, in 2017, as a Leshner Public Engagement Fellow, I ran into a similar problem on Capitol Hill. It took time for me to see the parallels and decide that the real lesson from that day is that before policy makers will act, the issue in question must mature and be seasoned in the public eye. That's why I decided to write this book.

If one carefully listens to the message beneath the words spoken by those staffers that day, a very wise set of instructions can be culled regarding how to proceed. Elected officials need their constituents to believe in a cause to enable them to make a bold move.

Let's face facts. Completely revamping the US healthcare system is not an incremental, minor tweak. It would reflect a fundamental transformation of a multitrillion-dollar medical, social, economic, and political powerhouse of an industry. The change would affect literally every American, and the healthcare industry has more constituents than one can count. There is so much money around, those constituents will have a huge influence and voice. That's why healthcare reform blew up in 1993 when the Clintons tried to push it. It's why the Affordable Care Act has been such a lightning rod for controversy, despite the fact that President Obama and his team adapted it from a Republican plan.

In retrospect, I should not have been surprised at the response I got from those Congressional staffers. And in fact, I subsequently realized that I was the one who messed up, not them. Because I came in asking what they could do for me. And what I should have been doing was the opposite. I should have been asking, what could I do to help them improve our system? The message beneath the words was: the issues you are raising are dangerous and controversial, and Congress can't work on them until the American people are ready for it. Had I been in a more receptive mood, rather than in a mood to make a pitch, I would have heard the message that day that the staffers needed help softening the ground up, maturing the dialogue.

It simply won't be possible for elected officials to accomplish the massive changes necessary to implement healthcare reform unless the public is already there. There are too many vested interests, too many competing ideas, too many ways to fail, and there is too much money at stake.

At the end of the day, what I've come to realize since that day on Capitol Hill is that the power to drive forward with implementing healthcare reform lies with you and me, more than with our elected officials.

True, you and I can't pass laws. You and I can't change regulations. But what you and I can do is debate, dialogue, and discuss, openly and in public. What you and I can do is message our elected officials that the issue of healthcare reform is maturing. That it is now much better cooked and seasoned than it was before. It is time to finish cooking the issue, take it out of the oven, and serve it. We can provide the political cover to leaders who want to lead but heretofore have been prevented from taking bold action by the controversy and heat generated by vested interests arguing against change.

We can make clear that we now understand our healthcare problems much better than before. And as a result of that better understanding, we realize that the arguments made against change are simply vested interests protecting their own incomes, at the expense of everyone else's well-being. Just as we convinced food manufacturers and retail outlets to sell antibiotic-free meat, we can show our elected officials that we are ready for and want change in our healthcare system.

So if you want to help make a difference, talk about healthcare. Talk about what you learned in this book with your family. Talk about it with your friends and neighbors. Sponsor a public meeting and invite an expert to come in to speak. Tweet about it. Put it on Instagram. Use whatever social media platform you prefer.

The point is, let us collectively educate and signal to Capitol Hill that the public is now ready to move forward with a significant improvement in our healthcare system. Let us signal to Capitol Hill that we are no longer willing to accept the excuses made by special interests that participate in the multitrillion-dollar healthcare industry regarding why we can't change and can't do better.

Based on the extensive, objective data and international comparisons I've shown you, I believe that the plan we should move forward with is an amalgamation of Medicare for All and Medicare for Those Who Want It.

I believe we should move forward with a universal, single-payer, national insurance plan, with no deductible or coinsurance, but with co-pays for specialty care and prescription drugs, funded by centrally collected taxes that everyone pays, but while still giving the individual a choice about whether they want to use the public insurance or buy their own private insurance. I actually really like Australia's tax that encourages people who can afford it to buy private insurance, and I fully support that approach for the US as well. The resolution to the seeming paradox between a single-payer plan and offering choices is to give government-sponsored insurance to all residents, but also allow and encourage a thriving private insurance market that people can choose to purchase into if they would like. Like the drivers who choose to drive in the FasTrak and toll lanes, they can pay for a private healthcare plan if they like, while still helping the rest of their fellow Americans cover the cost of the public plan. Let the public plan and private markets compete. Give people options. And let's move towards global budgets and away from fee-for-service.

I think this collective idea makes the most sense. I think it will offer the best coverage at the best price, and will help reform healthcare delivery to eliminate waste and improve outcomes. I also think it is the most politically palatable, minimizing triggering opposition by including aspects that should appeal to people on both sides of the aisle.

But you know what? At this point, I'll accept almost any universal system that can muster the political and social support behind it to get it done. I'd rather not make the *perfect* be the enemy of the good. I have no use for a philosophically optimal system that can never be implemented. I want something that can get done. So I'm keeping an open mind while advocating for what I think is best, and I'd encourage you to do that too.

⚕ ⚕ ⚕ ⚕ ⚕

Let me close by offering some motivational thoughts.

Doesn't it annoy you that Americans are getting ripped off to the tune of more than a trillion dollars per year in excess taxes and lost wages due to wasteful healthcare spending?

As a taxpayer, doesn't it annoy you that Americans' taxes are wasted on inefficient healthcare?

As someone who works hard for your family, doesn't it annoy

you to know that Americans' wages are 10 percent lower than they should be because of healthcare wastage?

As someone who worries about your family's health and well-being, doesn't it annoy you that healthcare costs are a leading cause of personal bankruptcy in the US?

As a worker or corporate manager in America, doesn't it annoy you that American businesses suffer crippling costs due to bloated healthcare, which places them at a marked disadvantage to international competitors that don't bear those costs?

As Chief Medical Officer of one of the largest public hospitals in the US, it annoys me that my hospital has to waste huge amounts of money by maneuvering through an unbelievably Byzantine maze of national healthcare complexity. This requires us to divert the attention of literally thousands of employees to continuously trying to figure out what care we are allowed to provide for whom and sending the rest away. Who bears the costs of all of this financial administrative work, which has nothing to do with caring for patients? You and me—the taxpayers. And that annoys me. Doesn't it annoy you?

It annoys me most of all that patients who depend on our healthcare system for their care have poor access to that care. They have to make choices between coming to the doctor, taking medications, and receiving treatments, versus eating. Or living indoors in a home. They are confused by the unnecessary, but quite intentional, complexity of our healthcare system. Our healthcare system is failing our families and our friends. We are broken. We are going bankrupt. We are dying.

Americans are indeed broken, bankrupt, and dying. And the

real tragedy of all of this is that it is totally solvable. We actually know how to solve it. We know how to cut trillions of dollars in cost while improving access to care. We know how to simplify things, so people don't get confused about their healthcare, and don't have to deal with frustrations in trying to get care. We know how to ensure access to healthcare for everyone. And how to keep healthcare from bankrupting people and families, or forcing them to choose between healthcare and eating, or living indoors. We simply choose to believe we can't change, helped along with that conviction by constant nudging from the financially vested, middling interests in the existing system.

Our problem is not a knowledge problem. It's a problem of will and politics. Those who say we don't know how to fix our healthcare system or that the solution is impossible to achieve and magical thinking…they are typically employed by or derive income or donations from, vested interests in our healthcare system that thrive off the waste.

You and I have the power to change this, together. We could provide much better healthcare, live longer, and have much better access to care, at hugely less cost to taxpayers, workers, and businesses by establishing a combined single-payer with an optional private insurance model. It is time for change. It is time to stand up and demand change from your elected officials, and from each other.

BIBLIOGRAPHY

CHAPTER 1

1. The Commonwealth Fund. "Home." https://www.commonwealthfund.org/.

2. Organisation for Economic Co-operation and Development. https://www.oecd.org/.

3. The Commonwealth Fund. "Mirror, Mirror: Comparing Health Systems Across Countries." https://www.commonwealthfund.org/series/mirror-mirror-comparing-health-systems-across-countries.

4. Tanzi, Alexandre. "Americans Lose in 2040 Global Life Expectancy Rankings." *Bloomberg*, October 20, 2018. https://www.bloomberg.com/news/articles/2018-10-20/americans-lose-among-2040-global-life-expectancy-rankings-map.

5. Barber, Ryan M, Nancy Fullman, Reed J D Sorensen, Thomas Bollyky, Martin McKee, Ellen Nolte, Amanuel Alemu Abajobir, et al. "Healthcare Access and Quality Index Based on Mortality from Causes Amenable to Personal Health Care in 195 Countries and Territories, 1990–2015: A Novel Analysis from the Global Burden of Disease Study 2015." *The Lancet* 390, no. 10091 (July 2017): 231–66. https://doi.org/10.1016/s0140-6736(17)30818-8.

6. Organisation for Economic Co-operation and Development. "Life

expectancy at birth." https://data.oecd.org/healthstat/life-expectancy-
at-birth.htm.

7. Moyers, Bill. *Bill Moyers Journal*. Podcast transcript, August 28, 2009.
https://www.pbs.org/moyers/journal/08282009/transcript1.html.

8. Organisation for Economic Co-operation and Development. "OECD
Insurance Statistics." https://www.oecd.org/daf/fin/insurance/
oecdinsurancestatistics.htm.

9. Organisation for Economic Co-operation and Development. "Health
Systems Characteristics." http://www.oecd.org/health/health-systems/
characteristics.htm.

10. Garfield, Rachel, Kendal Orgera, and Anthony Damico. "The Uninsured
and the ACA: A Primer – Key Facts about Health Insurance and the
Uninsured amidst Changes to the Affordable Care Act." Kaiser Family
Foundation. Last modified January 25, 2019. https://www.kff.org/
report-section/the-uninsured-and-the-aca-a-primer-key-facts-about-
health-insurance-and-the-uninsured-amidst-changes-to-the-affordable-
care-act-how-many-people-are-uninsured/.

11. Himmelstein, David U., Miraya Jun, Reinhard Busse, Karine Chevreul,
Alexander Geissler, Patrick Jeurissen, Sarah Thomson, Marie-
Amelie Vinet, and Steffie Woolhandler. "A Comparison Of Hospital
Administrative Costs In Eight Nations: US Costs Exceed All Others
By Far." *Health Affairs* 33, no. 9 (September 2014): 1586–94. https://doi.
org/10.1377/hlthaff.2013.1327.

12. Cheng, Tsung-Mei. "Health Care Spending in the US and Taiwan: A
Response to *It's Still the Prices, Stupid, and a Tribute to Uwe Reinhardt*."
Health Affairs, February 6, 2019. https://www.healthaffairs.org/do/10.1377/
hblog20190206.305164/full/.

13. Golshan, Tara. "The Answer to America's Health Care Cost Problem
Might be in Maryland." *Vox*, January 22, 2020. https://www.vox.com/
policy-and-politics/2020/1/22/21055118/maryland-health-care-global-
hospital-budget.

14. Sharfstein, Joshua M., Sule Gerovich, Elizabeth Moriarty, and David C.
Chin. "An Emerging Approach to Payment Reform: All-Payer Global

Budgets for Large Safety-Net Hospital Systems." The Commonwealth Fund. Last modified August 16, 2017. https://www.commonwealthfund. org/publications/fund-reports/2017/aug/emerging-approach-payment-reform-all-payer-global-budgets-large.

15. Scott, Dylan, Ezra Klein, and Tara Golshan. "Everybody Covered." *Vox*, February 12, 2020. https://www.vox.com/2020/1/13/21055327/everybody-covered.

16. Berwick, Donald M. "Elusive Waste." *JAMA* 322, no. 15 (October 15, 2019): 1458. https://doi.org/10.1001/jama.2019.14610.

17. Centers for Medicare & Medicaid Services. "FFS Data (2015-2018)." Last modified April 6, 2020. https://www.cms.gov/Medicare/Health-Plans/MedicareAdvtgSpecRateStats/FFS-Data.html.

18. Sisko, Andrea M., Sean P. Keehan, John A. Poisal, Gigi A. Cuckler, Sheila D. Smith, Andrew J. Madison, Kathryn E. Rennie, and James C. Hardesty. "National Health Expenditure Projections, 2018–27: Economic And Demographic Trends Drive Spending And Enrollment Growth." *Health Affairs* 38, no. 3 (March 2019): 491–501. https://doi.org/10.1377/hlthaff.2018.05499.

19. IHI Multimedia Team. "Like Magic? ('Every System is Perfectly Designed…')." Institute for Healthcare Improvement. Last modified August 21, 2015. http://www.ihi.org/communities/blogs/origin-of-every-system-is-perfectly-designed-quote.

CHAPTER 2

1. Hartman, Micah, Anne B. Martin, Joseph Benson, and Aaron Catlin. "National Health Care Spending In 2018: Growth Driven by Accelerations In Medicare And Private Insurance Spending." *Health Affairs* 39, no. 1 (January 1, 2020): 8–17. https://doi.org/10.1377/hlthaff.2019.01451.

2. Mnuchin, Steven T., R. Alexander Acosta, Alex M. Azar II, Nancy A Berryhill, and Seema Verma, MPH. "2019 Annual Report of the Boards of Trustees of the Federal Hospital Insurance and Federal Supplementary Medical Insurance Trust Funds." Boards of Trustees of the Federal

Hospital and Federal Supplementary Medical Insurance Trust Funds, April 22, 2019. https://www.cms.gov/Research-Statistics-Data-and-Systems/Statistics-Trends-and-Reports/ReportsTrustFunds/Downloads/TR2019.pdf.

3. The World Bank. "GDP (current US$)." https://data.worldbank.org/indicator/ny.gdp.mktp.cd.

4. World Population Review. "GDP Ranked by Country 2020." http://worldpopulationreview.com/countries/countries-by-gdp/.

5. World Population Review. "2020 World Population by Country." http://worldpopulationreview.com/.

6. Organisation for Economic Co-operation and Development. "Health Spending." https://data.oecd.org/healthres/health-spending.htm.

7. "2019 Employer Health Benefits Survey." Kaiser Family Foundation. Last modified September 25, 2019. https://www.kff.org/health-costs/report/2019-employer-health-benefits-survey/.

8. Tozzi, John. "Health Insurance Costs Surpass $20,000 Per Year, Hitting a Record." *Bloomberg*, September 25, 2019. https://www.bloomberg.com/news/articles/2019-09-25/why-is-health-insurance-so-expensive-20-000-a-year-for-coverage.

9. Hackbarth, Andrew D. "Eliminating Waste in US Health Care." *JAMA* 307, no. 14 (April 11, 2012): 1513. https://doi.org/10.1001/jama.2012.362.

10. Squires, David and Chloe Anderson. "U.S. Health Care from a Global Perspective." The Commonwealth Fund. Last modified October 8, 2015. https://www.commonwealthfund.org/publications/issue-briefs/2015/oct/us-health-care-global-perspective.

11. The Commonwealth Fund. "Mirror, Mirror: Comparing Health Systems Across Countries." https://www.commonwealthfund.org/series/mirror-mirror-comparing-health-systems-across-countries.

CHAPTER 3

1. Himmelstein, David U., Robert M. Lawless, Deborah Thorne, Pamela Foohey, and Steffie Woolhandler. "Medical Bankruptcy: Still Common

Despite the Affordable Care Act." *American Journal of Public Health* 109, no. 3 (March 2019): 431–33. https://doi.org/10.2105/ajph.2018.304901.

2. Himmelstein, David U., Deborah Thorne, Elizabeth Warren, and Steffie Woolhandler. "Medical Bankruptcy in the United States, 2007: Results of a National Study." *The American Journal of Medicine* 122, no. 8 (August 2009): 741–46. https://doi.org/10.1016/j.amjmed.2009.04.012.

3. Consumer Financial Protection Bureau. "Consumer Credit Reports: A Study of Medical and Non-Medical Collections." Last modified December 2014. https://files.consumerfinance.gov/f/201412_cfpb_reports_consumer-credit-medical-and-non-medical-collections.pdf.

4. Dobkin, Carlos, Amy Finkelstein, Raymond Kluender, and Matthew J. Notowidigdo. "Myth and Measurement — The Case of Medical Bankruptcies." *New England Journal of Medicine* 378, no. 12 (March 22, 2018): 1076–78. https://doi.org/10.1056/nejmp1716604.

5. Dranove, David, and Michael L. Millenson. "Medical Bankruptcy: Myth Versus Fact." *Health Affairs* 25, no. Suppl1 (January 2006): W74–83. https://doi.org/10.1377/hlthaff.25.w74.

6. Dickler, Jessica. "Most Americans Live Paycheck to Paycheck." *CNBC*, August 24, 2017. https://www.cnbc.com/2017/08/24/most-americans-live-paycheck-to-paycheck.html.

7. Konish, Lorie. "This is the Real Reason Most Americans File for Bankruptcy." *CNBC*, February 11, 2019. https://www.cnbc.com/2019/02/11/this-is-the-real-reason-most-americans-file-for-bankruptcy.html.

8. Epperson, Sharon and Jessica Dickler. "Next Government Shutdown: How to Build a Cash Cushion When Your Income is Cut Off." *CNBC*, February 9, 2019. https://www.cnbc.com/2019/02/08/how-to-build-a-cash-cushion-when-your-income-is-cut-off.html.

9. Kacik, Alex. "Operating Margins Stabilize, but Not-for-Profit Hospitals Still Vulnerable." *Modern Healthcare*, April 26, 2019. https://www.modernhealthcare.com/providers/operating-margins-stabilize-not-profit-hospitals-still-vulnerable.

10. "Drug Industry: Profits, Research and Development Spending, and Merger

and Acquisition Deals." United States Government Accountability Office, November 2017. https://www.gao.gov/assets/690/688472.pdf.

11. Flanagan, Cristin. "U.S. Hospitals Shut at 30-a-Year Pace, with No End in Sight." *Bloomberg*, August 21, 2018. https://www.bloomberg.com/news/articles/2018-08-21/hospitals-are-getting-eaten-away-by-market-trends-analysts-say.

12. The Commonwealth Fund. "Survey: 79 Million Americans Have Problems with Medical Bills or Debt." https://www.commonwealthfund.org/publications/newsletter-article/survey-79-million-americans-have-problems-medical-bills-or-debt.

13. Batty, Michael, Christa Gibbs, and Benedic Ippolito. "Unlike Medical Spending, Medical Bills In Collections Decrease With Patients' Age." *Health Affairs* 37, no. 8 (August 2018): 1257–64. https://doi.org/10.1377/hlthaff.2018.0349.

14. Norton, Mira, Liz Hamel, and Mollyann Brodie. "Assessing Americans' Familiarity with Health Insurance Terms and Concepts." Kaiser Family Foundation. Last modified November 11, 2014. https://www.kff.org/health-reform/poll-finding/assessing-americans-familiarity-with-health-insurance-terms-and-concepts/.

15. Garfield, Rachel, Kendal Orgera, and Anthony Damico. "The Uninsured and the ACA: A Primer – Key Facts about Health Insurance and the Uninsured amidst Changes to the Affordable Care Act." Kaiser Family Foundation. Last modified January 25, 2019. https://www.kff.org/report-section/the-uninsured-and-the-aca-a-primer-key-facts-about-health-insurance-and-the-uninsured-amidst-changes-to-the-affordable-care-act-how-many-people-are-uninsured/.

16. Kirzinger, Ashley, Cailey Muñana, Lunna Lopes, Liz Hamel, and Mollyann Brodie. "KFF Health Tracking Poll – June 2019: Health Care in the Democratic Primary and Medicare-for-all." Kaiser Family Foundation. Last modified June 18, 2019. https://www.kff.org/health-reform/poll-finding/kff-health-tracking-poll-june-2019/.

17. Wilper, Andrew P., Steffie Woolhandler, Karen E. Lasser, Danny McCormick, David H. Bor, and David U. Himmelstein. "Health Insurance

and Mortality in US Adults." *American Journal of Public Health* 99, no. 12 (December 2009): 2289–95. https://doi.org/10.2105/ajph.2008.157685.

18. Woolhandler, Steffie, and David U. Himmelstein. "The Relationship of Health Insurance and Mortality: Is Lack of Insurance Deadly?" *Annals of Internal Medicine* 167, no. 6 (June 27, 2017): 424. https://doi.org/10.7326/m17-1403.

19. Sommers, Benjamin D., Katherine Baicker, and Arnold M. Epstein. "Mortality and Access to Care among Adults after State Medicaid Expansions." *New England Journal of Medicine* 367, no. 11 (September 13, 2012): 1025–34. https://doi.org/10.1056/nejmsa1202099.

20. Hartman, Micah, Anne B. Martin, Joseph Benson, and Aaron Catlin. "National Health Care Spending In 2018: Growth Driven by Accelerations In Medicare And Private Insurance Spending." *Health Affairs* 39, no. 1 (January 1, 2020): 8–17. https://doi.org/10.1377/hlthaff.2019.01451.

21. Mnuchin, Steven T., R. Alexander Acosta, Alex M. Azar II, Nancy A Berryhill, and Seema Verma, MPH. "2019 Annual Report of the Boards of Trustees of the Federal Hospital Insurance and Federal Supplementary Medical Insurance Trust Funds." Boards of Trustees of the Federal Hospital and Federal Supplementary Medical Insurance Trust Funds, April 22, 2019. https://www.cms.gov/Research-Statistics-Data-and-Systems/Statistics-Trends-and-Reports/ReportsTrustFunds/Downloads/TR2019.pdf.

22. Congressional Budget Office. "Budget and Economic Data." https://www.cbo.gov/about/products/budget-economic-data#2.

23. "The 2019 Long-Term Budget Outlook." Congress of the United States Congressional Budget Office, June 2019. https://www.cbo.gov/system/files/2019-06/55331-LTBO-2.pdf.

24. Sisko, Andrea M., Sean P. Keehan, John A. Poisal, Gigi A. Cuckler, Sheila D. Smith, Andrew J. Madison, Kathryn E. Rennie, and James C. Hardesty. "National Health Expenditure Projections, 2018–27: Economic And Demographic Trends Drive Spending And Enrollment Growth." *Health Affairs* 38, no. 3 (March 2019): 491–501. https://doi.org/10.1377/hlthaff.2018.05499.

25. Centers for Medicare & Medicaid Services. "National Health Expenditure Accounts: Methodology Paper, 2017." http://www.cms.gov/NationalHealthExpendData/downloads/dsm-17.pdf.

26. Pizzella, Patrick and William W. Beach. "National Compensation Survey: Employee Benefits in the United States, March 2019." U.S. Bureau of Labor Statistics, September 2019. https://www.bls.gov/ncs/ebs/benefits/2019/employee-benefits-in-the-united-states-march-2019.pdf.

27. Adler, Loren and Brian Collens. "Gates, Mullen Echo Leaders of Debt Commissions: America's Fiscal Challenge is a Matter of Arithmetic." Bipartisan Policy Center. Last modified September 19, 2012. https://bipartisanpolicy.org/blog/gates-mullen-echo-leaders-debt-commissions-americas-fiscal-challenge-matter/.

28. Hackbarth, Andrew D. "Eliminating Waste in US Health Care." *JAMA* 307, no. 14 (April 11, 2012): 1513. https://doi.org/10.1001/jama.2012.362.

29. La Roche, Julia. "Buffett: 'Medical Costs are the Tapeworm of American Economic Competitiveness." *Yahoo! Finance*, May 6, 2017. https://finance.yahoo.com/news/buffett-medical-costs-tapeworm-american-economic-competitiveness-220647855.html.

30. Denney, Timothy. "Healthcare Costs are Harming U.S. Competitiveness." *International Policy Digest*, June 17, 2019. https://intpolicydigest.org/2019/06/17/healthcare-costs-are-harming-u-s-competitiveness/.

31. The Harris Poll. "New Poll: U.S. Business Leaders Would Increase Employee Wages and Technology Investments if They Could Lower Healthcare Costs." Last modified 2014. https://theharrispoll.com/a-new-poll-of-chief-financial-officers-cfos-at-large-u-s-companies-that-currently-provide-health-insurance-to-their-employees-finds-that-about-9-in-10-agree-that-if-their-companys-healthca/.

32. Kramer, Mark R. and John Pontillo. "End the Corporate Health Care Tax." *Harvard Business Review*, October 24, 2018. https://hbr.org/2018/10/end-the-corporate-health-care-tax.

CHAPTER 4

1. Papanicolas, Irene, Liana R. Woskie, and Ashish K. Jha. "Health Care Spending in the United States and Other High-Income Countries." *JAMA* 319, no. 10 (March 13, 2018): 1024. https://doi.org/10.1001/jama.2018.1150.

2. Klein, Jennifer. "The Politics of Economic Security: Employee Benefits and the Privatization of New Deal Liberalism." *Journal of Policy History* 16, no. 1 (January 2004): 34–65. https://doi.org/10.1353/jph.2004.0002.

3. PBS. "Healthcare Timeline." https://www.pbs.org/healthcarecrisis/history.htm.

4. Mihm, Stephen. "Employer-Based Health Care was a Wartime Accident." *Chicago Tribune*, February 2017. https://www.chicagotribune.com/opinion/commentary/ct-obamacare-health-care-employers-20170224-story.html.

5. *Employment and Health Benefits: A Connection at Risk*. Washington, DC: National Academies Press, 1993. https://doi.org/10.17226/2044.

6. Scofea, Laura A. "The Development and Growth of Employer-Provided Health Insurance." *Monthly Labor Review*, March 1994. https://www.bls.gov/opub/mlr/1994/03/art1full.pdf.

7. Spellberg, M.D., Brad. *Rising Plague: The Global Threat from Deadly Bacteria and Our Dwindling Arsenal to Fight Them*. New York: Prometheus Press, 2009.

8. Fuchs, Victor R. "How and Why US Health Care Differs From That in Other OECD Countries." *JAMA* 309, no. 1 (January 2, 2013): 33. https://doi.org/10.1001/jama.2012.125458.

9. Baker, Charles D., Arthur Caplan, Karen Davis, Susan Dentzer, Arnold M. Epstein, Bill Frist, Robert S. Galvin, et al. "Health of the Nation — Coverage for All Americans." *New England Journal of Medicine* 359, no. 8 (August 21, 2008): 777–80. https://doi.org/10.1056/nejmp0805637.

10. Denney, Timothy. "Healthcare Costs are Harming U.S. Competitiveness." *International Policy Digest*, June 17, 2019. https://intpolicydigest.org/2019/06/17/healthcare-costs-are-harming-u-s-competitiveness/.

11. Emanuel, Ezekiel J. "The Real Cost of the US Health Care System." *JAMA* 319, no. 10 (March 13, 2018): 983. https://doi.org/10.1001/jama.2018.1151.

CHAPTER 5

1. Sabatini, Nelson, Joseph R. Antos, Howard Haft, and Donna Kinzer. "Maryland's All-Payer Model—Achievements, Challenges, and Next Steps." *Health Affairs Blog*, January 31, 2017. https://www.healthaffairs.org/do/10.1377/hblog20170131.058550/full/.

2. Himmelstein, David U., Miraya Jun, Reinhard Busse, Karine Chevreul, Alexander Geissler, Patrick Jeurissen, Sarah Thomson, Marie-Amelie Vinet, and Steffie Woolhandler. "A Comparison Of Hospital Administrative Costs In Eight Nations: US Costs Exceed All Others By Far." *Health Affairs* 33, no. 9 (September 2014): 1586–94. https://doi.org/10.1377/hlthaff.2013.1327.

3. Golshan, Tara. "The Answer to America's Health Care Cost Problem Might be in Maryland." *Vox*, January 22, 2020. https://www.vox.com/policy-and-politics/2020/1/22/21055118/maryland-health-care-global-hospital-budget.

4. Hackbarth, Andrew D. "Eliminating Waste in US Health Care." *JAMA* 307, no. 14 (April 11, 2012): 1513. https://doi.org/10.1001/jama.2012.362.

5. Macrotrends. "Humana Revenue 2006–2019 | HUM." https://www.macrotrends.net/stocks/charts/HUM/humana/revenue.

6. Mishra, Manas and Askash B. "Health Insurer Humana's Full-Year Profit Forecasts Disappoints." *Reuters*, February 6, 2019. https://www.reuters.com/article/us-humana-results/health-insurer-humanas-full-year-profit-forecasts-disappoints-idUSKCN1PV1A2.

7. Humana. "2018 Annual Report." https://humana.gcs-web.com/static-files/a8b89abb-64e0-4fb1-ab70-b80ae1726eb0.

8. Berwick, Donald M. "Elusive Waste." *JAMA* 322, no. 15 (October 15, 2019): 1458. https://doi.org/10.1001/jama.2019.14610.

9. Himmelstein, David U., Terry Campbell, and Steffie Woolhandler. "Health Care Administrative Costs in the United States and Canada, 2017." *Annals of Internal Medicine* 172, no. 2 (January 7, 2020): 134. https://doi.org/10.7326/m19-2818.

10. Scott, Dylan. "Taiwan's Single-Payer Success Story—and Its Lessons for America." *Vox*, January 13, 2020. https://www.vox.com/health-care/2020/1/13/21028702/medicare-for-all-taiwan-health-insurance.

11. Cheng, Tsung-Mei. "Reflections On The 20th Anniversary Of Taiwan's Single-Payer National Health Insurance System." *Health Affairs* 34, no. 3 (March 2015): 502–10. https://doi.org/10.1377/hlthaff.2014.1332.

12. Mnuchin, Steven T., R. Alexander Acosta, Alex M. Azar II, Nancy A Berryhill, and Seema Verma, MPH. "2019 Annual Report of the Boards of Trustees of the Federal Hospital Insurance and Federal Supplementary Medical Insurance Trust Funds." Boards of Trustees of the Federal Hospital and Federal Supplementary Medical Insurance Trust Funds, April 22, 2019. https://www.cms.gov/Research-Statistics-Data-and-Systems/Statistics-Trends-and-Reports/ReportsTrustFunds/Downloads/TR2019.pdf.

13. Cubanski, Juliette, Tricia Neuman, and Meredith Freed. "The Facts on Medicare Spending and Financing." Kaiser Family Foundation. Last modified August 20, 2019. https://www.kff.org/medicare/issue-brief/the-facts-on-medicare-spending-and-financing/.

14. Dodge v. Ford Motor Co., 204 Mich. 459, 170 N.W. 668 (1919), https://h2o.law.harvard.edu/cases/3965.

15. IHI Multimedia Team. "Like Magic? ('Every System is Perfectly Designed…')." Institute for Healthcare Improvement. Last modified August 21, 2015. http://www.ihi.org/communities/blogs/origin-of-every-system-is-perfectly-designed-quote.

16. Terhune, Chad and Anna Gorman. "Insurers Make Billions off Medicaid in California During Obamacare Expansion." *Los Angeles Times*, November 5, 2017. https://www.latimes.com/business/la-fi-medicaid-insurance-profits-20171101-story.html.

17. Meltzer, Rose. "Big 8 Health Insurers Rake in More than $7B in Q3, Setting up Strong Finish to 2018." Fierce Healthcare. Last modified November 19, 2018. https://www.fiercehealthcare.com/payer/big-eight-insurers-set-to-finish-strong-year-raking-132-4-billion-total-q3.

18. National Association of Insurance Commissioners. "U.S. Healthy Insurance Industry | 2018 Annual Results." https://naic.org/documents/topic_insurance_industry_snapshots_2018_health_ins_ind_report.pdf.

19. Advisory Board. "Hospital Profit Margins Declined from 2015 to 2016,

Moody's Finds." Last modified May 18, 2017. https://www.advisory.com/daily-briefing/2017/05/18/moodys-report.

20. Kacik, Alex. "Operating Margins Stabilize, but Not-for-Profit Hospitals Still Vulnerable." *Modern Healthcare*, April 26, 2019. https://www.modernhealthcare.com/providers/operating-margins-stabilize-not-profit-hospitals-still-vulnerable.

21. Slovak, Julianne. "The Average Profit Margin of Pharmaceuticals." *AZ Central*, May 14, 2018. https://yourbusiness.azcentral.com/average-profit-margin-pharmaceuticals-20671.html.

22. Shrank, William H., Teresa L. Rogstad, and Natasha Parekh. "Waste in the US Health Care System." *JAMA* 322, no. 15 (October 15, 2019): 1501. https://doi.org/10.1001/jama.2019.13978.

23. Woolhandler, Steffie, and David U. Himmelstein. "Single-Payer Reform: The Only Way to Fulfill the President's Pledge of More Coverage, Better Benefits, and Lower Costs." *Annals of Internal Medicine* 166, no. 8 (February 21, 2017): 587. https://doi.org/10.7326/m17-0302.

CHAPTER 6

1. Scott, Dylan, Ezra Klein, and Tara Golshan. "Everybody Covered." *Vox*, February 12, 2020. https://www.vox.com/2020/1/13/21055327/everybody-covered.

2. Scott, Dylan. "Taiwan's Single-Payer Success Story—and Its Lessons for America." *Vox*, January 13, 2020. https://www.vox.com/health-care/2020/1/13/21028702/medicare-for-all-taiwan-health-insurance.

3. Mossialos, Elias Mossialos, Martin Wenzl Wenzl, Robin Osborn Osborn, and Dana Sarnak Sarnak. "International Profiles of Health Care Systems, 2015." Commonwealth Fund, January 21, 2016. https://doi.org/10.15868/socialsector.25100.

4. Squires, David and Chloe Anderson. "U.S. Health Care from a Global Perspective." The Commonwealth Fund. Last modified October 8, 2015. https://www.commonwealthfund.org/publications/issue-briefs/2015/oct/us-health-care-global-perspective.

5. International Health Care System Profiles. "Country Profiles." https://
    international.commonwealthfund.org/.

6. The Commonwealth Fund. "International Profiles of Health Care Systems,
    2015." Last modified January 21, 2016. https://www.commonwealthfund.
    org/publications/fund-reports/2016/jan/international-profiles-health-
    care-systems-2015.

7. Fuchs, Victor R. "How and Why US Health Care Differs From That in
    Other OECD Countries." *JAMA* 309, no. 1 (January 2, 2013): 33. https://
    doi.org/10.1001/jama.2012.125458.

8. The Commonwealth Fund. "Mirror, Mirror: Comparing Health Systems
    Across Countries." https://www.commonwealthfund.org/series/mirror-
    mirror-comparing-health-systems-across-countries.

9. Papanicolas, Irene, Liana R. Woskie, and Ashish K. Jha. "Health Care
    Spending in the United States and Other High-Income Countries." *JAMA*
    319, no. 10 (March 13, 2018): 1024. https://doi.org/10.1001/jama.2018.1150.

10. Cheng, Tsung-Mei. "Reflections On The 20th Anniversary Of Taiwan's
    Single-Payer National Health Insurance System." *Health Affairs* 34, no. 3
    (March 2015): 502–10. https://doi.org/10.1377/hlthaff.2014.1332.

11. Cheng, Tsung-Mei. "Health Care Spending in the US and Taiwan: A
    Response to *It's Still the Prices, Stupid, and a Tribute to Uwe Reinhardt.*"
    Health Affairs Blog, February 6, 2019. https://www.healthaffairs.org/
    do/10.1377/hblog20190206.305164/full/.

12. Scott, Dylan. "Two Sisters. Two Different Journeys Through Australia's
    Health Care System." *Vox*, January 15, 2020. https://www.vox.
    com/2020/1/15/21030568/australia-health-insurance-medicare.

13. Scott, Dylan. "The Netherlands Has Universal Health Insurance—
    and It's All Private." *Vox*, January 17, 2020. https://www.vox.com/
    policy-and-politics/2020/1/17/21046874/netherlands-universal-health-
    insurance-private.

CHAPTER 7

1. World Population Review. "US States—Ranked by Population 2020." http://worldpopulationreview.com/states/.

2. World Population Review. "2020 World Population by Country." http://worldpopulationreview.com/.

3. The World Bank. "GDP (Current US$)" https://data.worldbank.org/indicator/ny.gdp.mktp.cd.

4. Bureau of Economic Analysis, U.S. Department of Commerce. "Regional Data." https://apps.bea.gov/iTable/iTable.cfm?reqid=70&step=30&isuri=1&major_area=0&area=06000&year=2017&tableid=505&category=1505&area_type=0&year_end=-1&classification=naics&state=0&statistic=-1&yearbegin=-1&unit_of_measure=levels.

5. International Monetary Fund. "GDP, Current Prices." https://www.imf.org/external/datamapper/NGDPD@WEO/OEMDC/ADVEC/WEOWORLD.

6. American Association for the Advancement of Science. "The Fellowship." https://leshnerfellows.aaas.org/Home/About.

7. Pollin, Robert, James Heintz, Peter Arno, and Jeannette Wicks-Lim. "Economic Analysis of the Healthy California Single-Payer Health Care Proposal (SB-562)." Political Economy Research Institute. Last modified May 31, 2017. https://www.peri.umass.edu/publication/item/996-economic-analysis-of-the-healthy-california-single-payer-health-care-proposal-sb-562.

8. Organisation for Economic Co-operation and Development. "Health Spending." https://data.oecd.org/healthres/health-spending.htm.

9. Liu, Jodi, Chapin White, Sarah Nowak, Asa Wilks, Jamie Ryan, and Christine Eibner. *An Assessment of the New York Health Act: A Single-Payer Option for New York State.* RAND Corporation, 2018. https://doi.org/10.7249/rr2424.

10. Fuse Brown, Erin C. and Elizabeth Y. McCuskey. "Could States do Single-Payer Health Care?" *Health Affairs Blog*, July 22, 2019. https://www.healthaffairs.org/do/10.1377/hblog20190717.466249/full/.

11. Van Doorn, Philip. "The Most Profitable Companies Get the Best Stock Returns." *Market Watch*, October 10, 2014. https://www.marketwatch.com/story/24-of-the-most-profitable-companies-return-an-average-of-573-in-a-decade-2014-10-10.

CHAPTER 8

1. Neuman, Tricia, Karen Pollitz, and Jennifer Tolbert. "Medicare-for-All and Public Plan Buy-In Proposals: Overview and Key Issues." Kaiser Family Foundation, October 2018. http://files.kff.org/attachment/Issue-Brief-Medicare-for-All-and-Public-Buy-In-Proposals-Overview-and-Key-Issues.

2. Weissmann, Jordan. "Any Plan for Universal Health Care Coverage Will Anger Some Voters." *Slate*, January 3, 2020. https://slate.com/business/2020/01/pete-buttigieg-health-care-plan-retroactive-enrollment.html.

3. Himmelstein, David U. and Steffie Woolhandler. "The 'Public Option' on Health Care Is a Poison Pill." *The Nation*, October 7, 2019. https://www.thenation.com/article/insurance-health-care-medicare/.

4. Woolhandler, Steffie, and David U. Himmelstein. "The American College of Physicians' Endorsement of Single-Payer Reform: A Sea Change for the Medical Profession." *Annals of Internal Medicine* 172, no. 2_Supplement (January 21, 2020): S60. https://doi.org/10.7326/m19-3775.

5. Crowley, Ryan, Hilary Daniel, Thomas G. Cooney, and Lee S. Engel. "Envisioning a Better U.S. Health Care System for All: Coverage and Cost of Care." *Annals of Internal Medicine* 172, no. 2_Supplement (January 21, 2020): S7. https://doi.org/10.7326/m19-2415.

6. Erickson, Shari M., Brian Outland, Suzanne Joy, Brooke Rockwern, Josh Serchen, Ryan D. Mire, and Jason M. Goldman. "Envisioning a Better U.S. Health Care System for All: Health Care Delivery and Payment System Reforms." *Annals of Internal Medicine* 172, no. 2_Supplement (January 21, 2020): S33. https://doi.org/10.7326/m19-2407.

7. Butkus, Renee, Katherine Rapp, Thomas G. Cooney, and Lee S. Engel.

"Envisioning a Better U.S. Health Care System for All: Reducing Barriers to Care and Addressing Social Determinants of Health." *Annals of Internal Medicine* 172, no. 2_Supplement (January 21, 2020): S50. https://doi.org/10.7326/m19-2410.

8. Doherty, Robert, Thomas G. Cooney, Ryan D. Mire, Lee S. Engel, and Jason M. Goldman. "Envisioning a Better U.S. Health Care System for All: A Call to Action by the American College of Physicians." *Annals of Internal Medicine* 172, no. 2_Supplement (January 21, 2020): S3. https://doi.org/10.7326/m19-2411.

CHAPTER 9

1. Blendon, Robert J., John M. Benson, and Caitlin L. McMurtry. "The Upcoming U.S. Health Care Cost Debate — The Public's Views." *New England Journal of Medicine* 380, no. 26 (June 27, 2019): 2487–92. https://doi.org/10.1056/nejmp1905710.

ACKNOWLEDGMENTS

This book is in honor of, and thanks to, the countless colleagues and healthcare professionals who staff the frontlines of our broken healthcare system, and the many patients they serve 24 hours per day, 365 days per year. I would like to offer my special thanks and appreciation to my mentors, Drs. Eric Brass and Hal Yee, who taught me how to think critically, how to challenge dogma, and how to lead and manage. The team at Scribe Media has been truly amazing, and has made this the best experience I've ever had publishing a book. From the incredible design team, to thorough and efficient editing, to the handling of all aspects of publicity and outreach, I have been impressed at every turn. Special thanks to Emily Anderson of Scribe, the ringleader who oversaw the team. And finally, this book would not have been possible without my wife, Sue, and our kids, Catherine and Michael, whose love and support are a source of constant renewal.

ABOUT THE AUTHOR

DR. BRAD SPELLBERG is chief medical officer at the Los Angeles County + University of Southern California Medical Center, and the associate dean for clinical affairs at the Keck School of Medicine at USC.

Internationally respected as an expert in Infectious Diseases and Internal Medicine, Dr. Spellberg has authored more than two hundred scientific publications, including his award-winning *Rising Plague*, named Outstanding Academic Title in 2009 by *Choice* magazine. Dr. Spellberg is also prominently featured in the documentary film, *Resistance*, and in the PBS *Frontline* episode, "Hunting the Nightmare Bacteria."

INDEX

C

D

E

F

G

H

I

J

JAMA (Journal of the American Medical Association), 144, 150
Japan, 40, 68, 146, 149, 151, 235
Johnson rod, 166–167, 263

K

Kaiser Family Foundation, 72–73, 75, 100, 262
Klein, Ezra, 216
Kramer, Mark, 114
Kuwait, 40

L

LAC+USC Medical Center, 20, 23–24, 28, 44, 47, 61, 119, 234, 255
life expectancy, 39–40, 42, 59, 79
life span, 40, 58, 79, 81, 85, 145, 175, 218, 260
Lighty, Michael, 233–234
line item, 159, 162–164, 173, 238, 279, 285
long-term care, 28, 31–32, 145
Los Angeles, 11, 15, 20, 24, 27, 31, 47
Los Angeles County, 20, 47, 315

M

margin, hospital, 98–99, 183
Maryland, 51–53, 167, 216, 218
maternal, 70, 145
maternal mortality, 145
Medicaid, 24, 27, 41, 51, 54, 66, 70, 101, 103, 108–109, 113, 137, 181, 191, 193, 197–198, 236, 246–248, 270, 272
MediCal, 121, 181–182, 228, 266
Medicare, 31, 41, 51, 54, 66, 70, 105–106, 108–109, 175, 184, 191, 193, 197, 198, 201
Medicare for All, 262–263, 265, 276–278, 293
Medicare for Those Who Want It, 263, 265, 267, 278, 293
Mexico, 84, 187, 267
Montenegro, 40
mortality, 40, 102, 104, 145, 218
Mr. A, 23–25, 28, 30–33, 35, 43, 46–48
Mr. B, 28, 30–33, 35, 47
Mr. D, 61–64, 266
Mr. E, 87–95, 100, 105, 177
Mr. F, 119–122, 266–267
MRI, 114, 147
Ms. C, 44–47, 61, 173–174, 266
Ms. G, 157–165, 177
Ms. H, 185, 187, 267
Ms. I, 227–229
multi-payer, 136, 140, 203–204, 207, 212, 215, 217–220, 222–225, 239, 241, 243, 265, 269, 274–278

N

National Academy of Medicine, 42
National Health Service, 172, 189, 200, 205
Netherlands, 69, 79, 122, 146–149, 152–153, 170, 203–204, 207, 212, 214–215, 222–225, 239, 269
network, insurance, 43, 44–47, 58, 101, 117, 157, 159, 173, 219, 264
New Year's resolutions, 261
New York State Health Act, 244
New Zealand, 36, 40, 69, 79, 82, 204, 206, 209, 235, 275, 278, 282
Norway, 36, 69, 79, 82, 205–206, 235, 239

O

Oregon, 103
Organisation for Economic Co-operation and Development (OECD), 36, 40, 49, 68, 78, 80, 82, 84, 144
out-of-pocket, 66, 70–71, 73–74, 97, 107, 116, 123, 149, 152, 201–203
out-of-pocket spending, 71, 207
outpatient care, 53, 74, 105, 145–149, 174, 200, 206, 208
outpatient surgical procedures, 147
overpricing, 76
overtreating, 162
overtreatment, 76
overutilization, 142, 148

P

peer nation, 15–151, 147–148, 153–154, 184–185
per diem, 74, 192
pharmaceutical companies, 98, 162, 183, 252
pharmaceutical spending, 148, 153, 202, 205, 237–238, 243, 273, 286
physicians' salaries, 152
Political Economy Research Institute (PERI), 232
Pollin, Robert, 232–237, 239–244
Pontillo, John, 114
Portugal, 78–79
price controls, 125
private insurance, 54, 70, 94, 113, 120–122, 138–140, 148–149, 154, 159, 178, 180, 182, 184, 191–193, 195–198, 201–210, 214, 222–225, 242, 249–250, 252, 263–269, 273–279, 282–283, 288–289, 293, 296
profit, 138–139, 140, 168
public option, 154, 207–208, 263, 265, 268, 273, 277, 282
public vs. private spending, 66, 124, 287

R

RAND Corporation, 75, 244
Revenue Act, 130–131
Rising Plague, 3, 19–20, 290
Russia, 67

S

T

U

V

W

CPSIA information can be obtained
at www.ICGtesting.com
Printed in the USA
LVHW090139280221
680130LV00014B/55